SCHOOL OF THE PROPHETS

NEWMAN STUDIES JOURNAL
SECOND SERIES

1

SERIES EDITORS

Christopher Cimorelli

Elizabeth A. Huddleston

Kenneth L. Parker

SCHOOL OF THE PROPHETS

John Henry Newman's Anglican *Schola* and the Ecclesial Vocation of the Theologian

MICHAEL J. G. PAHLS

Foreword by Brian Robinette

NSJ Second Series
National Institute for Newman Studies
Pittsburgh, Pennsylvania

Copyright © 2024
National Institute for Newman Studies
Pittsburgh, Pennsylvania

The paper used in this publication meets the minimum requirements of American National Standards for Information Science– Permanence of Paper for Printed Library Materials, ANSI Z39.48-1992.

Cataloging-in-Publication Data is available from the Library of Congress

Book ISBN: 979-8-9906211-0-7 | Ebook ISBN: 979-8-9906211-1-4

Book design by Burt&Burt
Text set in Bagatela and Ivy Journal

TO TRACY, LILY, AND ABIGAIL

TABLE OF CONTENTS

Abbreviations • ix
Foreword • xi
Introduction • 1

CHAPTER 1
Adrift in the Schools of Private Judgement
29

CHAPTER 2
A School's Nascent Form:
Newman's Reform of the Tutorial System
and the Turn to "Traditionary Religion"
71

CHAPTER 3
Commending the Episcopate and Constructing
a Popular Church: Oxford's Apostolical Men
Amid England's Imperiled Ecclesial Structures
99

CHAPTER 4
Imagining and Inhabiting the
Prophetical Office of the Church
137

CHAPTER 5
The Pros and Cons of Proving Canon:
Tract 90 and the Fall of Newman's Anglican School
187

Conclusion • 235
Bibliography • 243
Index • 261

Abbreviations

Apo	*Apologia Pro Vita Sua*
Ari	*Arians of the Fourth Century*
Ath i, ii	*Select Treatises of St. Athanasius in Controversy with the Arians*
AW	*Autobiographical Writings*
Call	*Callista: A Tale of the Third Century*
Cons	*On Consulting the Faithful in Matters of Doctrine*
DA	*Discussions and Arguments on Various Subjects*
Dev	*An Essay on the Development of Christian Doctrine*
Diff i, ii	*Certain Difficulties Felt by Anglicans in Catholic Teaching*
Duke	*Letter to His Grace, the Duke of Norfolk*
Ess i, ii	*Essays Critical and Historical*
GA	*An Essay in Aid of a Grammar of Assent*
HS i-iii	*Historical Sketches*
Idea	*The Idea of a University*
Jfc	*Lectures on the Doctrine of Justification*
PN	*Philosophical Notebooks of John Henry Newman*
Pro	*Lectures on the Prophetical Office of the Church*
LD i-xxxii	*The Letters and Diaries of John Henry Newman*, ed. Charles Stephen Dessain et al. (Oxford and London, 1978-2008).
LG	*Loss and Gain: The Story of a Convert*
MD	*Meditations and Devotions of the Late Cardinal Newman*
Mir	*Two Essays on Biblical and Ecclesiastical Miracles*
Mix	*Discourses Addressed to Mixed Congregations*
OS	*Sermons Preached on Various Occasions*
PS i-viii	*Parochial and Plain Sermons*
SD	*Sermons bearing on Subjects of the Day*
SN	*Sermon Notes of John Henry Cardinal Newman*
Tracts i-vi	*Tracts for the Times*
TP	*The Theological Papers of John Henry Newman on Faith and Certainty*
TT	*Tracts Theological and Ecclesiastical*
US	*Fifteen Sermons Preached Before the University of Oxford*
VM i, ii	*The Via Media*
VV	*Verses on Various Occasions*

Foreword

In his 2015 address to the Second International Congress of Theology held in Buenos Aires, Pope Francis spoke passionately of the need to overcome the opposition between theology and pastoral ministry. Occasioned by the 50th anniversary of the Second Vatican Council's conclusion, the pope outlined three marks of the theologian that are crucial to fulfilling this aim.

First and foremost, the theologian is filiated. He or she intimately knows the people of the church, their language and customs, their histories and traditions, their roots. Secondly, the theologian is a believer. Nourished by a source experience of Christ's love, he or she shares in Christ's own filiation with the Father through the Holy Spirit. Thirdly, the theologian is a prophet. Alert to the ways tradition can become obscured, misdirected, or alienating for persons within and beyond the church, the theologian exercises a prophetic role by engaging in loving critique so that the tradition may be vivified by God's surprising future. In this way, the theologian responds to the eschatological hope to which the entire church is called.

In offering this preface to *School of the Prophets: John Henry Newman's Anglican Schola and the Ecclesial Vocation of the Theologian* by the late Michael J. G. Pahls (1971-2019), I can think of no better way to summarize his life and work than by highlighting these characteristics of the theologian. Readers of this volume will know (or come to know) of Michael's significant contributions to the study of John Henry Newman, whose recent canonization reminds us of the exemplary degree to which these characteristics were exhibited in him. Like his theological hero, Michael richly embodied the vocation of an ecclesial theologian, one whose scholarly acumen and pastoral sensibility were drawn together in closest unity for the ongoing conversion of the church.

Conversion is a prominent theme in Michael's scholarship because it was a strong theme in his life. Born in Anderson, Indiana to a Catholic household, Michael became involved in a Pentecostal worshipping community as a young adult and eventually studied theology and ministry at Central Bible College in Springfield, Missouri (now Evangel University). Intellectually restless and electrified by his wide-ranging reading in philosophy, biblical hermeneutics, and church history, Michael found himself drawn to the Reformed tradition where he could more thoroughly integrate pastoral practice with his growing theological learning. After obtaining a Master of Divinity at Trinity Evangelical Divinity School in Chicago, where studied with Dr. Kevin Vanhoozer, Michael served as a pastor-theologian in the Reformed Church of America for several years in the Chicago area.

Greatly enriched by his pastoral work, Michael still felt ecclesially restless on account of his growing liturgical sensibilities. Already quite active in local ecumenical dialogue, Michael's adventurous reading in church history, systematic theology, and sacramental theology drew him closer to the wellsprings of the Christian liturgical tradition, leading him to seek ordination in the Anglican Communion. Michael also began doctoral studies in historical theology around this time at Saint Louis University, where he would write his dissertation under the supervision of Dr. Kenneth Parker. With a strong affinity for Newman's account of doctrinal development, as well as the future saint's public journey of conversion, Michael would eventually write on Newman's account of the theologian's prophetic role in a dissertation leading to the present volume.

Just as Newman's conversion to Catholicism displays an intimate relation between theological reflection, pastoral practice, and collegial debate–all of which are hallmarks of the *schola theologorum* as conceived and promoted by Newman–so too would Michael's breadth of inquiry, his extensive ministerial experience, and his years-long conversations with friends and colleagues lead him to reclaim the Catholicism of his youth. Unsure of when (or whether) he would be able to resume his work in ordained ministry, Michael, along with his family, would be confirmed in the Catholic Church and there find an ecclesial home. While suspending his abilities to serve in ordained ministry was personally very difficult–a deferment he explicitly understood in eschatological terms–Michael was able to teach and research in various capacities during the last few years of his life, including at Christian Brothers University and at Saint Agnes Academy in Memphis, Tennessee.

Michael's theological learning was profound. A meticulous scholar, his facility with a broad range of biblical, historical, philosophical, and doctrinal materials regularly astonished his friends, colleagues, students, and parishioners alike. An elegant writer and speaker–skills he honed as a scholar-pastor–Michael understood that theology is fundamentally conversational. The most embracing forms of dialogue, *theological* conversation draws its participants into the surprise of discovery, the joy of mutual understanding, the challenge of self-critique, the impulse for ongoing conversion, and ultimately friendship with one another and with God. It was no doubt this vision of theology that drew him so strongly to Newman.

With expertise in the Oxford Movement, Michael published an array of articles, book chapters, and reviews dedicated to themes of ecclesial authority, doctrinal development, liturgy, and culture. Already before his untimely death, Michael was making good on the enormous promise of his gifts and abilities. But it is the present work that will undoubtedly mark his most important contribution to the field. Focused on the prophetic role of the theologian, Michael's book draws his readers into the innermost workings of Newman's developing understanding of the *schola theologorum*, which, while having its fullest formulation after Newman's conversion, gained its seminal form and earliest momentum during his Anglican period. With remarkable detail and scholarly range, Michael demonstrates the fundamental continuities between Newman's Anglican and Catholic thought while offering a compelling portrait of Newman's vision for ecclesial unity amid differences. Above all, Michael highlights the prophetic office of the theologian, which for Newman meant critically challenging various misdirections and misapplications *of* the tradition with creative fidelity *to* the tradition. As with the three marks of the theologian outlined by Pope Francis, this prophetic office can only be *for* the church if the theologian engages this task as a son or daughter *of* the church. Genuine critique arises out of prior belonging, and such belonging is ultimately rooted in filiation with the living God.

On a more personal note, and in keeping with the theme of filiation, it is with immense gratitude, and not a little grief, that I conclude these prefatory words to the book of a cherished friend. I have learned more about the craft of theology from Michael than anyone else, and this in the context of a profound friendship that spanned several seasons of life. To have known Michael so intimately for so long, and to have witnessed his growth into the vocation of the theologian, will count among the greatest blessings of my life. Though he departed from this life far too early, it is with boundless appreciation and joyful anticipation that I commend this stellar piece of theological scholarship to the reader, wishing somehow that you may know something of Michael's passion and fidelity from its pages. Thank you, Michael, for the gift of your work, and above all, the gift of your life's vocation as an ecclesial theologian.

Brian Robinette, Boston College

INTRODUCTION

John Henry Newman, The *Schola Theologorum*, and the Ecclesial Vocation of Theology

On 27 December 1874, John Henry Newman penned his *Letter to the Duke of Norfolk* as a response to Prime Minister William Gladstone's published attacks on the newly defined doctrine of papal infallibility. Gladstone argued that the definition promulgated by the dogmatic constitution, *Pastor Aeternus* (1870), would necessarily entail the "renunciation of moral and mental freedom" and provoke the "civil disloyalty" of English Catholics.[1] In his rejoinder, Newman took up Gladstone's charges one by one, allaying fears and correcting misunderstandings. By this he hoped to put the best possible face on the new dogma and mitigate

---

[1] Gladstone's article, "Ritual and Ritualism," was published in an October 1874 edition of the *Contemporary Review* 24 (1874): 663-81. It dealt primarily with controversies over ritualism in Anglicanism, but the controversy gave Gladstone the opportunity to decry "the effort to Romanise the Church and people of England." Later in the article, he gestured to the Roman Catholic conversion of longtime political associate, George Frederick Samuel Robinson in September 1874 and wrote, "no one can become her [the Roman Church's] convert without renouncing his moral and mental freedom, and placing his civil loyalty and duty at the mercy seat of another; and when she has equally repudiated modern thought and ancient history." *LD* xxvii, 122n3. Gladstone later repeated and expanded on these charges in his 1874 pamphlet, "The Vatican Decrees in their Bearing on Civil Allegiance." The episode up to the publication of Newman's "A Letter Addressed to His Grace the Duke of Norfolk on Occasion of Mr. Gladstone's Recent Expostulation" is ably chronicled by John R. Page, *What Will Dr. Newman Do?: John Henry Newman and Papal Infallibility 1865-1875* (Collegeville, MN: Michael Glazier/Liturgical, 1994), 249-318. The Gladstone pamphlet and Newman's letter appear together in Alvan Ryan, ed., *Newman and Gladstone: The Vatican Decrees* (Notre Dame, IN: University of Notre Dame Press, 1962).

ongoing neo-ultramontane interpretations advanced by the Cardinal Archbishop of Westminster, Henry Edward Manning.[2] Most intriguing in Newman's apologetic for the First Vatican Council was his appeal to the ongoing interpretive work of the *schola theologorum*, arguing that it alone would establish the true and final sense of the council's definition. In his dedicatory remarks, Newman wrote,

> I deeply grieve that Mr. Gladstone has felt it his duty to speak with such extraordinary severity of our Religion and of ourselves. I consider he has committed himself to a representation of ecclesiastical documents which will not hold, and to a view of our position in the country which we have neither deserved nor can be patient under. None but the *Schola Theologorum* is competent to determine the force of Papal and Synodal utterances, and the exact interpretation of them is a work of time. But so much may be safely said of the decrees which have lately been promulgated, and of the faithful who have received them, that Mr. Gladstone's account, both of them and of us, is neither trustworthy nor charitable.[3]

---

2 A pastoral letter, promulgated by Archbishop Manning on 13 October 1870 indicates how little his views on papal infallibility had changed despite the council's apparent mitigation of the neo-ultramontane position on the dogma. Manning includes under the umbrella of infallibility "all legislative or judicial acts, so far as they are inseparably connected with [the pope's] doctrinal authority; as, for instance all judgments, sentences, and decisions which contain the motives of such acts as derived from faith and morals." Manning continues, "Under this will come laws of discipline, canonization of Saints, approbation of religious Orders, of devotions, and the like; all of which intrinsically contain the truths and principles of faith, morals, and piety." Henry Edward Manning, *The Vatican Council and its Definitions: A Pastoral Letter to the Clergy* (London: Longmans, Green, and Co., 1870), 89-90. Distressed that such a broad interpretation of *Pastor Aeternus* would leave little if anything outside the scope of the pope's infallible prerogative, Newman penned a letter to Lady Simeon, a prominent member of Manning's diocese, regarding her own expressed concerns. He wrote, "The archbishop only does what he has done all along–he ever has exaggerated things, and ever has acted toward individuals in a way which they felt to be unfeeling . . . And now, as I think most cruelly, he is fearfully exaggerating what has been done at the Council . . . Therefore, I say confidently, you may dismiss all such exaggerations from your mind, though it is a cruel penance to know that the Bishop, where you are, puts them forth. It is an enormous tyranny." Newman to Lady Simeon (18 November 1870), *LD* xv, 230.

3 Newman, *Duke*, in *Diff* ii (London: Longmans, Green, and Co., 1900), 176.

While the specific nomenclature *schola theologorum* appears infrequently and comparatively late in the writings of Newman's Roman Catholic career, his conception of theology as a distinct *munus* of the church emerges in his earliest writings as an Anglican Tractarian.[4] A sensitive, contextualized reading of that Anglican work reveals how, from his polemic deployment of the theological "schools" at Antioch and Alexandria in *The Arians of the Fourth Century* (1833), to his ecclesiological account of theology's vocation in the *Lectures on the Prophetical Office of the Church* (1837), to the imaginative theological rectification of Anglicanism's Protestant lapses in *Tract 90* (1841), and throughout his collaborative theological work as part of the "Oxford Movement," Newman's conception of theology as a necessary vocation in the church is ever-present. This study will make use of this fundamental insight to thicken what are presently "thin" and contested accounts of his latter thinking as a Roman Catholic.

In keeping with a project of historical theology, the proposed way into this project will be to examine afresh Newman's conception of the office of theology as it appears contextually in his Anglican writings, beginning in the 1820s and continuing into the 1840s. I treat both lexical and conceptual witnesses in the larger corpus of his work, attempting to account for potential sources and developments in his thought during this formative period in Newman's life. Most importantly, I explore his Anglican-Tractarian efforts as an attempt to construct a functioning theological school at the University of Oxford. Ultimately, I argue that a fuller appreciation of these experiences, for good and for ill, is a necessary precondition for understanding his later Catholic writings on the subject.[5]

---

[4] I use "Oxford Movement" and "Tractarianism" interchangeably to describe the movement of certain High Church members of the Oxford theological faculty, who from 1833 organized to resource the Church of England in its early Christian and Catholic heritage. Among the many initiatives of the movement, publication of the ninety *Tracts for the Times* proved to be its central and most enduring legacy. Because all the *Tracts* excepting those authored by Edward Bouverie Pusey, were published under the name "Members of the Faculty," the movement came to be called "Tractarianism."

[5] In this regard, the argument here is an extension of the case made by Dwight Culler that Newman's *Idea of a University*, published and expanded through the

Proposed here is that beginning in the 1820s and continuing through his final work as a Tractarian, John Henry Newman developed a coherent conception of theology as a distinct "prophetical" office, positioned between the faithful and the episcopate as an interpreter of church teaching and as a witness to its necessary development. Thus, thickened by the work done in this study, it becomes clearer how the Catholic Newman could imagine the *schola theologorum*,–the ecclesial manifestation of what he called the "Prophetical Office of the Church"–as an instrument for the regulation of "the *whole* Church system," applying, clarifying, and sometimes even rectifying its self-understanding.[6]

FACTS REQUIRING FOUNDATION: NEWMAN'S *SCHOLA THEOLOGORUM*

The present state of scholarly research suggests that the time is particularly ripe for a fuller treatment of Newman's conception of the *schola theologorum* and his understanding of theology as a vocation. Even where the subject has been passively treated as a discrete part of his ecclesiology or in reflections on his theory of doctrinal development, those treatments have largely been driven by contemporary preoccupations regarding the proper relationship between Roman Catholic theologians and the Roman magisterium. Following the Second Vatican Council's decisive turn away from neo-Thomism, Roman Catholic theologians have since explored a new freedom to rearticulate Catholic teaching in new language. Where these projects have been judged to depart too drastically from historically attested expressions, the Sacred Congregation for the Doctrine of the Faith (successor to the early modern Congregation of the Holy Office of the Inquisition, hereafter CDF) has been tasked to investigate, correct, and occasionally suppress

---

1850s and achieving final form in the 1889 edition, was the fruit of his years at Oxford. A. Dwight Culler, *The Imperial Intellect: A Study of Newman's Educational Ideal* (New Haven, CT: Yale University Press, 1955). Cf., J. M. Roberts, "The Idea of a University Revisited," in *Newman After a Hundred Years*, eds. Ian Ker and A. G. Hill (London: Clarendon, 1990), 193-222.

6 Newman, *Pro* ii (London: Longmans, Green, and Co., 1877), xlvii-xlviii.

such teaching. Actions of the CDF have subsequently led to the discipline of notable theologians in recent decades.[7] Such high-profile controversies have, in turn, led to a renewed study of the role of Catholic theologians vis-à-vis the magisterium.[8] While Newman's writings on

---

[7] Among those disciplined the most famous are Swiss theologian Hans Küng who was stripped of his *missio canonica* after the publication of his *Infallible?: An Inquiry* (1971), which rejected the doctrine of papal infallibility. Brazilian liberation theologian Leonardo Boff was silenced for a year in 1985 following the publication of his *Church: Charism and Power* (1985). Boff eventually left both the priesthood and the Franciscan order under pressure from the CDF. Finally, although never suppressed or silenced, the Belgian Dominican theologian Edward Schillebeeckx was perpetually suspect for questioning the necessity of faith of an empty tomb in the resurrection in *Jesus: An Experiment in Christology* (1974), for holding "Protestant" views on the congregational selection of priests in his *The Ministry in the Church* (1980), and for expressing doubts as to the necessity of apostolic succession for sacramental validity in his *The Church with a Human Face* (1985). Most significant, however, has been the case of American moral theologian Charles Curran whose stalwart and repeated public dissent from traditional Roman Catholic moral teaching in sexuality led to his removal in 1967 from a tenured faculty position at the Catholic University of America. While Curran was reinstated after a five-day faculty-led strike, he was again removed in 1986 after the CDF declared him ineligible to function as a Catholic theologian. A fuller story of the conflicted relationship between Roman Catholic theologians and the magisterium of the Roman Catholic Church in recent days can be accessed in Larry Witham, *Curran vs. Catholic University: A Study of Authority, Freedom, and Conflict* (Riverdale, MD: Edington-Rand, 1991). With the resignation of Pope Benedict XVI and the ascent of Pope Francis to the Chair of St. Peter, there are signals that the lingering cloud of disfavor under which liberation theology has labored is beginning to dissipate. Two years into Francis's pontificate, it is impossible to predict what the outcome of this shift will mean for more recently targeted theologians, such as Jesuit liberation theologian Jon Sobrino and Catholic feminist theologians Elizabeth Johnson and Margaret Farley [footnote composed in 2015].

[8] Studies in this area are too many to exhaustively name, but several of the more important and/or highly regarded works (in chronological order of appearance) are the essays in Leo O'Donovan, ed., *Cooperation Between Theologians and the Ecclesiastical Magisterium* (Washington, DC: Canon Law Society of America, 1982); Francis A. Sullivan, SJ, *Magisterium: Teaching Authority in the Catholic Church* (New York/Ramsey, NJ: Paulist, 1983); Edmund Hill, OP, *Ministry and Authority in the Catholic Church* (London: Geoffrey Chapman, 1988); Ladislas Orsy, *The Church: Learning and Teaching: Magisterium, Assent, Dissent, Academic Freedom* (Wilmington, DE: Michael Glazier, 1987); Thomas P. Rausch, SJ, *Authority and Leadership in the Church: Past Directions and Future Possibilities* (Wilmington, DE: Michael Glazier, 1989); Richard R. Gaillardetz, *Witnesses to the Faith: Community, Infallibility, and the Ordinary*

the subject have played only a minor role in the much larger conversation, shared respect for him among Roman Catholic progressives and traditionalists alike has led to a revived appreciation for his thought generally.[9]

JOHN COULSON AND THE COMMON TRADITION

The first sustained work on the subject was that of John Coulson. He first presented his preliminary essay, "Newman on the Church–His Final View, Its Origins and Influence," at a symposium on Newman's legacy held in 1966 at Oriel College, Oxford. A revised version subsequently appeared as part of the 1967 collection, *The Rediscovery of Newman: An Oxford Symposium*.[10] Coulson then expanded his argument three years later in a monograph entitled *Newman and the Common Tradition: A Study in the Language of Church and Society*. In these two works, Coulson attempted a comparison of Newman's ecclesiological

---

Magisterium of Bishops (New York/Mahwah, NJ: Paulist, 1992); Richard R. Gaillardetz, *Teaching with Authority: A Theology of the Magisterium in the Church* (Collegeville, MN: Michael Glazier/Liturgical Press, 1997); David Stagaman, SJ, *Authority in the Church* (Collegeville, MN: Michael Glazier/Liturgical Press, 1999); and Richard R. Gaillardetz, ed., *When the Magisterium Intervenes: The Magisterium and Theologians in Today's Church* (Collegeville, MN: Liturgical Press, 2012). See also the exceptionally helpful collection of essays in two works edited by Charles E. Curran and Richard A. McCormick, SJ, *Readings in Moral Theology*, no. 3: *The Magisterium and Morality* (New York/Ramsey, NJ: Paulist, 1982), and *Readings in Moral Theology*, no. 6: *Dissent in the Church* (New York/Mahwah, NJ: Paulist, 1988).

9 To illustrate the point, one might consider the preconciliar works of Günter Biemer and Jan Walgrave. Biemer speaks of Newman's prophetical office as merely another type of tradition, handed on in other forms . . . in the liturgies, in the literature of controversy, in sermons and the like." When he discusses "the teaching church," he makes reference to the apostles, bishops, councils, and the papacy, but has nothing to say about theologians. *Überlieferung und Offenbarung: die Lehre von der Tradition nach John Henry Newman* (Freiburg: Herder, 1961) and Günter Biemer, *Newman on Tradition*, trans. Kevin Smyth, 1967), 47, 99-120. Jan-Hendrik Walgrave's, *Newman, Le Developpement du Dogme* (Tournai-Paris: Casterman, 1957) makes no mention of the *schola theologorum* or of theologians at all.

10 John Coulson, "Newman on the Church–His Final View, Its Origins and Influence," in *The Rediscovery of Newman: An Oxford Symposium* (London: Sheed and Ward/SPCK, 1967), 123-43.

vision with those of Samuel Taylor Coleridge and Frederick Denison Maurice. He arrived at a conclusion that Newman provides a coherent account of the church, "which allows us to respond to it as a whole–as an organic unity of persons through whom the verifying presence of Christ is transmitted–yet without resting on this response as self-evident."[11] Coulson did not argue that Newman was directly dependent on Coleridge or Maurice (he conceded that the former especially is unlikely), but he rather maintained that all three were witnesses to an old, ecumenical tradition that had persisted into the nineteenth century–and that despite the unfinished business of the First Vatican Council.[12]

Coulson first began with Newman's 1877 preface to a reissue of his 1837 *Lectures on the Prophetical Office of the Church*. This appeared under the general title of *The Via Media of the Anglican Church*.[13] Coulson argued that for all its simplicity of form and expression, it is there that one finds Newman's "description of the Church in its final form."[14] As he argued, Newman's burden was describing both how Christ is present to his church and how the church, as transmitter of Christ's presence, is ordered and regulated. For Newman's opponents among the neo-ultramontanists, no such account was necessary.[15] Christ simply governed and regulated his church immediately by an infallible vicar–namely the pope–who possessed a universal jurisdiction. On the other hand, so-called "Liberal Catholics" like Lord Acton posited the autonomous

---

[11] John Coulson, *Newman and the Common Tradition: A Study in the Language of Church and Society* (Oxford: Clarendon, 1970), 166.

[12] Coulson, *Newman and the Common Tradition*, 123-43.

[13] Newman, *VM* i, xv-xciv.

[14] Coulson, *Newman and the Common Tradition*, 165.

[15] By "neo-ultramontanism" here, I intend the belief of certain Roman Catholics prior to the First Vatican Council who contended that papal infallibility could not be restricted to *ex cathedra* papal definitions. Whereas ultramontanism simply entailed recognition of the pope's universal jurisdiction beyond the limits of his own diocese (hence, "beyond the mountains" or specifically "beyond the Alps"), neo-ultramontanists argued that papal infallibility applied *ipso facto* to any and all papal teachings and statements. Approaching the definition of papal infallibility by the council, neo-ultramontanists advocated the most extreme definition of papal infallibility possible.

individual conscience as the only alternative to a totalizing neo-ultramontanist regime. As Coulson argued, however, Newman thought both alternatives made the same mistake by treating the church exclusively in political terms and setting the divergent faces of the church–that is, bishops, theologians, and laity–against one another. Newman's solution, then, was to "show how the different and apparently contradictory faces of the Church may be reconciled . . . His problem [was] how to define the parts of the Church without compromising its antecedent unity."[16]

Coulson's study highlighted Newman's "strong and abiding sense of the presence of Christ" in solidarity with his church. In the 1837 *Lectures on the Prophetical Office*, the Anglican Newman distinguished between the prophetical tradition as "that which gives the church life" and the episcopal tradition as "that which gives the church form." By the 1877 preface, the Catholic Newman made use of the *triplex munus Christi*–the notion that Christ perfectly realized the ancient Hebrew offices of prophet, priest, and king–reflecting on how Christ ministered presently in his church.[17] The church rules by the regal office of the magisterium, it mediates the presence of Christ to the world by a sacerdotal priesthood, and the prophetic office regulates the entire system, ensuring that the church "functions as a living whole instead of an abstraction of discordant and self-conceived parts."[18]

Coulson's work has been foundational to almost all the subsequent treatments of the *schola theologorum* in Newman. His work thus represents an important touchstone for the present study. That said, it remains important to note that while Coulson gestured to a "common tradition," with certain features locatable in Anglicanism generally or in Newman's experience as an Anglican evangelical more particularly,

---

16 Coulson, "Newman on the Church," 124.

17 Although his overall project is far afield of Newman studies, Gerald McCulloh has authored an excellent introductory history of the *Munus Triplex Christi* as a tool for organizing theological thought. See his "A History of the *Munus Triplex* in Christian Thought," in *Christ's Person and Life-Work in the Theology of Albrecht Ritschl with Special Attention to "Munus Triplex"* (Lanham, MD: University Press of America, 1990), 86-144.

18 Coulson, "Newman on the Church," 135.

Coulson did not develop this insight in any discernible way. Instead, he created a hard distinction between the Newman of 1837 and the Newman of 1877 and thereby limited himself to those later writings and to Newman's contemporaneous attempts to steer a middle course between Manning and Acton. Where Coulson's study turns on discontinuity, I highlight the demonstrable *continuities* in Newman's Anglican and Roman Catholic thought.

PAUL MISNER AND NEWMAN'S DEVELOPMENT OF THE PAPAL OFFICE

Paul Misner's 1976 study, *Papacy and Development: Newman and the Primacy of the Pope*, is significantly indebted to Coulson.[19] Arising from his own doctoral dissertation, written under the direction of Heinrich Fries for the University of Munich, Misner's research is easily the most subtle and thorough treatment of the subject to date. In a chapter entitled "Interdependent Functions in the Church: The *Schola Theologorum* and the Extent of Papal Power," he wrote of how Newman became disaffected with the exercise of Anglican episcopal oversight in the early 1840s and observed that this disaffection led Newman to speak in terms of divergent functions within the church–the free exercise of its regal office being the necessary precondition of its priestly office. Beyond this, there is no further mention of Newman's Anglican experience.[20] Rather, Misner limited his analysis to semantic occurrences of "*schola theologorum*" or near semantic parallels as they occur in Newman's Roman Catholic writings of the 1860s and 1870s.

Misner handled Newman's concept of the theological office in a bare sixteen pages, rooting his discussion, like Coulson, in the 1877 Preface to the *Lectures on the Prophetical Office of the Church*. But Misner also incorporated Newman's 1875 *Letter to the Duke of Norfolk* and various testimonial quotes culled from Newman's correspondence. Here, Misner better showed how Newman's *schola theologorum* was not precisely reducible to actual theological schools (Alexandria, Paris,

---

[19] Paul Misner, *Papacy and Development: Newman and the Primacy of the Pope* (Leiden: E. J. Brill, 1976).

[20] Misner, *Papacy and Development*, 159-60.

Rome, etc.), but represented more an abstracted consensus "where amidst many disputed questions the theologians of the church in communion with Rome nevertheless agreed."[21] Misner thus recognized how Newman's distribution of the "notes" of the church risked artificiality, but he nevertheless advocated the framework for the ways it provided the church with an instrument of correction. As he argued,

> [T]his multiplicity of diverse forces in the church . . . excludes from the outset the tendency to reduce church life to one of its functions, a besetting sin of Ultramontanes. Infallible definitions, for instance, are undoubtedly the province of ruling power–but only as taking over and sanctioning the accomplishments of the prophetic office, when necessity induces it to make such a rare move.[22]

Misner concluded that Newman opened the door for the thoroughgoing revision of ecclesiology in the post-Vatican II era, and he offered praise for the way Newman introduced an element of "constitution" beside that of "rule" into his ecclesiology. Here, Newman recovered the balance that had been so seriously threatened in the neo-ultramontanist party.[23] This study builds on these important insights. Unlike Misner, I argue that Newman's impulse to name a constitutional instrument for the church's theological "correction"–or as I think it better conceived, "rectification"–is already present in Newman's Anglican work.

JOHN BOYLE AND THE TEACHING AUTHORITY OF THE CHURCH

John Boyle's brief concluding chapter on "Problems and Prospects" in his larger *Church Teaching Authority: Historical and Theological Studies* has likewise made important use of Newman's 1877 Preface and the *Letter to the Duke of Norfolk*.[24] Although lacking the care for details

---

21 Misner, *Papacy and Development*, 161.

22 Misner, *Papacy and Development*, 165.

23 Misner, *Papacy and Development*.

24 John Boyle, *Church Teaching Authority: Historical and Theological Studies* (Notre Dame, IN: University of Notre Dame Press, 1995).

evident in Coulson and Misner (on whose work he clearly depends), Boyle suggested that there was a "considerable" difference between the Anglican Newman who authored the 1837 *Lectures on the Prophetical Office of the Church* and the Roman Catholic Newman who wrote forty years later. Of the former, Boyle said only that the Anglican Newman introduced the distinction between the "episcopal or apostolical office" and the "prophetical office" with the latter constituting theologians who are "successors to the New Testament *didaskaloi* (teachers)."[25] Of the latter, Boyle made his judgment that there was a "considerable" difference between Newman's earlier and later selves to hang on the latter's introduction of a third, sacerdotal office. Here Boyle simply neglected Newman's own indication in the 1837 advertisement that the limitations of space alone prevented his treating "the Sacerdotal as well as the Prophetical office of the Church."[26] Boyle was on firmer ground, however, when exploring Newman's ascription of preaching to the apostolic office of bishops while reserving the function of teaching to the *schola theologorum*.[27]

Of Newman's contribution to the discussion, Boyle commended the necessity for an "active, ongoing interaction among the various offices of the church that Newman depicts" and added:

> Newman had a lofty view of the role of bishops and of the pope in the church. But he also saw the need for balance among the church's various roles and functions. That balance is not something fixed once and for all; the changing life of the church requires that one function be emphasized at one time and another function at a later one. Newman saw the needs of the Anglican communion as different from those of the Catholic church. The body of Christ lives by changing and adapting.[28]

As goes Misner's analysis, so also goes that of Boyle. The neglect of Newman's Anglican career led Boyle to assume a sharp discontinuity

---

25 Boyle, *Church Teaching Authority*, 171.
26 Newman, *Pro*, in *VM* i, xi.
27 Boyle, *Church Teaching Authority*, 171-72.
28 Boyle, *Church Teaching Authority*, 173.

in Newman's thinking that did not exist in fact. This postulation of fundamental difference effectively severs Newman from himself and leads to an under-contextualized portrait. This book seeks to broaden this context so as to let the whole Newman speak.

AVERY CARDINAL DULLES ON NEWMAN AND THE POSTCONCILIAR HIERARCHY

Catholics of a more conservative nature have likewise embraced Newman as the "Father of the Second Vatican Council," but they have envisioned that patrimony functioning to establish a "true [i.e., "conservative"] understanding of the Council, free from ["progressive"] distortions and exaggerations."[29] In this vein, Avery Cardinal Dulles limited his focus to the same writings as Coulson, Misner, and Boyle, but he explored them so as to emphasize the singular unsuitability of Newman's conception for the present-day church. As he wrote,

> Theologians, many of whom are laypeople, do not constitute anything like the medieval *schola theologorum*. We do not commonly think of theologians as judges of orthodoxy, as was common in the late Middle Ages, but rather as explorers whose hypotheses need to be critically assessed by the hierarchical magisterium. As for the Pope and the bishops, we expect them to be guardians of revealed truth and not to yield to considerations of expediency. We connect the priestly office with the public liturgy rather than, as Newman did, with private devotions. While Newman correctly identified different tendencies in the Church, his division of powers among bishops, theologians,

---

29 In this vein see Ian Ker, "The Father of Vatican II," 7. Elsewhere Ker specifically deployed Newman in defense of Benedict XVI's programmatic restriction of conciliar reception and interpretation: "If there has been one keynote of Benedict XVI's pontificate, it has been 'the hermeneutic', or interpretation, 'of continuity'. By that the Pope means that the post-Vatican II Church needs to be understood in continuity, rather than disruption, with the Church of the past. It is not that the Pope denies the significance of the achievements of the Second Vatican Council but that he insists that that Council did not somehow cancel out all the other Councils or constitute so radical a disruption as to be equivalent to a revolution. It is above all in this respect that I am sure that the Pope will see the beatification of Newman as being of great importance for the Church." See Ian Ker, "Newman can lead us out of our post-Vatican II turmoil," *The Catholic Herald (10 July 2009)*: http://www.catholicherald.co.uk/.

and laity is not easily assimilable today. His position, moreover, can scarcely be reconciled with the Second Vatican Council, which taught that bishops "in an eminent and visible way, take on the functions of Christ himself as Teacher, Shepherd, and High Priest and act in his person" (*Lumen Gentium* 21).[30]

As with the prior works treated above, there is much to consider in Dulles's cautionary approach to the difference between the historical and contemporary implications of Newman's thought. His account, however, falls prey to a nearly identical weakness. By failing to attend to Newman's own practical implementation of his thinking in the 1830s and 1840s, Dulles is left with only his naked skepticism as to how Newman's conception of the *schola theologorum* might work in the present. He thereby removed the necessary hermeneutical distance between Newman's "prophetical" office of theology and the "regal" office of the magisterium and thereby evacuated the prophetic role of Newman's theological *munus*. In Dulles's account, therefore, Newman's *schola theologorum* is reduced to a kind of "court prophesy" where the magisterium speaks only from itself, for itself, and–as is too often the case–*to* itself.

DREW MORGAN AND THE FALL OF NEWMAN'S ANGLICAN SCHOOL

Drew Morgan published "The Rise and Fall of Newman's Anglican School: From the Caroline Divines to the *Schola Theologorum*" in 2009.[31] In many ways, his is a response to a pre-published version of my own essay, "Development in the Service of Rectification: Newman's

---

30 Avery Dulles, "Newman and the Hierarchy," in *John Henry Newman* (New York: Continuum, 2002), 17. It is hard to avoid the note of condescension in his use of "laypeople" here in his haste to buttress the distinctive authority of the magisterium. That aside, however, Cardinal Dulles's treatment of Newman's *schola theologorum* in a subsequent chapter on "the roles of theologians and the laity" is better developed but is only minimally suggestive and leaves the reader with less guidance when exploring the theological and ecclesiological implications of Newman's thought. See, 99-115.

31 Drew Morgan, "The Rise and Fall of Newman's Anglican School: From the Caroline Divines to the *Schola Theologorum*," *Newman Studies Journal* 6, no. 1 (Spring 2009): 20-35.

Understanding of the *Schola Theologorum*."[32] As was the case in my article, Morgan argued that Newman and other members of the Oxford Movement conceived of their project as an Anglican "school," attempting to root the Church of England in the witness of early Christianity. Because that witness preceded the Reformation-era schism between Rome and England, Tractarians felt a great urgency to locate their school in continuity with the Caroline Divines of the seventeenth century. In Morgan's analysis, this impulse gave birth to the precariously positioned *via media* of Newman's 1837 *Lectures on the Prophetical Office of the Church*. He then located the "fall" of Newman's Anglican school in his dawning awareness that, despite his desire to read the fathers of the church chronologically as a means to establish the antiquity of Anglicanism, the Caroline Divines were far more interested to deploy the fathers against Roman Catholicism. Thus, it became clear that the *via media* existed only on paper, and, given how Newman was increasingly able to make peace with distinctively "Roman" doctrines and practices, he became a man "without a School, and more frighteningly . . . a man without a church."[33]

Morgan additionally replicated Coulson's error, making much ado of Newman's nonexistent shift from a two-office understanding of the church in the 1837 *Lectures* to a three-office understanding in the 1877 Preface, but he rightly acknowledged how Newman "continued to maintain the necessity and even a certain type of primacy for the theological schools."[34] As I later make clear, Morgan also depends too heavily on Newman's *Apologia Pro Vita Sua* and thus makes far more of

---

[32] Michael J. G. Pahls, "Development in the Service of Rectification: Newman's Understanding of the *Schola Theologorum*," in Kenneth L. Parker and Michael J. G. Pahls, eds., *Authority, Dogma, and History: The Role of the Oxford Movement Converts in the Papal Infallibility Debates* (Bethesda, MD: Academica, 2009), 195-211. Although this article appeared in print in 2009, the essay was composed for a doctoral seminar at Saint Louis University in fall 2005. Morgan footnotes my article as it appeared on a personal website in 2005.

[33] Morgan, "The Rise and Fall of Newman's Anglican School," 27.

[34] Morgan, "The Rise and Fall of Newman's Anglican School," 31. Morgan is quick to add in a footnote, however, that "This description references the three as developed offices of church polity and is not a denial of the *primacy* of Peter."

Newman's appeal to the Caroline Divines than I think is warranted by contemporaneous evidence.

DEVELOPMENT IN THE SERVICE OF RECTIFICATION

Morgan's use of my prior work in this area requires some mention of my revised and expanded essay, "Development in the Service of Rectification: Newman's Understanding of the *Schola Theologorum*," as it appeared in the 2009 volume *Authority, Dogma, and History: The Role of the Oxford Movement Converts in the Papal Infallibility Debates*.[35] In many ways the latter portions of that essay are a pilot for the present study, but a word or two on the first half of my argument are in order for their contribution to this *status quaestionis*. While each of the preceding works has contributed to a better understanding of what Newman's *schola theologorum* does, it is equally important to clarify what the Catholic Newman thought the institutional manifestation of his prophetical office might look like.

As did the previous authors, I began my essay in the 1877 Preface, with Newman sketching out a theoretical ecclesiology patterned on the *triplex munus Christi*. Within this scheme, Newman named the prophetical office of theology, the sacerdotal office of the ministerial priesthood, and the regal office of the ruling episcopate as the practical manifestations of these offices in the church. The latter would take the form of "a synod of bishops" in an Anglican ecclesiology and a "teaching magisterium" in Catholic ecclesiology. As the 1877 Preface indicates, Newman understood that the institutional form of the prophetical office was both prior to, and foundational for, the other two offices. While he recognized that "theology cannot always have its own way," Newman maintained that such instances were a breach of the norm, and he vigorously defended the independence of the prophetic office against its effacement by the regal office.[36]

---

[35] Kenneth L. Parker and Michael J. G. Pahls, eds., *Authority, Dogma, and History: The Role of the Oxford Movement Converts in the Papal Infallibility Debates* (Bethesda, MD: Academica, 2009), 195-211.

[36] Newman, *VM* i, xlviii.

My essay then made recourse to various places where Newman spoke of the practical shape and function of the *schola theologorum* in occasional writings of the 1860s and 1870s. There, Newman spoke of the *schola theologorum* in one sense as a "generalization, for the decisions of theologians throughout the world," but he immediately recognized their "natural tendency to collect into centers," thus manifesting "a distinct character of their own, severally."[37] Newman then became even more specific, naming the competing schools of Alexandria and Antioch–schools that dominated the narrative in his first Anglican work, *The Arians of the Fourth Century*, as noteworthy examples.[38] The various medieval schools at the Universities of Paris and Bologna, and perhaps even Oxford as well, were likewise not far from his thinking.[39]

As Newman well recognized, "local disturbances" within the church constantly arise and threaten to set various local branches at odds with one another. On such occasions, the *judicat securus* of the universal

---

[37] Newman to Henry Nutcombe Oxenham (9 November 1865), *LD* xx, 98-99. These were manifestations of what Thomas Aquinas called the *magisterium cathedrae magistralis*. Cf., *Quodl*. 3,q. 4, a.1 (9). In both early and medieval Christian history bishops, the pope numbered among them, played something of a peripheral role in doctrinal disputes, only intervening when necessary. Often, the resolution of debates was left entirely to theological faculties functioning with ecclesiastical warrant and authority. See here Yves Congar's classic studies, "A Semantic History of the Term Magisterium" and "A Brief History of the Forms of the Magisterium and Its Relations with Scholars," in Charles Curran and Richard McCormick, eds., *The Magisterium and Morality: Readings in Moral Theology*, no. 3 (New York/ Ramsey, NJ: Paulist, 1982), 297-313, 314-31.

[38] Newman to Henry Nutcombe Oxenham (9 November 1865), *LD* xx, 99.

[39] Here I made use of Jacques M. Gres-Gayer's helpful reference to the theological faculty of Paris as a "self-perpetuating corporation of scholars" possessing a formally granted power to "read, teach, interpret Holy Scripture in Paris and everywhere on earth" to draw out Newman's understanding. Jacques M. Gres-Gayer, "The Magisterium of the Faculty of Theology of Paris in the Seventeenth Century," *Theological Studies* 53 (1992): 425. As I demonstrate later in this study, there is warrant in Newman's reflections on James Ingram's *Memorials of Oxford* (1837) in an article for the *British Critic* 24 (1838): 133-46, to suggest this. There Newman wrote of his own Oxford manifesting "a revival of that ancient energetic spirit, that resolve to take part and to have a voice in the world's matters, which is a distinguishing mark of the University in history. Its members have long determined that Church and State shall neither do, nor suffer, without their having a share in the doing or suffering" (133-34).

church was consulted to define doctrine and resolve such disputes. As he imagined it, the *schola theologorum* existed as the critical tool for recognizing and defining that secure judgment. As Newman understood it, "the great Catholic school of divines dispersed all over the earth," existed to discern and interpret the church's revealed faith as it was professed by the faithful.[40] By their various processes of inquiry and debate, theologians functioned collaboratively in service to the church, settling the force and wording of dogma "just as the courts of law solve the meaning and bearing of Acts of Parliament."[41] Thus the prophetical office, acting in its institutional form as the *schola theologorum*, plays a vital role in the development and *developmental rectification* of church doctrine.

Finally, it is important to note how Newman proved quite expansive in the way he refused to restrict operations of the *schola theologorum* to a single school based in Rome. Though as a faithful Roman Catholic, Newman resisted any temptation to uncritically extend manifestations to jurisdictions outside the Roman communion–thus, in 1869 he explicitly excluded "Greece" [that is, the Orthodox churches] and "England" [that is, Protestant Anglicanism]–he nevertheless understood the *schola theologorum* as something incorporated into the life of the whole church.

RECONTEXTUALIZING NEWMAN: OXFORD MOVEMENT STUDIES SINCE 1994

As the preceding survey has shown, while several interpreters have made cursory recognition of Newman's Anglican writings and their passing influence on his Roman Catholic thought, the present state of inquiry into Newman's conception of the *schola theologorum* has remained focused on those latter writings. Because of this, they lack proper historical contextualization and integration with his prior work.[42] As such, the present *status quaestionis* is underdeveloped and

---

40 Newman to Magdalene Helbert (20 October 1869), *LD* xxiv, 355.

41 Newman to William Henry Cope (10 December 1871), *LD* xxv, 447.

42 That this is a genuine lacuna in Newman studies is clear from a perusal of studies in foreign language works as well as in English. The most exhaustive treatment

overly susceptible to tendentious and partisan uses of the most extreme sort.[43] Absent the proposed historical touchstone, vitally connecting Newman's Catholic understanding to his Anglican Tractarian work, interpreters have tended along two divergent and distortive paths. Progressive interpreters have tended to view Newman's conception through the lens of a contemporary schism between church and academy. Exaggerating Newman's concern for the independence of the conscience and positing a dissident role vis-à-vis the magisterium, these accounts sit uneasily with Newman's professed lifelong hostility toward theological liberalism. On the other hand, a preoccupation with Newman's rejection of modernism and zeal for ecclesial authority has led conservative champions of Newman to suppress his emphasis on theology as something distinct and counterpointed to the regal office. This is to risk the removal of the very features that make Newman's "prophetical office" prophetical. Finally, most treatments of the *schola theologorum* have largely appeared before the recently achieved "revisionist" consensus in Oxford Movement studies and thus do not reflect an adequate appreciation of its centrality to Newman's Tractarian project.

---

of Newman's Anglican ecclesiology (or as he puts it, ecclesiologies) to date is that of Alain Thomasset, *L'Ecclésiologie De John Henry Newman Anglican (1816-1845)*, in *Bibliotheca Ephemeridum Theologicarum Lovaniensium*, 197 (Leuven: Peters, 2006). Though Thomasset conducts a thorough examination of Newman's *Lectures on the Prophetic Office of the Church* in particular, he does so only to further his exploration of a developing ecclesiology in Newman from "Calvinist" to "Anglo-catholic" to a gradually emerging "Roman" theory. In his treatment of Newman and tradition, Günter Biemer can speak of "the teaching church" with reference to the apostles, bishops, councils, and the papacy, but has nothing to say about theologians. Günter Biemer, *Überlieferung und Offenbarung: die Lehre von der Tradition nach John Henry Newman* (Freiburg: Herder, 1961). The two most important treatments of Newman's theology and his understanding of doctrinal development, Jan-Hendrik Walgrave's *Newman: Le Développement du Dogme* (Tournai-Paris: Casterman, 1957) and Nicholas Lash's *Newman on Development: The Search for an Explanation in History* (Shepherdstown, WV: Patmos, 1975), contain little if any mention of theologians or the *schola theologorum* as a generative force for dogmatic progress.

43 Garry Wills's deployment of Newman's *schola theologorum* is noteworthy here for the way he exhausts the form, but it is important to note the clear continuity between his own view and those of more reputable expositors. See his *Papal Sin: Structures of Deceit* (New York: Doubleday, 2000), 261-74.

The last two decades have witnessed a remarkable shift in the interpretation of Tractarianism. Whereas traditional accounts of the movement's history tended either toward uncritical approbation of the Oxford Movement–a divinely appointed "revival" of catholic and apostolic Christianity–or manifested in strident repudiation as an illicit compromise with Roman Catholicism, recent scholarship has been far more judicious.[44] Close attention to large-scale sociopolitical dynamics in Europe and studies of under-examined biographical eccentricities among individual Tractarians have given rise to a newfound sensitivity to important theological differences that existed within the Oxford Movement and the older High Church party of the Church of England. This, in turn, has led to greater clarity when describing the precise continuities and discontinuities existing between the Oxford Movement and prior incarnations of Anglicanism.[45]

In his groundbreaking study of early nineteenth-century English society, J. C. D. Clark interpreted the Oxford Movement as a direct consequence of, and a reaction to, dissolution in the eighteenth-century hierarchical and theopolitical *ancien regime*.[46] The prodigious historical work of Peter Nockles, rooted in the research of his published Oxford thesis, *The Oxford Movement in Context: Anglican High Churchmanship, 1760-1857*, is self-consciously indebted to Clark's revisionist portrait,

---

[44] Partisan histories, written to defend the Tractarians, include first-generation accounts of the Tractarians or their immediate progeny like Richard William Church's *The Oxford Movement: Twelve Years, 1833-1845* (London: Macmillan and Co., 1891), and Henry P. Liddon's four-volume *Life of Edward Bouverie Pusey* (London: Longmans, Green, Co., 1893-97). Contrariwise, partisan histories of the "resentful" among the first-generation "reminiscencers" include J. A. Froude's "The Oxford Counter-Reformation," in *Short Studies on Great Subjects*, vol. 4 (New York: Charles Scribners, 1883), 151-236. Also of note are the manifold extant anti-Tractarian works. See here Owen Chadwick, "The Oxford Movement and its Reminiscencers," in *The Spirit of the Oxford Movement: Tractarian Essays* (Cambridge: Cambridge University Press, 1990), 135-53.

[45] A helpful survey of this revisionist work is available in Kenneth Hylson-Smith's monograph, *High Churchmanship in the Church of England* (Edinburgh: T&T Clark, 1993).

[46] J. C. D. Clark, *English Society, 1688-1832: Ideology, Social Structure, and Political Practice During the* Ancien Regime (Cambridge: Cambridge University Press, 1985). A second revised and expanded edition of Clark's study appeared in 2000.

and he describes the Oxford Movement as part of a general revival in Anglican High Churchmanship emerging after the French Revolution.[47] While Nockles recognizes certain valid claims made by Tractarianism on Anglican history–and this will be important to note later in this project–he deploys a hermeneutic of discontinuity to highlight the selective and tenuous character of those claims and highlighted their fundamental revision of the received Protestant self-understanding of the Church of England.[48] Whereas prior Anglicanism understood itself as a thoroughly Protestant *via media* between Roman Catholicism and Puritanism, Nockles demonstrates how the Tractarians recast the Anglican *via media* as a third way between Roman Catholicism and Protestantism as such. This observation adds crucial texture to the contemporary study of the Oxford Movement and enables Nockles to account for the progressive "parting of the ways" between the Tractarians and onetime-sympathetic traditional High Churchmen.

Most important for this project is Nockles's article, "An Academic Counter-Revolution: Newman and Tractarian Oxford's Idea of a University," wherein he applies the general insights of his dissertation to

---

[47] Peter Nockles, *The Oxford Movement in Context: Anglican High Churchmanship, 1760-1857* (Cambridge: Cambridge University Press, 1994). Nockles's 1982 D.Phil. thesis was originally titled "Continuity and Change in British High Churchmanship, 1792-1850." In addition to *The Oxford Movement in Context*, he has published a number of supporting articles and chapters. Most important to my research have been his "The Oxford Movement: Historical Background, 1780-1833," in *Tradition Renewed: The Oxford Movement Conference Papers*, ed., G. Rowell (Allison Park, PA: Pickwick, 1986), 24-50; "Oxford, Tract 90, and the Bishops," in *John Henry Newman: Reason, Rhetoric, and Romanticism*, eds., D. Nicholls and F. Kerr (Carbondale, IL: Southern Illinois University Press, 1991), 28-87; and "'Lost Causes . . . and Impossible Loyalties': The Oxford Movement and the University," in *The History of the University of Oxford*, vol. VI: *Nineteenth-Century Oxford*, part 1, eds., M. G. Brock and M. C. Curthoys (Oxford: Clarendon, 1997), 195-276.

[48] Nockles has cautiously ventured that "the *protean* quality of the texts of seventeenth-century Anglican divinity ultimately eluded Tractarian efforts to appropriate them definitively in support of all the Movement's doctrines and practices and to pass them off as the Church of England's 'official' teaching." Peter Nockles, "Survivals or New Arrivals? The Oxford Movement and the Nineteenth Century Historical Construction of Anglicanism," in *Anglicanism and the Western Christian Tradition: Continuity, Change, and the Search for Communion*, ed., Stephen Platten (Norwich: Canterbury, 2003), 190-91.

the Tractarians' efforts at academic reform in the 1830s and 40s. While Nockles does not explore the implications of this work for Newman's conception of the prophetical office of the church or of his Catholic conception of the *schola theologorum*, he instinctively recognizes the clear connections between Newman's Oxford and Tractarian experiences and his later Catholic reflection on the nature of university education. Nockles's work in this article is especially important for the way it charts the roads not taken throughout Newman's experience as a tutor at Oriel College, in Newman's failure to secure his own professorship at Oxford, and in the consequences of his Catholic turn immediately prior to the *Tract 90* controversy. While I focus much more on Newman's theological development over the course of his Anglican life, Nockles's work on the institutional and pedagogical aspects of Newman's academic "counterrevolution" has been foundational to my own.

Following closely in the wake of Nockles's broader project, Anglican theologian Paul Avis presses Nockles's case still further, making use of the latter's conclusions to defend the essential Protestant identity of the Church of England and to deny continuities between the Oxford Movement and historic Anglicanism altogether.[49] Appearing in 1989 and republished with extensive revision and expansion in 2002, Avis's case represents a stridently partisan account of Tractarianism that treats Newman's secession to Roman Catholicism in 1845 as both self-evidently necessary and as *prima facie* evidence of the movement's being an aberration. According to his account, both Tractarianism and the Anglo-Catholic Ritualism that followed in its wake represent a wholly constructed theological identity that must be interpreted according to a hermeneutic of *apostasis*.[50]

---

[49] Paul Avis, *Anglicanism and the Christian Church: Theological Resources in Historical Perspective*, revised and expanded ed. (London: T & T Clark, 2002).

[50] "Ritualism" here refers to a movement of liturgical renewal that arose in the wake of the Oxford Movement in the Church of England. Having established the general normativity of the Christianity in late antiquity and emphasizing the importance of the "real presence" of Christ in the Eucharist, "Ritualism" sought to recover the liturgical settings and actions of the Church of England as they existed prior to the English Reformation. The chief representative work of this movement is the now-classic *Ritual Notes on the Order of Divine Service* (Oxford: Mowbray,

The work of Clark and Nockles has been of incomparable benefit to the field of Oxford Movement studies. Their basic account of Tractarianism is thus achieving a near-hegemonic status. That being said, there remains a question of how we are to inflect their observed differences between Tractarian Anglo-Catholicism and traditional High Churchmanship. While Nockles's hermeneutic of discontinuity stands uncontested in this project, Avis's narrative of apostasy is not treated as a necessary corollary. Rather, a properly thickened account of Newman's conception of the theological office allows us to appreciate the self-conscious nature of his constructed, Catholic Anglicanism in *Tract 90* especially. As I argue, Newman in particular, recognized in the parliamentary reforms of 1828-1832 a waning influence of the English monarchy as a vital center of theological gravity in the Church of England. With this came the specter of the church's official disestablishment. It becomes natural by light of Newman's latter reflections on the *schola theologorum* to interpret Tractarianism as the attempt of *theologians* to rehabilitate Anglicanism's flagging theological *raison d'etre*. They did this by interpreting, clarifying, and even rectifying its historical self-understanding. Far from apostasy, these activities of hermeneutical recovery can be better understood as a self-conscious prophetic critique of sectarian tendencies within the Church of England and as the attempt to establish Anglicanism in a fuller, more richly integrated, catholicity.

TYRRELL'S GAUNTLET AND THICK DESCRIPTION: THE LETTER AND SPIRIT OF NEWMAN

The field of Newman studies has always witnessed a diverse and politicized scholarship. This is due in large part to the circumstances of his conversion from Anglicanism to Roman Catholicism at the midpoint of his life. The shadow cast by his own autobiographical account of that pilgrimage in the *Apologia Pro Vita Sua* (1864) has proved difficult to overcome. Barely a decade after Newman's death, the modernist Catholic, George Tyrrell, lamented in his own day the manner in which

---

1894). See Nigel Yates, *Anglican Ritualism in Victorian Britain, 1830-1910* (Oxford: Oxford University Press, 2000).

"Theologians of every colour, black, white, and grey, have tried to appropriate Newman, and to forbid any interpretation of his teaching but their own."[51] Prior to Vatican II, Roman Catholic authors tended to lionize Newman as a champion convert to their cause, emphasizing the radical nature of his break with Anglicanism and treating events prior to 1840 as unfortunate "preliminaries."[52] Catholic biographers since the Second Vatican Council have tended to treat his Anglican career much more positively, but with the proviso that these years represent an attractive way of being Catholic rather than authentically Anglican.[53] Non-Catholic authors, mostly (but not exclusively) of Anglican extraction, have likewise focused for partisan reasons either positively or negatively on Newman's Tractarian career, either celebrating his memory as the font of an Anglican renewal or castigating him as a self-deceived false prophet.[54] These general partisan tendencies like-

---

51 George Tyrrell, "Introduction," in Henri Brémond, *The Mystery of Newman* (London: Williams and Norgate, 1907), xiii. Wilfrid Ward was the principal object of Tyrrell's remarks here, but they were and are much more widely applicable.

52 In this vein, the chief exemplar is the early biography written by Wilfrid Ward, *The Life of John Henry Newman Based on His Private Journals and Correspondence*, 2 vols. (London: Longmans, Green, & Co., 1912). There Ward treats the entire course of Newman's Anglican career in a bare 78 of a total 537 pages!

53 Vincent Ferrer Blehl's *Pilgrim Journey: John Henry Newman 1801-1845* (New York: Paulist, 2001) treats Newman's Anglican period exclusively, but the portrait that emerges is of a Catholic saint becoming the Catholic he already was. This is something of an unsurprising feature given that from 1986 to his death in 2001, Blehl served as Postulator of the Cause for Newman's Roman Catholic canonization. See also a whole host of standard biographical treatments by Catholic members of the International Circle of Newman Friends: Ian Ker, *John Henry Newman: A Biography* (Oxford: Oxford University Press, 1988); Sheridan Gilley, *Newman and His Age* (London: Darton, Longman, and Todd, 1990); and Mary Jo Weaver, ed., *Newman and the Modernists* (Lanham, MD: University Press of America, 1985). See also Ian Ker's *The Achievement of John Henry Newman* (Notre Dame, IN: University of Notre Dame Press, 1990).

54 Works in the former category include contemporary Anglican treatments by Geoffrey Rowell, *The Vision Glorious: Themes and Personalities of the Catholic Revival in Anglicanism* (Oxford: Oxford University Press, 1983), and Arthur Middleton, *Fathers and Anglicans: The Limits of Orthodoxy* (Herfordshire: Gracewing, 2001), 267-306. The primary exemplar of the latter tendency is the work of Frank Turner, *John Henry Newman: The Challenge to Evangelical Religion* (New Haven: Yale University Press, 2002). Of this portrait, reviewer Lawrence Cunningham concludes:

wise distill into treatments of the salient features of Newman's intellectual contribution and into passive treatments of his conception of the *schola theologorum* since the Second Vatican Council (1962-1965). For postconciliar Roman Catholics of a progressive disposition, Newman is John XXIII (or Francis) ahead of time, and he is portrayed as a principal steward of the Catholic flame in the dark and repressive neo-ultamontanist insurgency with its representative "Pian" papacies.[55]

As the above survey of the scholarly field suggests, however, both Newman and the Oxford Movement arise from a history that leaves many ragged edges for the would-be historian and expositor. Tyrrell himself recognized this and suggested that Newman's own work validates divergent claims to his mantle: "Intransigents will not readily admit that the progressives have good right to appeal to his principles; nor the progressives that his sympathies were entirely opposed to them; nor the twilight moderates that he had nothing whatever in common with them either in one respect or the other."[56] Contrasting Newman's "spirit and method" with "the very substance and letter of [his] doctrine," Tyrrell decried attempts in his own day to impose the latter

---

"Turner does not much like Newman and takes every opportunity to demonstrate that dislike." See his "Review of *John Henry Newman: The Challenge to Evangelical Religion*," *Horizons* 30 (2003): 146.

55 This division has proved to be particularly stark in the uses made of Newman among Roman Catholic theologians as they have reflected on the "ecclesial role of the theologian" following upon the promulgation of 1968 encyclical, *Humane Vitae*. Traditionalist Catholics have long insisted on the infallible teaching authority of the pope as he gives voice to the church's "ordinary magisterium." Because the contents of "ordinary magisterial" teaching are not precisely delineated as when the pope solemnly defines an infallible dogma, questions have been raised regarding the propriety and limits of faithful dissent among theologians. Coupled with the well-publicized critique of papal infallibility in the work of Hans Küng and the censure of several prominent Roman Catholic theologians in the intervening decades, the Congregation for the Doctrine of the Faith issued its 1990 instruction, *Donum Veritatis: On the Ecclesial Role of the Theologian* (Vatican City: Libreria Editrice Vaticana, 1990). Responses to the instruction by theologians and national bishops' conferences are manifold, and a listing of them is beyond the scope of this project, but mention must be made here of the deployment of Newman in service, both to the traditionalist and progressive causes.

56 George Tyrrell, "Introduction," in Henri Brémond, *The Mystery of Newman* (London: Williams and Norgate, 1907), xvii.

on the world as "a rigid rule of correct judgment." Mocking those who were already campaigning to have Newman declared a Doctor of the Church, he urged, "It is the man, not the Cardinal, that we would fain preserve in our midst; the living Newman, not the poor 'Clothes-Screen' in marble, senile and decrepit, that solicits our tears on the Brompton Road."[57] Bewailing this trend, Tyrrell lamented, "His synthesis, now obsolete, has been canonised at the expense of his synthetic spirit."[58] On the other hand, Tyrrell had little patience for those who would cast off all commitment to historical traces in order to use Newman as a wax nose. Recognizing that Newman indeed "forged one or two weapons against [Latitudinarians] which have since (whether fairly or unfairly) been actually turned to their service," he thus reminded interpreters of Newman's direct and lifelong combat against Latitudinarianism. Here, Tyrrell warned, "Many to-day justly call Martin Luther 'father' whom Luther would have burnt."[59]

While remaining aloof from Tyrrell's skepticism as to the possibility of an adequate theological analysis, I am persuaded by his proposal that we undertake studies of Newman with an eye toward capturing his "spirit and method." Tyrrell commended what has in our own era been called a "post-critical" disposition to Newman, suggesting that his ideal expositor is one "who, having passed from the ardour of discipleship to the stage of cool-headed comprehension, could unite the advantages of the inside and the outside standpoint."[60] Numerous contemporary interpreters have noted Newman's developed conception of the *schola theologorum* in his later writings as a Roman Catholic; I argue that those analyses have largely been restricted to direct semantic references so that critical historical and conceptual parallels in Newman's earlier Anglican-Tractarian writings have gone unacknowledged. Whether

[57] Tyrrell, "Introduction," x.

[58] Tyrrell, "Introduction," ix.

[59] Tyrrell, "Introduction," xv.

[60] Tyrrell, "Introduction," x-xi. Cf., Michael J. G. Pahls, "Beyond Ideology and Utopia: Towards a Post-Critical Historical Theology," *Credo ut Intelligam* 2 (2009): 1-8. Here, a post-critical historical theology is framed by recourse to the philosophy of Paul Ricoeur.

rooted in a now-discredited confidence in the power of lexicography to account for conceptual development or simply a desire to narrow the scope of an otherwise unwieldy inquiry (and the two concerns are mutually supportive), the restriction of Newman's conception of the *schola theologorum* to his explicit uses of the terminology results invariably in a too-narrow and thin description.[61]

My proposed methodological alternative is to develop a "thick description" of Newman's thought. Rooted in the work of ordinary language theorist Gilbert Ryle, "thick description" means sufficiently

---

61 Theological lexicography was originally the child of Hermann Cremer who first published his *Biblisch-theologisches Wörterbuch der neutestamentlichen Gräcität* in 1867. This work went through ten editions between 1867 and 1915, and the entire project was revamped by Gerhard Kittel and later Gerhard Friedrich beginning in 1932. This work was translated into English by Geoffrey Bromiley as the nearly-ubiquitous *Theological Dictionary of the New Testament*, eds., G. Kittel and G. Friedrich, 10 vols. (Grand Rapids: Eerdmans, 1964-1976). Cremer's original task was flawed but still rooted in scientific lexicography. Under Kittel's direction, however, the work came to include not only "external" lexicography but "internal" lexicography as well. Internal lexicography, however, is not lexicography at all but the study of *concepts* on the basis of the terms used to express them. However reasonable this may seem at first, the method does not support the claims made for it. As the subsequent linguistic work (more properly called "semiotics") of Ferdinand de Saussure demonstrates, words do not refer to things or concepts except in contextual discourse. See his *Course in General Linguistics*, trans. R. Harris (Peru, IL: Open Court, 1986). As Shakespeare bears witness, apart from its contextual deployment (by someone, to someone, with reference to someone), the lexeme "rose" would by any other name smell as sweet (*Romeo and Juliet*, Act 2, scene 2). Because words cannot of themselves bear conceptual freight, a too narrow focus on semantic parallels can lead either to what James Barr has called an "illegitimate totality transfer"–loading a word with a multiplicity of meanings possible for that word or to an overdependence on semantic parallels to the exclusion of conceptual parallels, rooted in discursive context, with or without the use of a given terminology. For a fuller discussion, see Barr's *Semantics of Biblical Language* (Oxford: Oxford University Press, 1961), or the more recent work of Moisés Silva, *Biblical Words and Their Meaning: An Introduction to Lexical Semantics*, revised ed. (Grand Rapids: Zondervan, 1994). The overdependence on theological lexicography is not the sole domain of biblical studies, of course, and the search for semantic parallels is a feature of much historical-theological work where the account of conceptual development is a key value. Whether we want to lay blame for this at the feet of a hegemonic enthusiasm for such methods in the theological education of a generation ago or in the ease by which a limited focus on semantic parallels can help to circumvent contextual reading in an overlarge corpus, however, the general critique holds.

accounting for an action so as not to lose its intentionality.[62] Put differently, a description is sufficiently thick when it allows us to appreciate everything an actor is doing in the execution of an action. Thin description of an action–Ryle uses the example of a man writing his name–would be a minimal account only: "The man is inscribing the seven letters of his surname on a sheet of paper."[63] Such an account is thin because it omits the necessary context to discern his intended communicative action. Once we appropriately thicken the account–in Ryle's example, the man is "a statesman" and the sheet of paper "a drafted peace-treaty"–a thickened description of the action is made possible: "[The statesman] is bringing a war to a close by inscribing the seven letters of his surname."[64]

Thin descriptions are easy enough to identify because of the way that they undersell the full intentionality of an actor. The present *status quaestionis* described here is an ideal exemplar. I argue that Newman intended *more* than his Catholic uses of *schola theologorum* reveal. To thicken the account, therefore, I propose to begin with the accounts of Coulson, Misner, Boyle, and Morgan above to bring these reflections on the Catholic into creative dialogue with his work as an Anglican Tractarian. It is my contention that attending to these conceptual parallels, the Oxford Movement itself can be viewed as an attempted institutional manifestation of Newman's prophetical office and thus as a forerunner of his *schola theologorum*. The bare similitude of his Anglican activities to his latter Catholic reflection would seem to warrant such a move, but this connection gains considerable explanatory power when we consider how Newman himself republished *The Arians of the Fourth Century* in new edition in 1871 and republished his *Lectures on the Prophetical Office of the Church* in 1877 with the all-important Preface.

---

[62] See Ryle's essays "Thinking and Reflecting" and "The Thinking of Thoughts: What is 'le Penseur' Doing," in Gilbert Ryle, *Collected Papers*, vol. 2 (New York: Barnes & Noble, 1971), 465-79, 496. Of course, better known for his popularization of the concept of "thick description" is cultural anthropologist Clifford Geertz. See here Geertz's essay, "Thick Description: Toward an Interpretative Theory of Culture," in *The Interpretation of Cultures* (New York: Basic Books, 1973), 3-13.

[63] Ryle, "The Thinking of Thoughts: What is 'le Penseur' Doing," 496.

[64] Ryle, "The Thinking of Thoughts: What is 'le Penseur' Doing."

Here Newman himself brought his prophetical *munus* into direct dialogue with his conception of the *schola theologorum*.⁶⁵ By gesturing to this broader historical-theological context himself, Newman becomes a guide to a fuller, thicker understanding of his mature thought.

Sufficiency can be an asymptotic goal when attempting thick description. Any proposed attempt at such will be provisional and must therefore remain open to additional thickening. While I cannot hope to claim that my proposed dialogue between the Anglican Newman and the Catholic Newman will exhaust his intentionality, I am confident that this reading of the former by light of the latter and vice-versa will yield both a thicker portrait of Newman's Catholic conception of the *schola theologorum* and a more suggestive account of Newman's Anglican intentions than presently exists.

---

65 In his preface Newman wrote, "I say, then, Theology is the fundamental and regulating principle of the whole Church system. It is commensurate with Revelation, and Revelation is the initial and essential idea of Christianity. It is the subject-matter, the formal cause, the expression, of the Prophetical Office, and, as being such, has created both the Regal Office and the Sacerdotal. And it has in a certain sense a power of jurisdiction over those offices, as being its own creations, theologians being ever in request and in employment in keeping within bounds both the political and popular elements in the Church's constitution,–elements which are far more congenial than itself to the human mind, are far more liable to excess and corruption, and are ever struggling to liberate themselves from those restraints which are in truth necessary for their well-being." *VM* i, xlvii-xlviii.

CHAPTER 1

Adrift in the Schools of Private Judgment

In a rarely noticed portion of his 13 January 1839 sermon on *The Nature of Faith in Relation to Reason*, John Henry Newman speculated on the propensity of human beings to "form into schools."[1] The sermon itself attempted to account for faith as an exercise of reason. In the same way that ordinary reason proceeds from what is known–mediating the knowledge of beings, facts, and events otherwise imperceptible by immediate sense experience–so faith proceeds from testimony to mediate the knowledge of unseen divine things. At root for Newman was the role of unstated or even unexamined presuppositions–premises that factor decisively, but imperceptibly, in the reasoning process. As Newman wrote, "there must ever be something assumed ultimately which is incapable of proof . . . its cogency must be a thing taken for granted; so far as it is its own evidence, and can only be received on instinct or prejudice."[2] These assumptions, be they the general reliability of sense experience, the general stability of nature, or the reliability of memory, allow for a certain predictability in human decision-making and account better for differences in party spirit or personal opinion than baser charges of faulty reasoning. For Newman, these *a priori* differences create the condition for what he habitually described throughout his writings as "schools."

Human beings do not generally reason badly in Newman's estimation. Acknowledging a view, common enough in his own day as in our own, that differences of opinion arise "from a want of mental conformity with the laws on which just reasoning is conducted," he objected,

---

1 Newman, *US*, 3rd ed. (London: Rivingtons, 1872), 212.
2 Newman, *US*, 213.

"surely there is no greater mistake than this." Rather, "the experience of life contains abundant evidence that in practical matters, when their minds are really roused, men commonly are not bad reasoners." They "do not mistake when their interest is concerned" and have "an instinctive sense in which direction their path lies toward it, and how they must act consistently with self-preservation or self-aggrandizement."[3] Each does not reason in his or her own way, and human beings gather into "schools"–understood here as reasoning communities–"not merely from imitation and sympathy, but certainly from internal compulsion, from the constraining influence of their several principles."[4] In Newman's view, then, faith is not unreason or weak reason but "unearthly" and "divinely illuminated" reason. That is, the assumptions and values giving rise to schools come to Christians, and as will be presently clear in Newman's thinking, to theologians particularly, as a divine charism and vocation.

These observations, written as Newman rapidly approached the sunset of his Anglican career, raise two related questions. First, given Newman's repeated appeal to the *schola theologorum* throughout his Roman Catholic reflections on ecclesiology and the exercise of authority in the church, where did Newman develop the capacity to think of schools in this way? Second, exactly what were the "several principles" constraining and compelling Newman to disassociate from the given Anglican schools available to him at the dawn of the nineteenth century in order to form his own distinctive school that we now describe under the name "Tractarianism" and "Oxford Movement?" This chapter will suggest an answer to both questions.

Numerous authors have noted the critical roles that theological liberalism and Protestant evangelicalism played in Newman's early life.[5] Although these studies have traced the varied ways that the two

---

3 Newman, *US*, 211.

4 Newman, *US*, 212.

5 Although his work calls for significant correction in places, Frank Turner's work remains important for the way he consistently casts Newman's Anglican period as a reactive critique of evangelicalism. Frank Turner, *John Henry Newman: The Challenge to Evangelical Religion* (New Haven, CT: Yale University Press, 2002). See also his "Editor's Introduction," in *The Apologia Pro Vita Sua and Six Sermons* (New

star-crossed and yet converging traditions appear in his thinking, no study has yet drawn the proper implications of Newman's own connection between liberalism and evangelicalism on the one hand, and the various proto-Arian and orthodox schools that he names in *The Arians of the Fourth Century* on the other. Indeed, his identification of the catechetical school at Alexandria as a historical-theological precedent demonstrably grounded his aspirations to form a school of "traditionary religion" at Oxford.

To tell that story well, however, it is necessary to retrace Newman's steps as he made his way through multiple personal encounters with what he later regarded as the false "schools" of liberalism and evangelicalism. Here I will explore anew the ways that these experiences bequeathed to him a unique set of "severable principles" that he would winnow and apply as a Tractarian. Although he would undeniably carry much from both schools with him, Newman also came to identify "private judgment" as their point of common heretical origin, leading necessarily to a common, apostate end. Far from being the product of a late polemical revision of his early religious development, Newman's

---

Haven: Yale University Press, 2008), 1-118. See also, Michael McClymond, "Continual Self-Reflection: John Henry Newman's Critique of Evangelicalism," in *Tradition and Pluralism: Essays in Honor of William M. Shea*, eds. Kenneth L. Parker, Peter A. Huff, and Michael J. G. Pahls (Lanham, MD: University Press of America, 2009); Thomas Sheridan, *Newman on Justification* (New York: Alba House, 1967); David Newsome, "Justification and Sanctification: Newman and the Evangelicals," *Journal of Theological Studies* 15 (1964): 32-53; and T. C. F. Stunt, "John Henry Newman and the Evangelicals," *Journal of Ecclesiastical History* 21 (1970): 65-74 for Newman's evangelical background. Although he overplays the degree to which the Oxford Noetics could be described as liberals prior to the Hampden affair, Robert Pattison in *The Great Dissent: John Henry Newman and the Liberal Heresy* (Oxford: Oxford University Press, 1991) remains helpful. Finally, Peter Nockles is helpful for his contextualization of Newman's pre-Tractarian experience in the late eighteenth and early nineteenth centuries. In addition to his *Oxford Movement in Context*, see his "The Oxford Movement: Historical Background 1780-1833," in *Tradition Renewed: The Oxford Movement Conference Papers*, ed. Geoffrey Rowell (London: Darton, Longman and Todd, 1986), 24-50, and his "Survivals or New Arrivals? The Oxford Movement and the Nineteenth-Century Historical Construction of Anglicanism," in *Anglicanism and the Western Christian Tradition: Continuity, Change and the Search for Communion*, ed. Stephen Platten (Norwich: Canterbury Press, 2003), 144-91. [See also, Geertjan Zuijdwegt, *Evangelicals Adrift: The Making of John Henry Newman's Theology* (Washington, DC: Catholic University of America Press, 2022.)]

near identification of evangelicalism and liberalism appeared quite naturally in his journey as a considered theological judgment, developed in personal encounters that he saw reflected in his early professional, ecclesial, and political context.

RHETORICISING HISTORY: NEWMAN'S SOJOURN IN THE EVANGELICAL SCHOOL

By his own recollection, Newman was not the product of an evangelical household.[6] In the early chapters of his *Apologia Pro Vita Sua*, he wrote of his family's religious allegiance to "the national religion of

---

[6] Given the rather loose manner in which "evangelical" is used in the writings of and concerning John Henry Newman, I have adopted the "quadrilateral" approach of David Bebbington to speak with categorical specificity. In his study, Bebbington identifies "evangelicalism" as manifesting four main or essential features: 1) "Conversionism," or an experienced transformation of life, notionally if not temporally distinct from baptism, accompanied by personal assurance of one's salvation; 2) "Activism," or energetic labor to insure the conversion of others and to promote the social ethics of the Gospel; 3) "Biblicism," or devotion to the Bible as the sufficient source of spiritual truth and sole authority in matters of doctrine and ethics; and 4) "Crucicentrism," or giving special emphasis to the substitutionary-sacrificial role of Jesus and to his atoning death on the cross as the central action of God in accomplishing human salvation. See *Evangelicalism in Modern Britain: A History from the 1730s to the 1980s*, 2nd ed. (London: Routledge, 1989), 1-17. Bebbington's quadrilateral has been criticized in recent years as being vague and potentially distortive. It must also be remembered that his categories are intended to embrace an unwieldy 250 years of evangelical experience. See here D. A. Carson's attempt to define evangelicalism globally according to missiologist Paul Hiebert's "center-bounded set" model. *Evangelicalism: What is it and is it Worth Keeping* (Wheaton, IL: Crossway, 2012). That said, Bebbington's categories have proved exceptionally durable and compare favorably with other studies. Compare, for example, Bebbington's four features with Peter Toon's definition: "An Evangelical Anglican has a strong attachment to the Protestantism of the national Church with its Articles of Religion and Prayer Book. He believes that the Bible is authoritative in matters of faith and conduct and is to be read individually and in the home as well as in church. He emphasizes the doctrine of justification by faith but with good works and a specific (holy) life-style as the proof of true faith. He claims to enjoy a personal relationship with God through Christ, the origins of which are usually traced not to sacramental grace but to a conversion experience. And he sees the primary task of the Church in terms of evangelism or missions and so emphasizes preaching at home and abroad." *Evangelical Theology 1833-1856: A Response to Tractarianism* (Atlanta: John Knox, 1979), 5.

England" and its "Bible religion." This consisted "not in rites or creeds, but mainly in having the Bible read in Church, in the family, and in private."[7] Newman's account here comports well with what can be known of his life by other sources.[8] Newman's father, John, professed no partisan allegiances beyond those common to the Church of England and seemed quite willing to entertain any number of controversial ideas, weighing each of them according to their merits.[9] The adult John Henry additionally recalled being "brought up from a child to take great delight in reading the Bible" and acknowledged his indebtedness for these affections to his grandmother and to his Aunt Elizabeth, with whom he stayed as a boy.[10] Prior to his fifteenth year, Newman wrote of having formed "no religious convictions," and context suggests that we understand him as affirming no partisan convictions as an adherent of a particular Anglican school.

---

[7] Newman, *GA* (London: Burns, Oates and Co., 1870), 54. Newman, of course, did recall in his *Apologia* that he was possessed of "perfect knowledge" of his Catechism, found in the 1662 *Book of Common Prayer*. Cf., Newman, *Apo* (London: Longman, Green, Longmans, Roberts and Green, 1864), 55.

[8] Newman's nephew, J. B. Mozley, testified to his mother's recollection of no evangelical or Calvinistic influences in Newman's boyhood home: "You are at liberty . . . to refer to me as giving my *mother's* evidence that the teaching in the Cardinal's home was not either Calvinistic or Evangelical; I think it was soon after the publication of the 'Apologia' that she said this to me." John Henry Newman, et al., *The Correspondence of John Henry Newman with John Keble and Others, 1839-1845* (London: Longmans Green, 1917), 394.

[9] Francis Newman once described John Newman as "*somewhat free-thoughted, fond of seeing* what different people had to say for their opinions. A reader and admirer of the works of Barclay the Quaker, he could not bear John Newton, in whose parish, St. Benet Fink, he lived, on account of his connection with the slave trade, and perhaps his Calvinism. He was a Whig, despised the city companies, and never cared to take up his freedom, though it might have done him some little good in his bank. He was of independent mind, and looked at things from his own point of view, but, having no political influence, he did not say much." Newman, *Correspondence of John Henry Newman with John Keble and Others*, 394.

[10] Newman later wrote to his Aunt Elizabeth, "Whatever good there is in me, I owe, under grace, to the time I spent in that house [at Fulham] and to you and to my dear Grandmother, its inhabitants." Newman to Aunt Elizabeth Newman (25 July 1844), *LD* x, 303.

In the succeeding fifteen years of his life, however, Newman became deeply entangled in the partisan religious conflicts that characterized early nineteenth-century England. These developed throughout his sojourn into a distinctive set of partisan convictions that were uniquely his own. Passing through adolescence and into adulthood, he encountered the pitched battle between modernity's "heretical imperative" on one hand, and Christian orthodoxy on the other. This battle was initially waged in the fields of his own religious interiority as a convert to evangelicalism, but it later opened on to new fronts in the religious travails of his family, his country, and his church.[11] In briefly revisiting the details of his journey, it becomes easier to see what he jettisoned and what he retained. It also clarifies how he cast his own Anglican school as a solution to the errors he saw amid the competing schools of his day.

Newman's induction into the "evangelical school," as he sometimes called it, occurred as an embolism between perilous twin exposures

---

11 "Heretical imperative" is the terminology coined by sociologist, Peter Berger, in his *The Heretical Imperative: Contemporary Possibilities of Religious Affirmation* (New York: Anchor/Doubleday, 1979). As Berger uses the term, he intends that multitude of religious options presented by modernity that make the individual religious choice both necessary and possible. Berger uses the word "heretical" in the sense of "optional" rather than "deviant," but the observation that individual religious choice or "private judgment" supersedes dogmatic attempts to foreclose otherwise viable religious alternatives is very much what Newman had in mind. This corresponds, roughly, to the definitions of Avery Cardinal Dulles: "approximately ... the privatization of religion and its reduction to private sentiment," and Terrence Merrigan: "essentially a form of solipsism, a conviction that truth, especially in matters of religion, is a private affair." See Avery Dulles, *Newman* (New York: Continuum, 2002), 14 and Terrence Merrigan, "Newman and Theological Liberalism," *Theological Studies* 66 (2005): 608. Frank Turner has complained that Newman scholarship has yet to assign a substantial historical content or meaning to Newman's use of liberalism, and clarity is made difficult as we observe with Owen Chadwick that "what Newman denounced as liberalism, no one else regarded as liberalism." See Frank Turner, "Editor's Introduction," in Newman, *Apo* (New Haven, CT: Yale University Press, 2008), 57 and Owen Chadwick, *Newman: A Short Introduction* (Oxford: Oxford University Press, 1983), 74. While it is true that Newman was indiscriminate in his application of the label, Turner's virtual identification of liberalism and evangelical Protestantism in Newman's mind seems too strident. Rather, we must bear in mind that Newman's animus toward Evangelicalism was always rooted in the idea that it provided no sure defense against *unbelief*.

to theological liberalism.[12] Although Newman's precise understanding of the term "liberalism" bears further examination, his exposure to Thomas Paine's *Tracts against the Old Testament* and David Hume's *Essays* provoked in him certain habits of mind that he would later associate with the term.[13] Of the former author he confessed to the dangerous pleasure he found in thinking of the Paine's objections. He also wrote of certain writings in French–perhaps by Voltaire–denying the immortality of the soul. Newman recalled the intriguing power of their propositions, glossing his adolescent reaction as "How dreadful, but how plausible!"[14] This corresponded to sentiments Newman previously recorded in a private notebook from 1823:

> I recollect (in 1815 I believe) thinking I should like to be virtuous, but not religious. There was something in the latter idea I did not like. Nor did I see the *meaning* of loving God. I recollect (in 1815) contending

---

[12] The phrase "evangelical school" first appears in Newman's correspondence in a letter from Thomas Dyke Acland dated 25 May 1834, and it seems clear that it was not Newman's invention. Evidence of Newman's use of James Stephen can be dated from (16 March 1835), *LD* v, 47. Cf, also *LD* xi, 129, 131; *LD* ix, 575; and *LD* xxi, 313.

[13] The reference of evangelicalism here as a "school" derives from the overall argument of this chapter, but it remains noteworthy that Newman himself referred to the evangelicalism and liberalism of his own experience as "schools." In his elegiac essay on John Keble, published shortly after his conversion to Roman Catholicism in 1846, he praised Keble's expressions of devotion to the Blessed Virgin in the verses of "Orphanhood" in *The Christian Year*. Newman noted, however, the ways that Keble softened his language to assuage Protestants. He then complained of "the *Evangelical school*, which never allows the mention of one doctrine of religion without a recapitulation of all the rest." See Newman, "Art. VIII.–*Lyra Innocentium: Thoughts in Verse on Christian Children, their Ways and their Privileges*," *The Dublin Review* 20 (March and June 1846): 451. This essay was latter republished under the title "John Keble" in the anthology *Ess* ii (London: Longmans, Green, & Co., 1871), 421-53. Describing his early introduction to Keble in the *Apologia*, he wrote of the latter's perceptible shyness of him due to "the marks which I bore upon me of the *of the* evangelical and liberal schools," Newman, *Apo*, 76-77. Of his use of "church" as published in the *Parochial and Plain Sermons*, Newman wrote "I meant,–in common with all writers connected with the Tract Movement, whatever their shades of opinion, and with the whole body of English divines, except those of the Puritan or Evangelical School,–the whole of Christendom, from the Apostles' time till now." Newman, *Apo*, 442.

[14] Newman, *Apo*, 58.

against Mr. Mayers in favour of Pope's "Essay on Man." What, I said, can be more free from objection than it? does it not expressly inculcate "Virtue alone is happiness below?"[15]

Newman's later reflections on his spiritual disposition during the period also emphasize his impiety and wickedness. Those judgments specifically centered on sins of intellectual pride and self-sufficiency–sins he often spoke of as telltale faults of theological liberalism. He confessed to being "very bad-tempered, vain, proud, arrogant, prone to anger and vehement."[16]

Newman's "first conversion" followed closely on the heels of his father's bank failure in March 1816 and upon his own severe illness a few months later.[17] The former required that the Newman family adopt an austere manner of life as the elder John Newman took unsteady employment as a brewer in Alton. The retirement of remaining debts required the sale of both the family home in London and their country cottage in Norwood. The latter illness was severe enough to put young John Henry in fear of his life and seems to have shaken him out of any adolescent notions of self-sufficiency. Writing in 1869, Newman reflected, "I have had three great illnesses in my life, and how have they turned out! The first keen, terrible one, when I was a boy of 15, and it made me a Christian–with experience before and after, awful, and known only to God."[18]

Resulting from the onset of his family's financial struggles, Newman's parents decided that he would remain at Ealing during the summer holidays. During those difficult days he came under the tutelage of Walter Mayers, an evangelical Calvinist clergyman and

---

[15] Newman, *AW*, 169.

[16] Newman, *AW*, 174.

[17] Newman spoke of his turn "to a spiritual life" as taking place between 1 August and 21 December of that year. Newman, *AW*, 150. On his father's business affairs, see Anne Mozley, ed., *Letters and Correspondence of John Henry Newman During His Life in the English Church*, vol. 1, 21. Newman himself later corrected Mozley's characterization of the hardships experienced by his father: "My Father's bank never failed. It stopped–but paid by the end of the month its creditors in full." Newman to Thomas Mozley (9 June 1882), *LD* xxx, 94.

[18] Newman, *AW*, 268.

the classics master at the school. As the result of his extended ministrations, Newman embraced an evangelical faith, and in the years following his entrance at Trinity College, Oxford, Mayers became an ever-present confidant and advisor.[19] Newman's father was deeply suspicious of this influence and very critical of his young son's fervent

---

[19] There is some question as to whether this was indeed an authentic evangelical awakening because Newman himself recognized that his experience was free of the progressive stages of conversion named in various "morphologies of conversion" contained in what he would much later call "the language of books." C. Stephen Dessain has concluded from this absence that, "Newman was never a real Evangelical, and had never been through the conventional experiences of conviction of sin, terror, despair, followed by full assurance of salvation," C. Stephen Dessain, "Newman's First Conversion," *Newman Studien* 3 (1957): 50. Based on Newman's social affinities and durability of the actual experience in Newman's reflection, however, John Linnan has argued that "Newman experienced what can only be called an Evangelical conversion, and that in spite of his latter attempt to disassociate himself from that group, by every reasonable criterion, the conversion of 1816 was not only a true and real conversion but also a conversion of the Evangelical sort." John Linnan, *The Evangelical Background of John Henry Newman: 1816-1826*, vol. 2 (Louvain, 1965), 346. The question has always been whether Newman's self-understanding was coherent enough to give him cognitive rest as an evangelical. Posing the question in this manner, the evidence allows us to answer with only a qualified "yes." On one hand, Newman certainly made a sincere attempt to assimilate both his early life and doctrinal understanding to the established categories of evangelicalism. On the other hand, Newman's dissatisfaction with these categories emerged quite quickly and grew progressively stronger as he matriculated from Ealing to Oxford where he acquired new theological vocabulary to articulate his experience. Here Dessain made his best point, arguing that Newman "accepted Christianity in the purest form then available to him, the doctrine of the Blessed Trinity (the Theology), and the Redemption (the Economy), together with grace and the belief in heaven and hell. The dogmas about the Church and the Sacraments would be accepted when they were seen by one who had not sinned against the light to cohere with and follow from the rest." Dessain, "Newman's First Conversion," 51. Newman's early letters and diaries contain numerous instances of correspondence with Mayers as he sought to refine his own religious opinions. As early as January 1817, Newman questioned Mayers, who as an evangelical believed that one must undergo a personal conversion in addition to receiving the sacrament of baptism, how it could be that children dying in infancy could be saved. See, Newman to Walter Mayers (January 1817), *LD* i, 30. Even after Mayers left Ealing in 1822 for parish ministry, Newman consulted Mayers in 1833 regarding the desirability of taking orders and preached his first sermon at Mayer's parish in Over Worton, near Banbury, on 23 June 1824. *LD* i, 177. Newman's letters and diaries evince their ongoing correspondence until Mayers's death in 1828.

evangelical piety.[20] Perhaps of greater importance than Mayer's personal ministrations, however, were the authors that he commended to Newman. Of these, three are especially important to note, both for their lingering influence on Newman's evolving theological outlook and for his eventual repudiation of the evangelical school.

There is little doubt that Thomas Scott's autobiographical account of his religious development in the 1779 volume, *The Force of Truth*, dominated Newman's earlier and latter self-conception.[21] Born to a grazier family in Lincolnshire, Scott first encountered evangelical Calvinism in the person of John Newton, while serving as curate of a parish in Weston Underwood. In January 1774, he learned that Newton had visited two of his own dying parishioners. Lingering guilt over the incident roused him from clerical indolence, and Scott began a spiritual journey that led him from heterodox, "Socinian" views of God into a robust Trinitarian orthodoxy.[22] Recording the history of his religious

---

[20] On 6 January 1822, Newman recalled his father's misgivings: "It is very proper to quote Scripture, but you poured out texts in such quantities. Have a guard. You are encouraging a nervousness and morbid sensibility, and irritability, which may be very serious. I know what it is myself perfectly well. I know it is a disease of mind. You must exert yourself and do every thing you can. Depend upon it, no one's principles can be established at twenty. Your opinions in two or three years will certainly, certainly change. . . . Take care, I repeat. You are on dangerous ground. The temper you are encouraging may lead to something alarming. Weak minds are carried into superstition, and strong ones into infidelity." Newman, *AW*, 179; Cf., *LD* i, 117.

[21] A contemporary portrait of Thomas Scott is available in Arthur Pollard, "Scott, Thomas (1747-1821)," in *Oxford Dictionary of National Biography*, online ed., ed. Lawrence Goldman (Oxford: Oxford University Press): http://www.oxforddnb.com/view/article/24919. A fuller, contemporaneous biography was written by Scott's eldest son, John Scott, *The Life of the Rev. Thomas Scott, D.D.* (Boston: Samuel T. Armstrong and Crocker and Brewster, 1822). Scott's own autobiographical *The Force of Truth* was originally published in 1779, but the work went through at least ten editions in the succeeding twenty years. Newman had what was in all probability his personal copy from childhood shelved in his library at the Birmingham Oratory. Citations of the work here are from that edition. See Thomas Scott, *The Force of Truth*, 10th ed. (Brookfield: E. Merriam & Co., 1817).

[22] "Socinian" here refers generally to the doctrine of the Racovian Catechism of 1602 and derives from the name of its principal author, Fausto Sozzini (Faustus Socinus). Socinians historically rejected the preexistence of Christ, the doctrine of original sin, and the propitiatory view of the atonement. Socinians also

opinions in words that could have easily been penned by Newman himself in later years, Scott's testimony to his conversion is worth quoting at length for its appeal to Christian antiquity as a sure guide to spiritual and theological integrity.

> My esteem for Mr. N[ewton] was also now very much increased; and though I had hitherto concealed this part of my sentiments from him, yet I knew his to be very different. I was not indeed willing to be taught by him in other matters: yet, in this respect, finding his opinion the same which in all former ages of the Church hath been accounted orthodox, while that which I held had always been branded as heretical; my fears of a mistake were thus exceedingly increased. In this perplexity I applied to the Lord, and frequently besought him to lead me to a settled conclusion what was the truth in this important subject. After much meditation, together with a careful examination of all the Scriptures which I then understood to relate to it, accompanied with earnest prayer for divine teaching, I was at length constrained to renounce, as utterly indefensible, all my former sentiments, and to accede to that doctrine which I had so long despised.[23]

In his *Apologia* Newman recalled Thomas Scott as "the writer who made a deeper impression on my mind than any other, and to whom (humanly speaking) I almost owe my soul."[24] These words warrant serious consideration, not only for the expressiveness of Newman's elegiac recollections, but more importantly for Newman's lifelong praise of Scott as an exemplar of personal holiness and of the dogged pursuit of theological truth.[25] These values are amply reflected in two of

---

limited divine foreknowledge to necessary truths, denying that future contingent truths were properly knowable. See, Thomas Rees, trans., *The Racovian Catechism* (London: Longmans, Hurst, Rees, Orme, & Brown, 1818). See also, Sarah Mortimer, *Reason and Religion in the English Reformation: The Challenge of Socinianism* (Cambridge: Cambridge University Press, 2010). Although "Socinianism" developed into a general descriptor for virtually any dissenting belief in both Britain and North America, Scott's narrative reveals a much greater precision in his use of the term.

23 Scott, *The Force of Truth*, 97-98.

24 Newman, *Apo*, 60.

25 Note especially here Newman's letter to James Hewitt, Lord Lifford dated 12 September 1837 wherein Newman boasts of his ability even then to "bear to stand

Scott's "proverbs" that Newman remembered in later years: "Holiness rather than peace" and "Growth the only evidence of life."[26] Scott's deep suspicion of Calvinistic antinomianism provoked in Newman a scrupulosity that frequently bordered on a manic censoriousness.[27] Still, long after abandoning Scott's Protestant and evangelical viewpoint, Newman continued to praise his "bold unworldliness and vigorous independence of mind."[28] Indeed, this commitment to Thomas Scott's

---

an examination." He continues, writing of how "From the age of 15, when first I knew them, I was attracted by the earnestness, manliness and independence of his character; he seemed to me one who was willing to stand on God's side against the world, and I never have lost this impression of him. He is the fairest specimen that can be taken of the so called Evangelical school, from the very practical character of his works. I am perfectly well acquainted with his Force of Truth, his Essays, his Son's life of him, and above all his Commentary." From this it seems clear that Newman likely adapted the letter to compose his remarks on Scott in the *Apologia*. See *LD* vi, 129. Cf., *LD* i, 165; *LD* iii, 260; *LD* v, 45, 390; *LD* xii, 368; *LD* xix, 365; and *LD* xxxii, 261-62. Note also that Newman's library at the Birmingham Oratory contains copies of Scott's *The Force of Truth: Essays on the Most Important Subjects in Religion*, 7th ed. (London: 1814); *A Treatise on Growth in Grace*, 6th ed. (London: 1824); *The Holy Bible with explanatory notes*, new edition, 6 vols. (London: 1812); and J. Scott, *The Life of the Rev. Thomas Scott* (London: 1822). *LD* vi, 129.

26 Newman, *Apo*, 61. From this, it is perfectly clear why Newman could cite the influence of William Law's (1686-1761) *A Serious Call to a Devout and Holy Life* (1729) alongside the influence of Scott. Newman remembered Law's decidedly Arminian work as of a character "very opposite" to Calvinism, but the shared concern for holiness is the common denominator. Newman, *Apo*, 62. Noted also is the work of John Linnan demonstrating Newman's particular regard for holiness in the latter's preaching at St. Clement's, Oxford. See John Linnan, "The Search for Absolute Holiness: A Study of Newman's Evangelical Period," *The Ampleforth Journal* 73 (1968): 161-74.

27 A poignant example of this can be found in a diary entry of April 1823 wherein Newman gives full voice to his sense of the gravity of sin in comparison with others: "But, when he talks of our natural sin as an *infirmity*, and I as a *disease*, he as an imperfection, and I as a poison, he as making man imperfect as the Angels may be, I as making him the foe of God and an object of God's wrath, here we can come to no agreement with each other, but one or other of us must fearfully mistake the Scriptures." Newman, *AW*, 171.

28 Newman, *Apo*, 60. Thomas Scott's religious development did not cease with his evangelical conversion. Following closely upon his submission to Trinitarian orthodoxy, he wrote of his ongoing struggles to receive the Calvinist doctrines of total depravity, personal election, the limited intent of Christ's atonement, and

vision of personal holiness, expressed in a fundamental antithesis between the church and the world, is so ubiquitous in the whole of Newman's life as to be considered indelibly characteristic.[29]

Newman nearly always mentioned Joseph Milner alongside Scott when he spoke of his inheritance from the evangelical school. This is all the more curious given Newman's particular disregard of Milner as a critical historian.[30] Indeed, having read *The Decline and Fall of the Roman Empire* during the long vacation of 1818, Newman reserved his highest historiographical praise for Edward Gibbon, whom he begrudgingly celebrated for "his happy choice of expressions, his vigorous compression of ideas, and the life and significance of his every word."[31] Milner, nevertheless, exerted a powerful influence on Newman's religious affections as he read the multivolume *History of the Church of Christ* (1794-1809). So much was this the case that Newman later gushed at his being "nothing short of enamoured" as he "read the long extracts from St. Augustine, St. Ambrose, and the other Fathers which I found there." He read these as "being *the* religion of the primitive Christians."[32]

To appreciate the long-term effects of Milner's work on Newman, it is worthwhile to consider that Milner composed his work as a corrective to the German Lutheran historian, Johann Lorenz von Mosheim.

---

perseverance. Scott wrote of these collectively as the "doctrine of personal election, and those [tenets] which immediately depend on it and are connected with it." Although Scott did finally accede to these as well, he both relegated them to secondary importance and retained a strong concern to suppress what he called antinomian abuses of these doctrines manifesting in "licentiousness." Scott, *The Force of Truth*, 91, 106.

29 They are demonstrably present as well in his 1832 sermon, "Personal Influence, the Means of Propagating the Truth." I argue in a later chapter that this sermon is preferable to Keble's sermon on "National Apostasy" for dating the proper commencement of Newman's Tractarian school.

30 Cf., *LD* v, 45; *LD* vi, 129; *LD* xii, 368.

31 Newman to John William Bowden (October 1819), *LD* i, 67. Cf., Newman, *AW*, 40-41, 44. Newman would much later remember Gibbon as "perhaps the only English writer who has any claim to be considered an ecclesiastical historian." Newman, *Dev* (London: James Toovey, 1845), 5.

32 Newman, *Apo*, 62. Emphasis mine.

Milner was quite critical of Mosheim for the latter's preoccupation with heresy and schism. In his mind this was as absurd as thinking that the history of English highwaymen was the history of England.[33] In contrast, Milner set out to tell the story of the church as a legacy of unbroken and genuine evangelical piety, replete with occasional "effusions of divine grace" as "the attendant and shadow of transcendent sanctity."[34] In doing so, Milner crafted an apologetic narrative for evangelical Anglicans to emulate. In the early church he celebrated Cyprian, Ambrose, and Augustine. When treating the early medieval period, he eulogized Gregory the Great and traced the lives of several missionaries. Anselm and Bernard were the focus of the twelfth century, but Milner's evangelical anti-Catholicism then manifested in a portrait of Thomas Aquinas as a semi-Pelagian. Alternatively, he celebrated the marginal Cathari, Waldenses, and Lollards as true apostolic successors and heralds of the evangelical Protestant doctrines of grace. Milner concluded his narrative with Luther, the Reformation, and the Anglican reformers as the proper heirs of a glorious Christian antiquity.[35]

Newman emulated Milner's general tendency to conscript history in service to polemic and devotional ends. Hugh McDougall has usefully written that Newman was never a historian in the pure sense of the word. Rather, he was an "apologist" who "used history, [but] never served it."[36] Newman, then, might be usefully described as a historian of Providence, ever prosecuting a moral and theological case through the rhetorical deployment of–or in Stephen Thomas's coinage, the "rhetoricisation" of–history.[37] For Newman, the profit of history was

---

[33] Joseph Milner, *The History of the Church of Christ: Volume the First Containing the Three First Centuries* (London: 1794), x.

[34] Newman, *Apo*, 83.

[35] A useful discussion of Milner's legacy can be found in George Reginald Balleine, *A History of the Evangelical Party in the Church of England* (London: Longmans, Green, & Co, 1908), 76-77.

[36] Hugh McDougall, "Newman–Historian or Apologist?," *CCHA Study Sessions* 35 (1968): 97.

[37] The term "rhetoricisation" is the amazingly apt coinage of Stephen Thomas, *Newman and Heresy: The Anglican Years* (Cambridge: Cambridge University Press, 1991), 204, 252.

to be found in demonstrating saints' "bold unworldliness and vigorous independence of mind" where it was to be found. As he argued in 1837, "If the voluminous remains of that period, including the works of Ambrose, Austin, Jerome, Chrysostom, Basil, Gregory of Nyssa, Gregory Nazianzen, Athanasius, and Cyril of Jerusalem, will not afford a standard of Catholic doctrine, there seems little profit to be gained from Antiquity at all."[38] He developed this outlook during his evangelical sojourn but along with his zeal for the virtue of holiness, it too became an indelible feature of his whole life's thought.[39]

This tendency also appears in a third work that Newman specifically recalled having read in these early years. Thomas Newton's *Dissertations on the Prophesies* (1758), an exposition of the so-called "prophetic" passages of the Bible from a historicist point of view, remains a masterpiece of hermeneutical ingenuity for the ways that its author identified contemporaneous events and persons as they lay barely concealed among the ancient visions of the Old and New Testament.[40] For Newton, the prophetic promise that God would make a "great nation" of Ishmael (Genesis 21:18) referred directly to the flourishing of Islam under the Ottoman Empire.[41] The fourth trumpet of the Revelation, darkening a third of the sun, the moon, and the stars (Revelation 8:12), became in Newton's hand a prophesy of Italy becoming a province of

---

38 Newman, *Pro* (1837), 206.

39 McDougall, "Newman–Historian or Apologist?," 98.

40 Historicist interpreters generally see biblical prophesies as predicting the major movements of Christian history, most of which have been fulfilled up to the time of the interpreter. Typically, historicism is highly ideological in nature so that, for example, Protestant versions of historicism associate prophesies of weal with the Reformation and subsequent Protestant triumphs while associating prophesies of woe with periods of dissolution and defeat (i.e., invasions of the Christianized Roman Empire by the Goths and the Muslims, the corruptions of the medieval Catholicism and the pope and the rise of Napoleon). G. K. Beale has provided a helpful discussion and evaluation of historicist approaches to biblical prophecy generally and to the Revelation in particular, in his commentary on the book. See G. K. Beale, *The Book of Revelation*, New International Greek Testament Commentary (Grand Rapids: Eerdmans, 1999), 44–49.

41 Thomas Newton, *Dissertations on the Prophesies, Which Have Been Remarkably Fulfilled and are at This Time Being Fulfilled*, 2nd ed., vol. 1 (London: J & R Tonsond, 1759), vol. 1, 52–54.

the Eastern Empire, with Rome being governed over by a duke under the Exarch of Ravenna from the years 584 to 751.[42] Especially critical for Newman was Newton's declaration that John the Revelator's "beast with ten horns" (Revelation 13:1ff.) was Catholic Rome. The Antichrist, prophesied by John, the Prophet Daniel, and the Apostle Paul, was none other than the pope.[43] Of this latter conclusion, Newman later testified to its enduring effects on him: "My imagination was stained by the effects of this doctrine up to the year 1843; it had been obliterated from my reason and judgment at an earlier date; but the thought remained upon me as a sort of false conscience."[44] Newman reportedly first read Newton's work in the autumn of 1816 and subsequently commended it to his Aunt Elizabeth as "extremely ingenious and also *satisfying*."[45] Though he came to entertain doubts regarding Newton's conclusions here and there, he continued to appeal to them in succeeding years.[46] By endowing otherwise mundane events of the historical past with a contemporary theological significance, Newton's apocalyptic outlook lent a perceptible prophetic urgency to Newman's rhetoricisations of history. Newman's later enthusiastic embrace of theology as a "prophetical office" and of theologians as the proper successors of John, Daniel, and Paul, owes much to Newton's early influence.

Newman's break with the "Peculiars," or "Xs," as his friend, Richard Hurrell Froude, liked to call them, became clear as he gradually internalized the principles and proclivities of new mentors. Still, it remains important to pause and reflect on the enduring role that this early sojourn in the evangelical school played in his imagination over the succeeding years. James Pereiro has helpfully drawn attention to the

---

42 Newton, *Dissertations on the Prophesies*, vol. 3, 390.

43 Newton, *Dissertations on the Prophesies*, vol. 1, 488; vol. 2, 394-425; vol. 221-23.

44 Newman, *Apo*, 63.

45 Newman to Elizabeth Newman (30 October 1816), *LD* i, 27.

46 In a letter to his sister, Jemima, dated 8 March 1824, Newman briefly asked her to communicate to his aunt that "some part of Newton on the Prophecies, his explanations for instance of the 11th of Daniel and the beginning of the Apocalypse are reckoned *incorrect*." *LD* i, 173. Newton's work was subsequently published in *The Works of the Right Reverend Thomas Newton* (1782), and Newman again obtained the work from the Oriel College Library on 19 November 1824. He kept this work through the Christmas holiday and returned it on 20 January 1825.

ways that "people born into traditional middle-of-the road or High Church Anglican families ... discovered and embraced 'living religion' in their contact with Evangelicals" and how those experiences generated a sense of the Church of England's "devotional and ascetical deficiency" by contrast.[47] Evangelicalism's concern to fill the existential gap between an individual and his religion by emphasizing personal holiness and spiritual immediacy closely parallels its apocalyptic tendency to collapse the distance between contemporary Christian experience and the Christian past. As a young student of the evangelical school, Newman learned to never detach himself from history in the manner of scientific historians that flourished on the Continent in the wake of Barthold Niebuhr's *Römische Geschichte* (1812). As Hugh McDougall has observed, "[Newman] could move from the fifth to the seventeenth to the nineteenth century with blithe indifference to the intervening periods. For Newman it was as though all Christian history were contemporary history."[48]

THE "NEW SCHOOL" AT ORIEL AND THE LIBERAL TENDENCIES OF A CREEDLESS CHURCH

As his father predicted in 1822, the distinctive features of Newman's evangelicalism rapidly fell away following his admission to the Oriel

---

[47] James Pereiro, *'Ethos' and the Oxford Movement: At the Heart of Tractarianism* (Oxford: Oxford University Press, 2008), 57.

[48] McDougall, "Newman–Historian or Apologist?," 101. Benjamin King has additionally pointed to Newman's concession to Rome that "the mental creations of her theologians ... not start from a novel and simply original tradition, but should be substantially one with the teaching of St Athanasius, St Augustine, St Anselm and St Thomas, as those great doctors in turn one with each other," *LD* xxix, 212. Thus, King argues that "Newman propounds a synthesis of the 'great doctors' as if they represented a single metaphysical system." Benjamin John King, "'In Whose Name I Write': Newman's Two Translations of Athanasius," *Journal for the History of Modern Theology/Zeitschrift für Neure Theologie Geschichte* 15, no. 1 (2008): 38. Cf., Benjamin King, *Newman and the Alexandrian Fathers: Shaping Doctrine in the Nineteenth Century* (Oxford: Oxford University Press, 2009), 222. As my analysis shows, however, Newman could also entertain such synchronic, as opposed to diachronic and developmental, readings of Christian history as a convinced Anglican evan- gelical.

College fellowship on 4 April 1823.[49] In the Summer of 1823, Newman came under the sway of Richard Whately and numerous other members of the High Church Oxford faculty known popularly as the "Noetics."[50] Although observing that the Noetics were little more than friends and that they were never all in Oriel residence at the same time, Frank Turner also admitted to a broad set of principles that lends coherence to their overall outlook.[51] The term "Noetic" itself derives from the Greek γνῶσῐς and refers to a general ethos that privileged intellectual originality over rigor. Newman later remembered how the Noetics characteristically "called everything into question" and how they "disallowed authority as a judge in matters intellectual."[52] In their general ecclesiastical attitudes they championed ecclesiastical moderation, rejecting the bibliocentrism and Calvinism of the evangelicals, while remaining critical of High Church clericalism on the other.[53] Additionally, the Noetics advocated an exclusively spiritual role for the church vis-à-vis the state, the doctrinal authority of apostolic tradition, and the sacramentality of the church. Contemplating them by way of these principles, Newman certainly thought of them as a coherent *school* and continued to reference them in this way throughout his life.[54]

49 It is also worthwhile to note Walter Mayers's marriage on 21 December 1824 occasioned a marked decline in his influence on Newman.

50 "Noetics" was the name given to men based in Oriel College in the 1820s. The central figures were Edward Copleston, John Davison, Edward Hawkins, Renn Dickson Hampden, Thomas Arnold, Baden Powell, Joseph Blanco White, and Samuel Hinds. The Noetic school of the 1820s was not uniformly liberal or Unitarian in its instincts despite the later attempts of Tractarians to paint them as such. H. C. G. Matthew, "Noetics, Tractarians, and the Reform of the University of Oxford in the Nineteenth Century," *History of Universities* 9 (1990): 195-225. As Peter Nockles argues, however, following the Peel election of 1829 especially, at least some of the Noetic school–Hampden and Powell, particularly–began to trend toward liberalism. Peter Nockles, "An Academic Counter-Revolution: Newman and Tractarian Oxford's Idea of a University," History of Universities 10 (1991): 149.

51 Turner, *John Henry Newman*, 77.

52 Newman, *AW*, 73.

53 Turner "Editor's Introduction," 77-78.

54 Note again his reference to the "evangelical and liberal schools" in *Apo*, 77. In his "Autobiographical Essay," Newman also spoke of the Noetics as being "*neither*

As Peter Nockles has written, Newman's Oxford was distinctive for its curricular emphasis on Aristotle, for the smaller scale of its colleges, for the close relationship of tutor to pupil, and for its historic religious traditions, associations, and ethos.[55] Owing its preeminence to large-scale curricular reforms earlier in the decade, Oriel College stood out for the way it chose and nurtured its fellows.[56] As R. W. Church, himself a provost of Oriel, remembered it, the examination "was altogether a trial, not of how much men knew, but of how they knew and what they could do."[57] This twin emphasis on distinction and originality won Newman election to Oriel despite his otherwise disastrous performance in the examinations of late 1820.[58] This honor would reocca-

---

High Church nor Low Church, but . . . a new school, or, as their enemies would say, a *clique*." Later in the same work he spoke of them as comprising "what may technically be called the Oriel school." Newman, *AW*, 73, 74.

[55] Peter Nockles, "The Oxford Movement in an Oxford College: Oriel as the Cradle of Tractarianism," in *The Oxford Movement: Europe and the Wider World, 1830-1930* (Cambridge: Cambridge University Press, 2012), 15. Nockles explores this territory in an extended fashion in his "An Academic Counter-Revolution," 137-97.

[56] Heather Ellis has carefully contextualized the conserving tendencies motivating the Examination Statute of 1800 (with its revision in 1807) against a larger concept of intergenerational conflict. Her depiction of the contrast between the senior men of Oriel, defending Britain's *ancien régime*, while its junior men pursued twin courses of more subversive and radical reform–one liberal and one reactionary–makes good sense of the situation. See Heather Ellis, *Generational Conflict and University Reform: Oxford in the Age of Revolution* (Leiden: Brill, 2012), 139-86. The nature of the reforms and their importance to the ascendancy of Oriel are detailed by K. C. Turpin, "The Ascendency of Oriel," in *The History of the University of Oxford*, volume VI: *Nineteenth-Century Oxford*, part I, ed., M. G. Brock and M. C. Curthoys (Oxford: Clarendon, 1997), 183-92. Cf., Ernest Nicholson, "Eveleigh and Copleston: The Pre-Eminence of Oriel," in *Oriel College: A History*, ed., Jeremy Catto (Oxford: Oxford University Press, 2013), 247-90, and W. R. Ward, *Victorian Oxford* (London: Frank Cass, 1965), 1-20.

[57] R. W. Church, *Life and Letters of Dean Church*, ed., Mary C. Church (London: Macmillan, 1894), 20. Cf., Liddon, *The Live of Edward Bouverie Pusey*, vol. 1, 67.

[58] Many years later, Newman later remembered his failure, writing, "He had over-read himself, and being suddenly called up a day sooner than he expected, he lost his head, utterly broke down, and, after vain attempts for several days, had to retire, only first making sure of his B.A. degree. When the list came out, his name did not appear at all on the mathematical side of the paper, and in classics it was found in the lower division of the second class of honours, which at that time went

sion the dangerous "liberal" tendencies he had detected in his earlier, pre-evangelical thinking.

Richard Whately paved the way for Newman's professional advancement by naming him vice principal of St. Alban's Hall, Oxford, when he himself became principal. From Whately, Newman also learned to appreciate the necessity of the church's sacred independence from the *saeculum*. As expressed in his anonymously published *Letters on the Church* (1826), Whately argued that unlike the Jewish theocracy of the Hebrew Bible, the church possessed no "secular power" by divine mandate.[59] He strongly contended that "it is a sacrilege to exercise secular power in religious concerns, and to attempt enforcing the doctrines and duties of Christianity by the sword of civil government."[60] Rejecting any pretense to the "power of the sword," Whately argued that the church should, rather, recover its proper spiritual authority. He thus advocated a clear separation between powers of church and state:

> The connexion, then, such as it now subsists, between the state and the church, which some, both statesmen and churchmen, from confused or partial and imperfect views of the subject, are so anxious to maintain, is not only in principle unjustifiable, but is, in every point, inexpedient for both parties; each of whom would obtain the very objects proposed (and others besides) much more easily and effectually if the system were altered.[61]

Newman recalled in the *Apologia* that Whately inspired his appreciation of "the existence of the Church, as a substantive body or corporation; next to fix in me those anti-Erastian views of Church polity, which were one of the most prominent features of the Tractarian movement."[62] It

---

by the contemptuous title of the 'Under-the-line,' there being as yet no third and fourth classes." Newman, *AW*, 47.

[59] Richard Whately, *Letters on the Church. By an Episcopalian* (London: 1826). This work was republished in the United States as *Christianity Independent of the State* (New York: Harper and Brothers, 1837). Quotations here are from this latter edition. There is little reason to doubt the consensus opinion on Whately's authorship of the work as he cites it in *Apo*, 69-70.

[60] Whately, *Christianity Independent of the State*, 37.

[61] Whately, *Christianity Independent of the State*, 147.

[62] Newman, *Apo*, 69.

remains important to remember, however, that Whately's view also exhibited a corollary emphasis. On his account, the church possessed no warrant to impose its creed by law. Although he was personally no theological liberal, this suspicion of authoritative theological boundaries became in Newman's estimation a necessary precondition for theological liberalism and its manifold infidelities. Newman's stumbling upon this connection in his own experience led eventually to his break with the Noetic school.

Under the tutelage of Edward Hawkins, Newman came to repudiate the evangelical doctrine of *sola scriptura* in favor of a broader appreciation for the role of tradition in the church. Hawkins's *Dissertation upon the Use and Importance of Unauthoritative Tradition as an Introduction to the Christian Doctrines* (1818) was a lifelong touchstone in Newman's thinking for the way that it set the traditional Protestant doctrine of private judgment in an ecclesial context, with teachers and mentors being essential to a proper reading of the Bible.[63] Hawkins also influenced Newman's views on the efficacy of the sacraments. The question of baptism, a concern to Newman in 1817, continued to plague him as late as 1824. His evolving views on that subject serve as a useful barometer for his general religious development away from evangelicalism.

On 24 August 1824, Newman recorded his ruminations on the evangelical doctrines of grace while reading John Bird Sumner's *Apostolic Preaching Considered in an Examination of St. Paul's Epistles* (1815). He had turned to the work at Hawkins's suggestion and wrote of how it threatened to drive him "either into Calvinism or Baptismal Regeneration." At this point Newman resolved to "steer clear of both, at least in preaching," but still, the question lingered:

> I am always slow in deciding a question; and last night I was so distressed and low about it that the thought even struck me I must leave the Church. I have been praying about it.... I do not know what will

---

[63] Importantly for Newman's latter disposition, Hawkins posited the argument that Christ and his apostles provided for the continuity of tradition in "a perpetual succession of ministers and teachers." Edward Hawkins, *A Dissertation upon the Use and Importance of Unauthoritative Tradition as an Introduction to the Christian Doctrines* (London: SPCK, 1819), 32.

be the end of it. I think I really desire the truth, and would embrace it wherever I found it.[64]

While lodging in the same house as fellow tutor, Edward Bouverie Pusey, in December 1824, the two shared many conversations on the subject of religion. Reflecting on one such occasion in his 16 December journal entry, Newman wrote that they discussed the nature, origin, and application of salvation, "I arguing for imputed righteousness, he against it, I inclining to separate regeneration from baptism, he doubting its separation etc."[65] By the thirteenth of the following month, however, Newman expressed a very different outlook:

> I think, I am not certain, I must give up the doctrine of imputed righteousness and that of regeneration as apart from baptism . . . It seems to me the great stand is to be made, *not* against those who connect a spiritual change with baptism, but those who deny a spiritual change altogether. . . . All who confess the natural corruption of the heart, and the necessity of change (whether they connect regeneration with baptism or not) should unite against those who make it (regeneration) a mere opening of new prospects, when the old score of offences is wiped away, and a person is for the second time put, as it were, on his good behaviour.[66]

---

64 Newman, *AW*, 202; *LD* i, 185n2.

65 Newman, *AW*, 203; *LD* i, 204n1.

66 Newman, *AW*, 203. By "those who deny a spiritual change altogether," Newman refers obliquely to Charles Lloyd (1784-1829) who was canon of Christ Church, Oxford, and the Regius Professor of Divinity. Newman had attended between 1824 and 1826 a series of discussion forums led by Lloyd for students preparing for ordination. Unlike the Noetics, contemporaneous descriptions of Lloyd place him directly in the High Church camp. See John Overton, *The English Church in the Nineteenth Century* (London: Longmans, Green, and Co., 1894), 45. Newman identified him as one of the "high-and-dry" school, professing "to hold to theology, and [laying] great stress on a doctrinal standard, on authoritative and traditional teaching," while also attributing to him "far larger views than were then common." Newman, *AW*, 70. Although it is difficult to determine the extent of his influence on Newman, Middleton's judgment seems sound: "the Professor's wide learning, his historical, biblical, and liturgical knowledge, together with his Catholic outlook, must have greatly helped in the mental and spiritual development of the young Fellow of Oriel College, not yet freed from the grip of Evangelicalism." Robert

Upon hearing his change of mind, Pusey indulged in some good-natured humor, chiding him for his "becoming more high church," but this seems to have only been a mediating position as can be seen in Newman's concluding remark: "I still rather hesitate–at least I do not like to apply the term 'regeneration' to the privileges of baptism, though I do not use it on the other side."[67] Still, as Newman would himself later recall in his 1874 *Autobiographical Memoir*, the break had far-reaching consequences for he had "in fact got hold of the Catholic doctrine that forgiveness of sin is conveyed to us, not simply by imputation, but by the implanting of a habit of grace."[68]

Newman also encountered Joseph Butler's *Analogy of Religion* (1736) during this period. In the *Apologia* he remembered its pivotal influence on his thought and celebrated, "Its inculcation of a visible Church, the oracle of truth and a pattern of sanctity, of the duties of external religion, and of the historical character of Revelation."[69] The work instilled in Newman two primary duties:

> First, the very idea of an analogy between the separate works of God leads to the conclusion that the system which is of less importance is economically or sacramentally connected with the more momentous system, and of this conclusion the theory, to which I was inclined as a boy, viz. the unreality of material phenomena, is an ultimate resolution... Secondly, Butler's doctrine that Probability is the guide of life, led me, at least under the teaching to which a few years later I was introduced, to the question of the logical cogency of Faith.[70]

Butler's *Analogy of Religion, Natural and Revealed* (1736) enabled Newman to configure Christian conversion and assurance as a "change of thought" emerging from converging and consistent probabilities. Although this did not eliminate the affections, under Butler's teaching

---

Middleton, *Newman at Oxford: His Religious Development* (Oxford: Oxford University Press, 1950), 48.

67 Newman, *AW*, 204, Cf., *LD* i, 206n1.

68 Newman, *AW*, 78.

69 Newman, *Apo*, 67.

70 Newman, *Apo*, 67–68.

Newman became more and more distrustful of religious enthusiasms, enjoined by evangelicals as useful measures of progress in the Christian life. Thus, in the *Autobiographical Memoir*, Newman's third-person narrative chronicled the evangelical school's waning influence on his self-conception:

> Mr. Newman then, before many months of his clerical life were over, had taken the first step towards giving up the evangelical form of Christianity; however, for a long while certain shreds and tatters of that doctrine hung about his preaching, nor did he for a whole ten years altogether sever himself from those great religious societies and their meetings, which then as now were the rallying ground and the strength of the Evangelical body. Besides Sumner, Butler's celebrated work, which he studied about the year 1825, had, as was natural, an important indirect effect upon him in the same direction, as placing his doctrinal views on a broad philosophical basis, with which an emotional religion could have little sympathy.[71]

By 1827, Newman again spoke of a lapse wherein he found himself "drifting in the direction of liberalism." He characterized this in the *Apologia* as his beginning to "prefer intellectual excellence to moral."[72] This personal lapse had doctrinal implications too, as he confessed to musings on the Trinity that tended toward Arianism. Recalling a sermon he delivered on 15 April 1827, Newman criticized the Athanasian creed as being "unnecessarily scientific." He also admitted of a certain "disdain for antiquity" that "showed itself in some flippant language against the Fathers in 'Encyclopedia Metropolitana'" and of coming under the influence of Conyers Middleton and his rejection of postbiblical miracles.[73] Newman embraced Middleton's line of critique,

---

71 Newman, *AW*, 78.

72 Newman, *Apo*, 72.

73 In his *Free Inquiry into the Miraculous Powers, Which are Supposed to have Subsisted in the Christian Church, from the Earliest Ages Through Several Successive Centuries* (London: Mamby and Cox, 1749), Middleton suggested both that ecclesiastical miracles must be accepted or rejected as a whole and that Christians must distinguish between the credible testimony of the church fathers to their historic beliefs and practices, on one hand, and their less credible historical witness to the miraculous on the other.

assuming with it the tendency to ascribe the supernatural claims of early Christianity to superstition.[74] This trend toward "liberalism" in Newman's thinking was apparently so pronounced that it aroused the concerns of Whately and his soon-to-be friend and confidant, Hurrell Froude. Oncoming events of a far more personal nature would soon shake him out of this brief flirtation.

MARY, CHARLES, AND FRANCIS: PRIVATE JUDGMENT AND APOSTASY

On 26 November 1827, Newman suffered a physical and emotional collapse resulting from the extraordinary burdens on his time and attention. In addition to his normal responsibilities, he had been supplementing his income during the Long Vacation by privately tutoring two Oriel undergraduates, Charles Golightly and Henry Wilberforce. In addition to this, preparation for his work as a public examiner kept him busy with seven to eight hours of reading each day.[75] By the beginning of term, Newman also received word of a crisis in his Aunt Elizabeth's financial affairs and spent from the end of October to mid-November scrambling to secure funds to cover the deficit. The overwhelming

---

[74] Newman, *Apo*, 72. Here Newman refers to Middleton's *A Free Inquiry into the Miraculous Powers*.

[75] A. Dwight Culler has summarized the stakes involved in Newman's preparations to be an examiner, writing, "It was like preparing for his own examination all over again, only in some ways it was worse. Indeed, if the undergraduates had only known it, it was really the examiner who was on trial, for in his case a dozen books would not do. He must master all the varying dozens which would be brought up during the entire year, and in the examination itself he must keep at it day after day before an audience which would only be too delighted to see him slip and fall. Moreover, the questions which a student has only to answer he must produce; and before a continuing audience and in the presence of his own colleagues he must produce them in some variety–otherwise he would be the laughing stock of the university. This was no idle fear. So great was the dread of exposure among the younger dons that there was a real difficulty, we are told, in finding six tutors a year who were willing to undertake the office." A. Dwight Culler, *The Imperial Intellect: The Study of Newman's Educational Ideal* (New Haven, CT: Yale University Press, 1955), 58-59.

weight of responsibility occasioned a mental and physical collapse, and Newman was taken by Robert Wilberforce to recuperate at Highwood.

On 5 January 1828 Newman suffered yet another blow when his sister, Mary, died suddenly just after her nineteenth birthday.[76] Newman remembered his sister fondly to Wilberforce: "She was gifted with that singular sweetness and affectionateness of temper that she lived in an ideal world of happiness, the very sight of which made others happy."[77] Recounting the moments of her passing to Hawkins, Newman recalled how "she consoled us by being able collectedly and calmly (on being told of her imminent danger) to review her life and faith, to confess the incompleteness and insufficiency of her obedience, and her full belief that in her Savior only could her sins be pardoned and her soul saved."[78] He also shared how "she owned to us that she could not fully satisfy her mind as to the *certainty* of her salvation, and was in some fear–but her entire hope was in Christ."[79] Years later, Newman remembered how these twin events "rudely awakened [me] from my dream."[80] Just as his former illness of 1816 had broken him of an adolescent flirtation with liberalism, so this new brush with mortality exposed the limits of his mental and spiritual reserves. Interestingly, it seems to have finally secured his opinion against evangelicalism, particularly in its doubts about the sacramental powers of baptism. The security of a determinate sacramental assurance, both of Mary's salvation and of his own, seems to have better withstood his scrupulosity than the evangelical school's fleeting signs of grace in his soul. The question now was whether the Noetic school could stand as a workable alternative.

The answer was not slow in coming. At nearly the same time, two of Newman's brothers were undergoing spiritual crises all their own. In both, Newman was again confronted in a personal way with the

---

[76] On Newman's relationship with his sister, see especially the recent work of Edward Short, *Newman and His Family* (London: Bloomsbury, 2013), 209-32.

[77] Newman to Robert Isaac Wilberforce (14 January 1828), *LD* ii, 49-50.

[78] Newman to Edward Hawkins (18 January 1828), *LD* ii, 51.

[79] Newman to Edward Hawkins (18 January 1828), *LD* ii, 51.

[80] Newman, *Apo*, 72.

twin catastrophic ends of evangelicalism and liberalism.[81] Through his fraternal-pastoral ministrations to Charles and Francis Newman, John Henry perceived both a rejection of ecclesial authority and a shared confidence in the reliability of private judgment. The domestic counterpoint to movements in his own soul enabled Newman to comprehend the essential affinity of the evangelical and Noetic schools for one another. This would finally blossom into a firm conviction that evangelicalism was wholly insufficient to stave off the liberal apostasy lying dormant among the Noetics. The insight would become a principal breakthrough, without which his Tractarian school would remain unintelligible and unnecessary.

Newman's father declared bankruptcy on 1 November 1821, and in January of the following year, the family's belongings were sold in front of their home on Southampton Street, Bloomsbury.[82] Bankruptcy proceedings continued for nearly a year, leaving John Newman a broken man. He rapidly declined and died two years later. Faced with these domestic challenges, John Henry assumed the conventional role of eldest son and quickly became the primary source of financial support for his immediate family and aunt. He supplemented the funding that came with his Oriel fellowship with income earned from private tutorial work.[83] Adding monies from his Oriel tutorship, his annual income amounted to £650 by 1826. This was further supplemented by a small income from his vicarate at St. Mary's, which began in 1828.[84]

Charles was something of a black sheep in the family. Prior to his death, John Newman gave up any hope that Charles would prosper in

---

[81] On Newman's relationships with his Francis and Charles, see Short, *Newman and His Family*, 115-208. See also William Robbins, *The Newman Brothers: An Essay in Comparative Intellectual Biography* (Cambridge, MA: Harvard University Press, 1966).

[82] The declaration of bankruptcy, as published in *The Gazette*, can be found in Sean O'Faolain, *Newman's Way: The Odyssey of John Henry Newman* (New York: Devin-Adair, 1952), 76.

[83] During the Long Vacation of 1822, Newman took only four hours of sleep per night. He had four pupils at the start of 1823 and was considering applications by two more. To this he added such paternal duties as overseeing the education of his sisters. O'Faolain, *Newman's Way*, 82-83.

[84] O'Faolain, *Newman's Way*, 82-83.

the world, and the young man responded by gradually severing ties with his family and tying his fate to the politics of radical socialism. By 1823 Charles was a professed atheist and a devotee of the Welsh socialist, Robert Owen of Lanark.[85] Despite John Henry's successful effort to secure employment for him with the Bank of England in 1825, Charles resigned in 1832. The subsequent strain guaranteed that correspondence between the two would be infrequent, but the discourse that did pass between them illustrates well John Henry's transition away from evangelicalism and his enduring commitment to the virtues of personal holiness and doctrinal orthodoxy.

During a long walk from Tunham Green to Knightsbridge (Town to Strand) in August of 1823, the brothers argued long over John Henry's attempts to bring about Charles's conversion. In typical evangelical fashion, John Henry commended the constant and attentive reading of the Bible and earnest prayer for illumination. His diary recorded his urging that Charles "strive to live up to the dictates of conscience and what the mind acknowledges to be right." In doing so, the elder brother assured that persons "would not fail of heaven" regardless of the sect or communion to which they belonged.[86] Following up on this conversation with Charles by letter, John Henry Newman emphasized again the role of personal conscience and the sincere pursuit of truth:

> Now it will be found, I presume, even on a slight examination, that the generality of men have *not* made up their religious views in this sincere spirit ... This is not the frame of mind in which they can hope for success in any worldly spirit, why then in that most difficult one of religious truth?[87]

---

[85] Owen vigorously held to three fundamental tenets. First, he was a natural determinist and denied that individuals are ultimately free or responsible. Second, he believed that "all religions are based on the same ridiculous imagination" and reduce a human being to the status of "a weak, imbecile animal; a furious bigot and fanatic; or a miserable hypocrite." Third, he zealously advocated socialism, with villages governed by a central committee in much the same way that Marx did. See here Frank Podmore, *Robert Owen: A Biography*, 2 vols. (London: Huchinson & Co., 1906), esp. 1:246-47.

[86] Newman, *AW*, 192-93.

[87] Newman to Charles Robert Newman (12 December 1823), *LD* i, 170.

Months later, John Henry pursued a different tack with Charles, who was by this time very much under Robert Owen's influence:

> I wish it to be distinctly understood that I consider the rejection of Christianity to arise from a fault of the heart, not of the *intellect*; that unbelief arises, not from mere error of reasoning, but either from pride or from sensuality . . . A dislike of the *contents* of Scripture is at the bottom of unbelief; and since those contents must be rejected by fair means or foul, it is plain that *in order to do this* the evidences must in some form be attacked.[88]

Reflecting his study of Butler on 14 April the same year, he located Charles's pride in an excessive reliance on unaided human rationality:

> [T]he grand evidence your conduct supplies, is, your assuming that unassisted reason is competent to discover moral and religious truth. If this were the case, I confess it would be a great argument *in limine* against any revelation at all. To my knowledge this was a principle with you a year and a half ago; and if you have held it from that time to this, doubtless you never entered into the spirit of Christianity: whose fundamental doctrine it is that the mind cannot arrive at religious truth 1st without revelation, 2nd without God's dispersing its prejudices in order to its *receiving* that *revelation*. Had you felt not only the desirableness of religious truth, but also our inability to attain it of ourselves, you would not have been seduced into your present opinions. Nor till you have recourse to the Author of Nature himself for direction, humbly, sincerely, perseveringly can you expect to possess real knowledge and true peace. For the fulfillment of that joyful event, I offer for you, my dear Charles, continual prayers. May the time come at last, however tardily! Amen.[89]

The two brothers resumed their controversy again in 1830. This time, John Henry Newman penned a lengthy letter along with a "memorandum on revelation." There, he rehearsed again the controversies between them, now four years old. With some minor additions, reflecting a recently begun study of early Christianity, he argued again for

---

[88] Newman to Charles Robert Newman (24 March 1825), *LD* i, 219.
[89] Newman to Charles Robert Newman (14 April 1825), *LD* i, 228.

the critical distinction between the contents of revelation, involving doctrine, and the contents of the Bible, which do not.[90] From there, the correspondence between John Henry and Charles became even more infrequent and cool.

Like his eldest brother, Francis Newman was a young protégé of Walter Mayers and imbibed the latter's evangelicalism from his own days as a student at Ealing. With the financial support of John Henry Newman, Francis studied at Worcester College, Oxford, and attained a double first in 1826. He was elected to a Balliol College fellowship later that same year, but in 1827 he was befriended by Benjamin Wills Newton, a fellow of Exeter College, Oxford, who had experienced a profound evangelical conversion through the ministrations of the sectarian Calvinist, Henry Bellenden Bulteel. That same year, Francis befriended Joseph Philpot who was recently returned from Ireland where he served as a tutor to the sons of Chief Justice Edward Lord Pennefather. While residing in Ireland, Philpot too experienced an evangelical conversion under the ministrations of John Nelson Darby, Lord Pennefather's brother-in-law.

Under the influence of these radical Calvinist associations, Francis took Philpot's place as a private tutor in Ireland and likewise came under Darby's influence. By the time of his return to Oxford, Francis adopted Darby's rejection of infant baptism. He likewise rejected all ecclesiological distinction between the lay and clerical estates. The resulting inability to assent to the Church of England's Thirty-nine Articles required him to resign his Balliol fellowship in 1830. Soon thereafter, Francis left Oxford again to work at a nonconformist faith mission in Baghdad under the supervision of Plymouth Brethren founder, Anthony Norris Groves. This succession of lapses from Evangelical Anglicanism to nonconforming evangelicalism to liberal skepticism was nearly seamless. By 1833, he was rumored to be entertaining unsound views concerning the doctrine of eternal punishment, and in 1835 Francis became an openly-professed Unitarian.

John Henry Newman's religious controversies with Francis began during the latter's sojourn in Ireland. These were largely taken up with

---

[90] Newman to Charles Robert Newman (19 August 1830), *LD* ii, 266-83.

the question of scriptural authority, primarily as it regarded the practice of infant baptism. Their mother had written distressing letters concerning Francis's independence of thought and John Henry responded to her distress by composing, in February 1827, a long essay of sixty-six pages defending the sacramental practices of the Church of England.[91] The doctrinal row between the two men deepened in 1829 as the elder worked to persuade the Oxford Church Missionary Society Auxiliary to refuse monies collected from St. Ebbe's Church under the ministrations of Henry Bulteel and Richard Waldo Sibthorp. Newman was then co-secretary and was anxious that the society steer clear of the strongly Calvinistic preaching associated with the two men. Upon failing in this initial endeavor, John Henry Newman published his *Suggestions in Behalf of the Church Missionary Society* (1830)–a work that was stridently critical of the society's evangelical associations. Newman challenged its independence from the Church of England, particularly in the division of the country into "districts of its own appointing" and in the maintenance of oversight by "a committee of management in London" as opposed to the church's traditional diocesan oversight by

---

[91] Harriet Newman to Newman (23 April 1828), *LD* ii, 67. This long letter to his mother was cribbed from William Wall's *The History of Infant Baptism*, which Newman obtained from the Oriel College Library and held in his possession from 15 November 1834 to July 1836. See here, Kenneth Parker, *Newman's Oriel College Senior Library Record*: https://digitalcollections.newmanstudies.org/library-records. In his own memoir, Francis recalled his own disposition on the question, writing, "The arguments from Scripture had never recommended themselves to me. Even allowing that they might confirm, they certainly could not suggest and establish the practice. It now appeared that there was no basis at all; indeed, several of the arguments struck me as cutting the other way. 'Suffer little children to come unto me,' was urged as decisive: but it occurred to me that the disciples would not have scolded the little children away, if they had ever been accustomed to baptize them." Concluding the subject, he added "Prepossessions being thus overthrown, when I read the apostolic epistles with a view to this special question, the proof so multiplied against the Church doctrine, that I did not see what was left to be said for it. I talked much and freely of this, as of most other topics with equals in age, who took interest in religious questions; but the more the matters were discussed, the more decidedly impossible it seemed to maintain that the popular Church views were apostolic." Francis Newman, *Phases of Faith, Or, Passages from the History of My Creed* (London: J. Chapman, 1850) 6-11. Cf., Thomas Sheridan, *Newman on Justification* (New York: Alba House, 1967), 127-34; and Robbins, *The Newman Brothers*, 14-39.

bishops.[92] As a solution, he advocated instead that clergy be recruited for membership so that they might by their votes bring the society under the clear authority of the Church of England. With the support of Francis Newman, Henry Bulteel brought a motion the next month to depose Newman as secretary.

When Francis announced that he would be leaving for his mission to Baghdad, John Henry Newman responded with a mixture of exasperation and resigned hopes that the experience might be of some benefit. In a letter to his sister Jemima, he complained of Francis's "dissatisfaction with every thing as it is," conceding that "I doubt not it will be a relief to his mind to be free from the irritation which I believe the sight of every thing around him occasions." Despite his observation that Francis's otherwise dangerous impulses might have been brought to good use abroad, Newman concluded,

> There is only one grave and painful scruple that I have–If he goes out without *any* authority from the Church (or not even any dissenting body), I think he is (abstractedly) committing a sin–tho' even then I should use our Lord's words 'Forbid him not' etc. but *how* he means to go, I suppose time will show us.[93]

Almost six years later, on 17 November 1835, he reported that Francis had undertaken a preaching ministry altogether outside the Church of England and that he had broken with Newman socially. There he pointedly denounced his brother's "verging toward liberalism," adding in summary "That wretched Protestant principle about Scripture, when taken in by an independent and clear mind, is almost certain to lead to errors I do not like to name."[94]

This latter conflation of evangelical confidence in private judgment and a liberal drift into unbelief was anything but accidental. A proper understanding of the connection as the common end of the evangelical and Noetic schools is critical to any proper understanding of Newman's efforts to construct a viable alternative. In jousting with Charles,

---

92 Newman, *VM* ii, 10-11.
93 Newman to Jemima Newman (27 May 1830), *LD* ii, 226-27.
94 Newman to Richard Hurrell Froude (17 November 1835), *LD* v, 164.

Newman discovered the inadequacy of a direct appeal to revelation in the face of liberalism's aggressive confidence in unaided reason. In his dispute with Francis, Newman came to perceive how the rejection of ecclesiastical authority left no definitive check on a person's drift from despising the church to the despising of Christianity altogether. This fundamental weakness–inherent in both the evangelical and Noetic schools–grounded Newman's read of his nation's religious landscape and made his turn to the founding of a new school necessary.

CONSPIRING LIBERALISM: ORIEL AND ENGLAND

Newman's first decade at Oriel also coincided with a tumultuous period in the life of England and its established church.[95] Not yet a generation had passed since the French Revolution. Germany's conservative institutions were hurriedly accommodating these forces as well, and England was becoming more patient of the political enfranchisement of dissenting sects.[96] In 1828, parliament ended the Test and Corporation Acts, under which dissenters held office by annual indemnity or by hypocritical compliance with requirements that they be communing members of the Church of England. The following year, parliament passed the Roman Catholic Relief Act, granting Roman Catholics the right to serve as parliamentary members.

At Oxford, however, matters were very different. Students were, upon their matriculation, required to subscribe to the Thirty-nine

---

[95] H. C. G. Matthew has written well of the importance of seeing the two together: "The University of Oxford in the first half of the nineteenth century faced *in micro* the challenge which the British governing class faced *in macro*: was it possible to preserve both Anglican hegemony and to remain 'National'?" H. C. G. Matthew, "Noetics, Tractarians, and the Reform of the University of Oxford," *History of Universities* 9 (1990): 195.

[96] On Germany, see C. E. McClelland, *State, Society, and University in Germany, 1700-1914* (Cambridge: Cambridge University Press, 2008), ch. 4. Regarding the broader currents in England, see J. C. D. Clark, *English Society 1660-1832* (Cambridge: Cambridge University Press, 2000), 501-64. A different perspective, one that counters the *ancién regime* thesis of Clark, can be found in Boyd Hilton, *A Mad, Bad, Dangerous People?: England 1783-1846* (Oxford: Clarendon, 2006), 24-30.

Articles and to take an oath upon the Act of Supremacy. All resident members of the university were, by definition, members of the Church of England. Nonresident members enforced this hegemony by exercise of their permanent right to vote in the university's convocation. Furthermore, the university acted as the national church's seminary because more of its graduates served as clergy than any other profession.[97] It is not too much to say that religion was the dominant subject of the curriculum, with the reactionary Examination Statute of 1800 requiring that "every examination, on every occasion, the Elements of Religion, and the Doctrinal Articles . . . must form a part."[98] Thus, as H. C. G. Matthews has written, "the establishmentarian constitution defined the character of the university in a way that, even before the reforms of 1828-1832, they had in considerable measure largely ceased to do in wider English civil society. In Oxford, the rhetoric of the Anglican confessional constitution fused precisely with the reality."[99]

Newman had supported his mentor, Edward Hawkins, in a successful election to the Oriel provostship at the beginning of 1828. Hawkins had run, perhaps ironically, against Newman's future Tractarian collaborator, the High Churchman, John Keble, whom he knew only as a venerable figure of Oriel. In a letter to Keble dated 19 December 1827, Newman justified his allegiances, explaining that Hawkins's

> general views so agree with my own, his practical notions, religious opinions, and habits of thinking, that I feel vividly and powerfully the advantages the College would gain when governed by one who pursuing ends to which I cordially approve would bring to the work powers of mind to which I have long looked upon with great admiration.[100]

Keble, on the other hand, appeared to Newman as harboring different views on "the mode of governing a College" and "the desirableness

---

[97] H. C. G. Matthew, "Noetics, Tractarians, and the Reform of the University of Oxford," 195.

[98] G. R. M. Ward and James Heywood, eds., *The Oxford University Statutes: The University Statutes from 1767 to 1850* (London: William Pickering, 1851), 33.

[99] Matthew, "Noetics, Tractarians, and the Reform of the University of Oxford," 197.

[100] Newman to John Keble (19 December 1827), *LD* ii, 44-45.

of certain reforms in the University at large."[101] As a consequence of Hawkins's election, Newman succeeded him as vicar of the University Church of St. Mary the Virgin, a post he held until the collapse of his own school at Oxford in 1841 and in the Church of England in 1843.

A critical mark of the Noetics being "moderate" and "comprehensive" was their general support for the political enfranchisement of Roman Catholics. While under the influence of Whately, Newman petitioned annually for Catholic Emancipation and was in the minority, voting against the Petition to Parliament against Catholic Claims in the Oxford Convocation of 1828.[102] By 1829, however, he had come under the sway of Froude and Keble, and so Newman broke with his senior colleagues at Oriel to join a coalition of younger conservative dons in their opposition to the reelection of Sir Robert Peel to his Oxford seat in Parliament. At root in the controversy was Peel's own reversal of his policy against the Catholic Relief Act.[103] Peel was, in all other matters, a reliable conservative of the Tory Party, defending the traditional social and political order for nearly twenty years. Faced in 1828 with the election of Daniel O'Connell to the parliamentary seat at County Clare, and thus an imminent threat of civil war in Ireland, Peel threw his support in favor of Catholic Emancipation. For his part, Newman feared the admission of non-Anglicans to Parliament because the alliance between the Church of England and the state exposed the church to further meddling on the part of persons who had no stake in its interests. According to Newman's account, this was a foreboding "symptom" of a darker conspiracy rooted in "a systematic hatred to our Church borne by Romanists, Sectarians, Liberals, and Infidels."[104] The indiscriminate conflation of these forces clearly reflects the opinion

---

[101] Newman to John Keble (19 December 1827), *LD* ii, 44-45.

[102] Newman, *Apo*, 72.

[103] A detailed chronicle of the progress of Catholic emancipation from 1827-1832 can be found in Clark, *English Society*, 527-47. See also Hilton, *A Mad, Bad, Dangerous People?*, 384-97; Bernard Ward, *The Eve of Catholic Emancipation: Being the History of the English Catholics During the First Thirty Years of the Nineteenth Century* (London: Longmans, Green, & Co., 1912); Bernard Ward, *The Dawn of the Catholic Revival in England 1781-1803*, 2 vols. (London: Longmans, Green, & Co., 1909).

[104] Newman to Samuel Rickards (6 February 1829), *LD* ii, 119.

formed in controversy with his brothers. Two schools were now erecting battlements at Oxford, and the soul of the nation was at stake.

Adding further gravity to Peel's reversal was the heavy influence of Arthur Wellesley, the first Duke of Wellington.[105] In a letter to his sister, Jemima, Newman expressed his resentments as arising from a desire to protect the theological integrity and durability of the University of Oxford.

> Mr Peel changes his mind on the Catholic Question, resigns his seat–and is not re-proposed by his Society. Meddling individuals put him up again, the Anti Catholic leaders (old Die-in-the-breach) and others shrink back, the Town lawyers say it will be a bad thing for the success of their *Political Schemes* if he is not re-elected acknowledging the while *Oxford* will lose credit by his re-election, and all the influence of Government and the Aristocracy is brought into play. Now is not it hard that because a Minister chooses *deliberately* to change his opinion, that Oxford must *suddenly* in a few days change too?–And changing with a *Minister* incur the imputation of changing from interested motives? It is rather too much that MP's change is to be sheltered by our change and that we are to whitewash him by our own disgrace. What is the reputation of the whole cabinet, great Captain and all, put together compared with that of Oxford, built up (as it is) in the lapse of centuries. [sic] Oxford has never turned with the turn of fortune. Mistaken we may have been, but never inconstant . . . Better to be bigoted than time-serving.[106]

In the same letter, Newman recognized that the question of Catholic Emancipation was a foregone conclusion for the society at large, but he believed that his beloved Oxford might still raise a standard against the "grand attack on the Church in progress from the Utilitarians and

---

[105] Newman derisively spoke of Wellesley, a former military, as "The great Captain," mocking the arrogance of his thinking "that we should turn round at the word of command," following Peel's resignation in February 1829. Newman to Harriet Newman (17 February 1829), *LD* ii, 122. Cf.; Newman, *Apo*, 72-73.

[106] Newman to Jemima Newman (4 March 1829), *LD* ii, 127.

Schismatics." He cast himself and his university coreligionists as "appointed Guardians and Guides of Christ's Church."[107]

From this it becomes clear how resonant convictions in Newman's own soul, in the experience of religious conflict with his younger brothers, and in this collaborative defense of Oxonian theological integrity, were leading to a break with the Noetics and the formation of a new school. Hawkins and the older Oriel dons supported the government and even went so far as pledging the support of the college to Peel. Newman and Froude responded by becoming the most active and zealous members of the Oxford committee pledged to support the candidacy of Peel's opponent, Sir Robert Inglis. That Keble too expressed his voice against Peel was, for Newman, "like some beautiful and sublime poetical incident and quite touching."[108] Writing to his mother on 13 March 1829, however, he lamented,

> We live in a novel era–one in which there is an advance toward universal education. Men have hitherto depended on others, and especially on the Clergy, for religious truth; now each man attempts to judge for himself... Christianity is of faith, modesty, lowliness, subordination; but the spirit at work against it is one of latitudinarianism, indifferentism, republicanism, and schism, a spirit which tends to overthrow doctrine, as if the fruit of bigotry, and discipline as if the instrument of priestcraft.[109]

In this extraordinary letter, Newman identified by name those whom he regarded as enemies of the church and of Christian truth:

> 1. [T]he uneducated or partially educated mass in towns, whose organs are Wooler's, Carlisle's publications etc. They are almost professedly deistical or worse. 2. The Utilitarians, political economists, useful knowledge people–their organs the Westminster Review, the London University, etc. 3. The schismatics, in and out of the Church, whose organs are the E[c]lectic Review, the Christian Guardian, etc. 4. The Baptists, whose system is consistent Calvinism, for as far as I can

---

[107] Newman to Jemima Newman, *LD* ii, 128.
[108] Newman to Samuel Rickards (18 February 1829), *LD* ii, 123.
[109] Newman to Mrs. Newman (13 March 1829), *LD* ii, 129-30.

see, Thomas Scott etc are inconsistent, and such inconsistent men would in times of commotion split, and go over to this side or that. 5. the high circles in London. 6. I might add the indifferentists, but I do not know enough to speak, like men who join Roman Catholics on one hand and Socinians on the other. Now you must not understand me as speaking harshly of individuals; I am speaking of bodies and principles.[110]

In the end, Hawkins failed to supply his promised support. The election was held on 26 February 1829, and at the close of the poll, 755 members of convocation had voted for Inglis, while 609 votes went to Peel. Three days later Newman wrote to his mother expressing his jubilation:

We have achieved a glorious Victory ... We have proved the independence of the Church and of Oxford. So rarely is either of the two in opposition to Government, that not once in fifty years can independent principle be shown; yet in these times, when its existence has been generally doubted, the moral power we shall gain by it cannot be overestimated.[111]

The identification of the Church of England's interests with those of Oxford is of paramount importance for the way it functioned as the decisive and increasingly exclusive constant in Newman's subsequent thought as a Tractarian. Oxford would become, as Richard Church later put it, "the fulcrum" from which Newman's school would "move the Church."[112]

Newman's religio-political realignment in 1829 and the resulting defeat of Peel represent the moment of conception for Newman's new school. It marks a final convergence of values that had been fomenting since his adolescence. Despite the temptation of some to spy opportunism in Newman's turn away from what he regarded as "false schools"

---

[110] Newman to Mrs. Newman, *LD* ii, 130.

[111] Newman to Mrs. Newman (1 March 1829), *LD* ii, 125.

[112] Richard William Church, *The Oxford Movement: Twelve Years, 1833-1845* (London: Macmillan and Co., 1891), 154. Cf., Nockles, "An Academic Counter-Revolution," 148.

of evangelicalism and liberalism, there is a manifest coherence in his personal, domestic, and public developments of the period.[113] For all the partisan flourish of J. H. L. Rowlands's evaluation, his discernment of the essential consistency in Newman's matriculation is fair.

> Newman's behaviour throughout was never inconsistent. It was a matter of conscience, nurtured by the teaching of the Church, against a wicked and fallen world, epitomized by politicians who were prepared to sacrifice the traditions of an ancient Christian polity. The Conservatives had accommodated their principles to the spirit of the age. Newman seriously believed that the influence of the Church and the University was being threatened. In the first public event with which he had been concerned, Newman felt that he had done his duty to preserve the integrity of Church and University.[114]

Critical here is the way that the church and university operated in a relationship of mutual implication in Newman's mind. As the Peel affair revealed, however, the university might also act in a prophetic fashion, advocating on behalf of the unique vocation of the church when the great "principalities and powers" of society and state collaborated to subvert her witness. The university too needed strengthening for the day of battle, and Newman would in 1829 move immediately to fortify Oriel College, attempting to better establish its roots in the soil of piety, holiness, and sound learning according to the example of ancient Christianity.

---

[113] Always the skeptic when it came to Newman's deeper motives, Frank Turner has painted the activities of Newman between 1828 and 1829 as something of a Machiavellian power grab–a quest to fashion a political coalition between the university MAs and the country parsons to oppose the senior members of the university and their connections in London. In this, however, Turner confuses the desire to "do something" with the desire to "be something" and this may be the key misstep from which the many missteps of his biographical portrait spring. Rarely does Turner grant that Newman actually believed what he professed, and, when he does, the concession is always framed by jabs at the manifest ridiculousness of Newman's belief. See Turner, *John Henry Newman*, 126-27.

[114] J. H. L. Rowlands, *Church, State, and Society: The Attitudes of John Keble, Richard Hurrell Froude, and John Henry Newman, 1827-1845* (Worthing: Churchman Publishing Ltd., 1989), 140.

NEWMAN'S ONE GREAT MISCHIEF

Newman's 1879 speech on the occasion of his receiving the *biglietto*, naming him a Cardinal of the Roman Catholic Church, is remarkable for the way he chose to summarize a lifetime's work: "I rejoice to say, to one great mischief I have from the first opposed myself. For 30, 40, 50 years I have resisted to the best of my powers the spirit of liberalism in religion."[115] As he continued, such liberalism was

> inconsistent with any recognition of any religion, as *true*. It teaches that all are to be tolerated, but all are matters of opinion. Revealed religion is not a truth, but a sentiment and a taste; not an objective fact; not miraculous: and it is the right of each individual to make it say just what strikes his fancy. Devotion is not necessarily founded on faith. Men may go to Protestant Churches and to Catholic, may get good from both and belong to neither. They may fraternize together in Spiritual thoughts and feelings, without having any views at all of doctrine in common, or seeing the need of them. Since then, religion is so personal a peculiarity and so private a possession, we must of necessity ignore it in the intercourse of man with man.[116]

This was, of course, completely consistent with his self-presentation in the *Apologia* as a "battle . . . with liberalism" by which he meant "the anti-dogmatic principle and its developments."[117]

The historical integrity of these statements has been called into question by Frank Turner, who treated them as yet another of Newman's rhetoricisations–this time of his own personal history. As Turner put it, Newman's portrayal of his life as a long struggle against "liberals" and "liberalism" was a deliberate appeal, both to conservative Anglicans who were scandalized by the liberal Protestantism of the collection, *Essays and Reviews* (1860), and to ultramontanist Catholics

---

115 Newman, *The Speech of His Eminence, Cardinal Newman on His Reception of the Biglietto* (Rome: Libraria Spithöver, 1879), 6.

116 Newman, *The Speech of His Eminence*, 7.

117 Newman, *Apo*, 120.

who had long suspected him of being a closeted liberal himself.[118] Even when treating the standard justifications of Newman's use of "liberalism" as supplied by Avery Cardinal Dulles and Terrence Merrigan—"the privatization of religion and its reduction to private sentiment" or "a form of solipsism, a conviction that truth, especially in matters of religion, is ultimately a private affair," respectively—Turner scolds their neglect of "historical and religious contexts in which Newman wrote and recalled personalities and events of the Tractarian era."[119]

Among the many objectives of this chapter, I have aimed to supply the necessary historiographic warrant for the basic definitions supplied by Dulles and Merrigan. Identifying evangelicalism and liberalism as twin "false schools" not only occasioned Newman's first imaginings of a potential alternative, but as later chapters will show, his clear perception of the ends of private judgment would serve as a kind of moral-intellectual compass, alerting him to potential hazards as he ventured toward a fuller conceptualization and development of his school in the oncoming years.

---

[118] Turner, "Editor's Introduction," in *Apo*, 57. Turner is not new in raising the question of what, exactly, Newman meant by "liberalism." Owen Chadwick once frankly admitted that "what Newman denounced as liberalism, no one else regarded as liberalism." See his Chadwick, *Newman*, 74.

[119] Dulles, *Newman*, 14; Terrence Merrigan, "Newman and Theological Liberalism," *Theological Liberalism* 66 (2005): 608.

CHAPTER 2

A School's Nascent Form
Newman's Reform of the Tutorial System and the Turn to "Traditionary Religion"

In his work, *'Ethos' and the Oxford Movement*, James Pereiro demonstrates that the concept of *ethos* lay at the heart of Tractarianism. The concept is thereby critical to understanding Newman's reform of the Oriel tutorial system as it became his school's nascent form. Rooted in Aristotle's *Nicomachean Ethics* and in Butler's *Analogy of Religion*, the Tractarians' catholic ethos was not understood primarily as an aesthetic or a sentiment. Rather, it was embodied in specific habits of heart and mind.[1] Summarizing its general themes, Pereiro writes of how this

> *ethos* was conceived as a moral temper involving openness to God's action in the soul. At the human level, this openness to God rests on a humble disposition of mind and heart–opposed to the self-sufficiency of Rationalism or the righteous confidence, of private judgment–and on a generous spirit, capable of following a radical ideal. Those dispositions enable the individual to submit to God's guidance, manifested in light for the intellect to perceive truth, and grace to enable the soul to discover and follow the path presented to it.[2]

Given the context of his early sojourn in the evangelical and liberal "schools," I argue here that Newman thought of the "Apostolical" ethos

---

1 James Pereiro, *'Ethos' and the Oxford Movement: At the Heart of Tractarianism* (Oxford: Oxford University Press, 2008), 85-92.

2 Pereiro, *'Ethos' and the Oxford Movement*, 108.

as the peculiar manifestation and fruit of an Apostolical *school*, exemplifying and promoting among its collective members what he would come to speak of as "the divinity of Traditionary Religion."[3] His conception of such a school followed immediately upon his rejection of a competing "liberal" ethos held in common by the schools of his day, but this was more than a simple pendular reaction on Newman's part. Newman's Apostolical ethos gave rise to his decided conviction that academic work was an expression of his priesthood. This cannot be stated too strongly: Newman saw his role at Oxford as the proper exercise of an ecclesial and pastoral *munus*. His labors to this end would commence within the portals of Oriel College, but they would soon open on a wider field, implicating Newman directly in a broader contest with what he spoke of as the "enthralling powers" of heterodox modernity. In these nascent years of the Tractarian movement, John Henry Newman first embarked upon the vocational work of a *theologian*.

THE TUTOR AS A MINISTER OF CHRIST

When Newman was ordained a priest of the Church of England on 29 May 1825, he took solemn vows to faithfully and diligently "minster the doctrine and sacraments, and the discipline of Christ" and "teach the people committed to [his] cure."[4] Unfortunately, in coming to the Oxford tuition, he encountered a culture where the compatibility of a clerical vocation with the life of a scholar was a matter of dispute. In the days of Elizabeth I and James I, when undergraduates came to the university at a very early age, the tuition was a pastoral office. There the tutor was not primarily a lecturer but a priest, acting *in loco pastoralis*, regulating students' expenses, forming their moral character,

---

[3] Newman, *Ari*, 88. Pereiro habitually refers to this as a "catholic" ethos, but as later chapters will demonstrate, the use of "catholic" with regard to early Tractarianism is misconceived. Certainly, it is "Apostolical" as Froude and then Newman habitually referred to the product of their explorations in early Christian history, but "catholicity" took on a special meaning in Newman's understanding after following his encounter with Nicholas Wiseman's essay, "The Anglican Claim of Apostolical Succession," and his study of Monophysitism in 1839.

[4] "The Ordering of Priests," in *The Book of Common Prayer* (1662).

and ministering to their religious needs. During the next two centuries, however, the system developed so that tutors increasingly supplanted professors in the actual instruction of undergraduates.[5] By the turn of the nineteenth century, a corresponding abeyance of moral and pastoral responsibility for students posed a dilemma for clergy who took their ordination vows seriously.

Newman doubtless learned to conceive the tensions created by this widening breach under the ministrations of Walter Mayers. In his work at Ealing, Mayers deeply felt the conflict between classical studies and his pastoral work. He finally overcame these tensions by dedicating himself fully to the traditional pastoral responsibilities of the tuition.[6] John Keble too felt uneasy when he gave up his parish ministry to teach at Oxford in 1818. He likewise reconciled himself to the work by taking a pastoral view of the tutor's role. Writing to his friend, J. T. Coleridge, Keble reflected,

> I thought at first it would be a very uncomfortable thing for me to give up my Cure and become an Academic again; but I get more and more reconciled to it every day. You consider tuition as a species of pastoral care, do you not? Otherwise it might seem questionable, whether a clergyman ought to leave a cure of souls for it. And yet there are some people at Oxford who seem to imagine that College Tutors have nothing to do with the morale. If I thought so, I would never undertake the office.[7]

---

[5] Dwight A. Culler, *The Imperial Intellect* (New Haven: Yale University Press, 1965), 49.

[6] The biographer wrote, "In this sphere of labour he continued about eight years, during which period his conduct was marked by that *consistency* which peculiarly distinguishes the true Christian from the body of mere professors, and which, alas! is but too rare in the present day, even amongst those whom charity would rank as the disciples of Christ. His mind, however, was considerably exercised by conscientious scruples in reference to the large portion of time devoted to tuition." See "A Brief Memoir of the Late Rev. Walter Mayers," in *Sermons by the Late Rev. Walter Mayers, A.M.* (London: James Nisbet, 1831), iv.

[7] John Keble to John Coleridge (29 January 1818), in John Taylor Coleridge, *A Memoir of the Rev. John Keble, M. A.: Late Vicar of Hursley*, 2nd ed., vol. 1 (New York: Pott and Amery, 1869), 72-73.

When Newman approached the canonical age of twenty-three, he carefully considered the question of whether he even ought to be ordained. In a journal entry dated 8 June 1823, he first wrote of consulting the writings of Thomas Scott, who generally advised "Not soon." Newman received similar advice from Edwin Hawkins, but for very different reasons: "Why bind yourself with a vow, when there is no necessity, and which *may* mean something incompatible with staying at College and taking pupils." Samuel Rickards too expressed doubts concerning "the propriety of College Tutors being clergymen."[8] By March 1825, however, Newman committed to live his priestly vocation as a scholar and resigned both his curacy at St. Clement's and his appointment at St. Alban's in order to accept the appointment as a tutor at Oriel.[9] A prayer preserved in his journal entry for 21 February 1826, however, still indicates a sense that he was entering upon contested territory:

> And now, O Lord, I am entering with the new year into a fresh course of duties (viz. the Tutorship). May I engage in them in the strength of Christ, remembering I am a minister of God, and have a commission to preach the gospel, remembering the worth of souls, and that I shall have to answer for the opportunities given me of benefitting those who are under my care.[10]

Writing to his sister, Harriet, a month later he again, almost defensively, spoke of his new role as a pastoral charge:

> I have a great undertaking before me in the Tutorship here. I trust God may give me grace to undertake it in a proper spirit, and to keep steadily in view that I have set myself apart for His service for ever. There is always the danger of the love of literary pursuits assuming too prominent a place in the thoughts of a College Tutor, or his

---

[8] Newman, *AW*, 192; *LD* i, 165n1. For a more detailed treatment of Newman's discernment of his clerical vocation, see Donald Capps, "John Henry Newman: A Study of Vocational Identity," *Journal for the Scientific Study of Religion* 9 (1970): 33-51.

[9] As he accepted his role as Whately's vice principal at St. Alban's, he reflected "I have all along thought that it was more my duty to engage in College offices than in parochial duty." Newman, *AW*, 205; *LD* i, 221n1.

[10] Newman (21 February 1826), *AW*, 209. Cf., *LD* i, 287.

viewing his situation merely as a secular office, a means of a future provision when he leaves College.[11]

Still again, just four weeks into his role as tutor, Newman's sense of revulsion at a creeping laxity in his soul was palpable. One perceives Newman's sense of systemic pressures to forego pastoral work in favor of a purer, more scholastic conception of his role. In the fires of this internal conflict, one catches the first hint of his intentions to remake the system.

> The College is filled principally with men of family, in many cases, of fortune. I fear there exists very considerable profligacy among them. There is much too in the system which I think wrong. I hardly acquiesce in the general reception of the Sacrament, which is expected, or even in the practice of having evening chapel. I think the Tutors see too little of the men, and that there is not enough direct religious instruction. It is my wish to consider myself as the minster of Christ. May I most seriously reflect, that, *unless* I find that opportunities occur of doing spiritual good to those over whom I am placed, it will become a grave question, whether I *ought* to continue in the Tuition.[12]

In correspondence and journal entries over the succeeding two years, Newman dutifully recorded the trials and tribulations suffered by himself and fellow tutors, Hurrell Froude and Robert Wilberforce, as they increasingly brought their pastoral influences to bear on the young men of Oriel. A. Dwight Cutler has done admirable work exposing both sides of these events, noting how the encounters Newman described as "rows as thick as blackberries" and as the efforts of "a new coachman" enduring "trouble with [his] *horses*" were experienced by his pupils as an overbearing censoriousness.[13] By May of 1827, Newman's sense of frustration translated itself in expressions toward those who

---

[11] Newman to Harriet Newman (21 March 1826), *LD* i, 280-81.

[12] Newman, *AW*, 209; Cf., *LD* i, 286-87n4.

[13] Culler, *The Imperial Intellect*, 53-58. Newman to Harriet Newman (1 November 1826), *LD* i, 305; Newman to Mrs. Newman (20 June 1827), *LD* ii, 20. To the latter correspondence, Newman's mother replied, with strong encouragement, "It gives me great pleasure to see you appear so strong at the end of a troublesome term. I

proved immune to his zeal. Finding himself far from the pastor who left the ninety-nine to save the one, Newman was positively jubilant when writing to his mother about having "hunted from the college two men."[14] Clearly something had to change.

THE SOLE OBJECT OF ALL TEACHINGS: RELIGION AND NEWMAN'S REFORM OF THE TUTORIAL SYSTEM AT ORIEL

From 14 to 16 August 1828, Newman accompanied Froude and Robert Wilberforce in a visit to the rectory of John Keble. During this meeting, he discovered that Keble's views on the administration of a college were very different from the views of Oriel's senior men, Edward Hawkins and Edward Copleston.[15] Discussions between the four consolidated Newman's opinion against the existing college lecture system and led to his proposing a new reform–one that would counter rather than abet what he saw as Oriel's ongoing spiritual decline.

Under the existing Oxford system, new members of each college were admitted three times in the year, sometimes more often, so that courses commenced anew at least three times a year. In a small college like Oriel, the system was interrupted, with students of different standing attending the same lecture.[16] Although the university required the assignment of a tutor to every undergraduate upon matriculation, the tutors shared the work of instruction in common. By the design of Hawkins and Copleston, this insured a certain continuity and quality of instruction where evenness of exposure prevented the weaknesses of a single tutor from falling entirely on his own students.

---

hope you will have effected a 'radical reform' by your vigorous measures, and that you are properly seconded." Mrs. Newman to Newman (26 June 1827), *LD* ii, 21.

14 Newman to Mrs. Newman (7 May 1827), *LD* ii, 15.

15 Newman later appended the diary entries of these days, writing "this was the first symptom of our growing intimacy. Old Mr Keble was then alive–and Keble was at his house." (14 August 1828), *LD* ii, 88.

16 Newman had complained of this as early as 1824. Cf., Thomas Vowler Short, *A Letter Addressed to the Very Reverend Dean of Christ Church on the State of the Public Examinations in the University of Oxford* (Oxford: Oxford University Press, 1822), 31.

Newman came to believe that this system of distribution diminished the personal relationship between the tutor and his assigned students.[17] His proposed reform of the lecture system was founded, as he wrote to Hawkins, "on these principles–that the Tutors have full authority to arrange their lectures together without consulting the Provost . . . and secondly, that each Tutor is essentially responsible for the instruction of the Pupils committed to him on entrance."[18] Over the previous two years, Newman came to realize that certain students would not desire a personal or pastoral relationship, so his plan grouped selected men in small private classes, each under their own tutor. The lectures would be conducted "quite familiarly and chattingly," while grouping the other, "bad men," in larger public classes to be distributed among the tutors according to the established system.[19]

Newman's plan also distinguished between subjects for which a more intimate grouping was desirable and those for which it was not. Private lectures "in which each Tutor lectures his own pupils" would cover "moral subjects" (that is, divinity, ethics) or history. As an alternative, they might prepare pupils for the public lectures. The lectures, "undertaken by the Tutors indiscriminately" would cover "Senior Greek Play," "Junior Greek Play," "Greek lecture for idle men," "Latin," "Rhetoric," "Latin Prose," "Latin Poetry," "Analytical Mathematics" (1 and 2), "Euclid in Michaelmas Term, Articles in Lent, [and] Logic in Easter and Act."[20] The subjects for which it was not worth the trouble to form small classes were those "which are, either *necessarily* read (as Euclid Articles, Logic) or *generally* (as Greek Plays, Greek and Latin Authors)– or *often*–(as Mathematics and Rhetoric)." Finally, Newman also

---

[17] In a letter from Edward Copleston to Hawkins (3 May 1830), Copleston laid out the system this way: "My *beau ideal* was that a Tutor should see all his own pupil's exercises and remark upon them–that he should talk to him about the lectures he was attending whether in his own classes or no–be ready to assist his difficulties– observe his conduct–and see more especially that his religious instruction went on." *LD* ii, 214. Cf., David Watson Rannie, *Oriel College* (London: F. E. Robinson, 1900), 203.

[18] Newman to Edward Hawkins (28 April 1830), *LD* ii, 208.

[19] Newman to Samuel Rickards (6 February 1829), *LD* ii, 117-19.

[20] Newman to Edward Hawkins (28 April 1830), *LD* ii, 208-209.

provided for the "interchange of pupils between Tutors for the sake of mutual convenience," giving a certain pastoral flexibility to the overall arrangement. The underlying principle of the system remained: each tutor retained responsibility for his own students and could keep them all (that is, even the bad ones) exclusively for himself.[21]

In his "Memorandum" on the Oriel Tuition dated 9 July 1830, Newman recounted his role as the "chief mover" of the reform, adding that Froude and Wilberforce "entered entirely into the views" so that it became the "unanimous act" of all three.[22] They then approached the senior tutor, Joseph Dornford, during their Christmas vacation of 1828 with the plan. For his part, Dornford only complained that the revisions would increase their workload, but he seems to have been content with implementing the plan at the beginning of Hilary Term on 14 January 1829.[23] They deliberately kept Hawkins in the dark regard-

---

[21] Newman to Edward Hawkins (28 April 1830), *LD* ii, 208-209.

[22] Newman's placement of himself at the center of their reforming efforts is suggestive for the way it anticipates his unique role in the Oxford Movement. While Peter Nockles has rightly criticized those who would reduce Tractarianism to the person and work of Newman, this should not diminish his central importance to the movement. Indeed, Nockles's appreciation of the variegated contributions of individual Tractarians and of English High Churchmen beside them helps to illumine where Newman's developing vision for their school led him along a distinctive, and ultimately divergent, path. Nockles, *Oxford Movement in Context*, 2ff.

[23] On 26 December 1828, Dornford wrote to Newman: "And now for your new plan of Lecturing–there is much in it that I like and at a first glance it seemed open to no objections–but now it appears to me that it is much better adapted to 200 men than to 50, and that in order to give effect to it each Tutor must give *so many* private lectures, that it will add very much to the labor; and that we shall in fact be reversing the system of division of labor, by putting *several* Tutors to do separately what *one* might do for the rest. If you say that we may avoid this by exchanging pupils with one another, then I think we are in fact coming back to the present system and virtually converting the private lecture into a public one. However there can be no objection I think if you all feel strongly about it to make the experiment and see how it *works*–and I perfectly agree with you here that we are not at all bound to consult anyone but ourselves on the adoption of it." *LD* ii, 206-207. In his 1874 *Autobiographical Memoir*, Newman recalled, "Mr Dornford, who was now the senior of the Tutorial body was far from indisposed to the view of his three colleagues." Newman, *AW*, 90; Cf., *LD* ii, 118n1.

ing the plan.[24] This small note is important, and not only for the way it illustrates Newman's initiative in these reforms. As will be clear in the subsequent chapters, Newman's manner of proceeding in the tuition reform would become a defining characteristic over the succeeding years. While one certainly cannot speak as though other actors in the Tractarian school were incidental to its work, Newman nevertheless remained its prime mover, with Hurrell Froude and John Keble exercising the most immediate influence on his thinking. When other parties proved less willing to follow his lead or to suborn his actions, Newman found ways to subvert their influence or marginalize them altogether.

When Hawkins finally became aware of their actions, he invited Newman to send "a short sketch" of the plan.[25] Upon his expressed commendation of the old system, Newman attributed its successes to the recourse students made, at their own expense, to private tuition–something that he, as a onetime private tutor himself, knew only too well. Thus, Newman's reforms embodied a dual rationale: one pastoral and one economic. On one hand, he complained that the "mere lecturing" required under the old system was "incompatible with due attention to that more useful private instruction, which has imparted to the office of Tutor the importance of a clerical occupation."[26] On the other hand, given that the inadequacies of the old system made necessary the expensive use of private tutors, "why not," he argued, "recognize it, control it, and make it economical?"[27]

At this point, an extended controversy ensued, with multiple conversations and letters passing between the involved parties.[28] In the

---

[24] In his 6 February 1829 letter to Samuel Rickards, Newman wrote, "we do not wish this to be talked about." *LD* ii, 118. Although he would later defend the integrity of his actions on the basis of the University Statue giving tutors the right to govern their own affairs, he seems to have been aware that Hawkins would neither approve, nor tolerate the plan. Cf., Culler, *The Imperial Intellect*, 68-69.

[25] Properly advised of Hawkins's disapproval of the reforms, Dornford was unwilling to persist and fell behind his provost following a full college meeting held on 24 April 1830.

[26] Newman to Edward Hawkins (8 June 1830), *LD* ii, 233.

[27] Newman to Edward Hawkins (29 April 1830), *LD* ii, 211-12.

[28] Newman's disposition toward Hawkins seems to have changed by 17 February 1829 where the latter is described to his sister, Harriet, as "our meddling

end, Newman staked his position on the university statutes having directly entrusted undergraduates to the care of a particular tutor. He additionally appealed to the practice of other colleges where tutors enjoyed a nearly unlimited right to arrange the lectures according to their own lights. Newman regarded this to be "a certain inherent discretionary power similar to that contained in the Pastoral Charge."[29] When Hawkins pressed his demand that they return to the old system, Newman initially considered resignation. Under the strong encouragement of Froude, however, he elected to continue the controversy until Hawkins agreed to amend future editions of the university calendar so that tutors would be renamed "*Assistant Tutor*" in all cases save that of

---

provost." *LD* ii, 122. The controversy is detailed in Newman to Edward Hawkins (6 April 1830), *LD* ii, 203; Edward Hawkins to Joseph Dornford (2 November 1829), *LD* ii, 207; Edward Hawkins to Newman (28 April 1830), *LD* ii, 208-209; Edward Hawkins to Newman (28 April 1830), *LD* ii, 209-11; Newman to Edward Hawkins (29 April 1830), *LD* ii, 211-12; Edward Hawkins to Newman (29 April 1830), *LD* ii, 212; Edward Copleston to Edward Hawkins (I) (3 May 1830), *LD* ii, 213-14; Edward Copleston to Edward Hawkins (II) (3 May 1830), *LD* ii, 214-15; Joseph Dornford to Newman (3 May 1830), *LD* ii, 215; Newman to Edward Hawkins (5 May 1830), *LD* ii, 216; Edward Hawkins to Newman (5 May 1830), *LD* ii, 216; Richard Hurrell Froude to Edward Hawkins (12 May 1830), *LD* ii, 218; Edward Hawkins to Richard Hurrell Froude (12 May 1830), *LD* ii, 218n1; Edward Hawkins to Robert Isaac Wilberforce (22 May 1830), *LD* ii, 222-23; Edward Hawkins to Newman (15 May 1830), *LD* ii, 228-33; Newman to Edward Hawkins (8 June 1830), *LD* ii, 233-34; Robert Isaac Wilberforce to Edward Hawkins (9 June 1830), *LD* ii, 234-35; Richard Hurrell Froude to Edward Hawkins (10 June 1830), *LD* ii, 235-36; Newman to Edward Hawkins (13 June 1830), *LD* ii, 237-38; Edward Hawkins to Newman (9 June 1830), *LD* ii, 239-41; Newman to Edward Hawkins (15 June 1830), *LD* ii, 241-42; Richard Hurrell Froude to Edward Hawkins (15 June 1830), *LD* ii, 243; Newman to Edward Hawkins (I) (12 October 1830), *LD* ii, 294; Edward Hawkins to Newman (12 October 1830), *LD* ii, 294; Newman to Edward Hawkins (II) (12 October 1830), *LD* ii, 295; Newman to Joseph Dornford (I) (23 October 1830), *LD* ii, 296; Newman to Joseph Dornford (II) (23 October 1830), *LD* ii, 296; Edward Hawkins to Newman (23 October 1830), *LD* ii, 296-97; Newman to Joseph Dornford (24 October 1830), *LD* ii, 297; Newman to Edward Hawkins (24 October 1830), *LD* ii, 297-98; Edward Hawkins to Newman (29 October 1830), *LD* ii, 298; Newman to Edward Hawkins (30 October 1830), *LD* ii, 300; Newman to Edward Hawkins (13 April 1831), *LD* ii, 326; Edward Hawkins to Newman (16 April 1831), *LD* ii, 326.

29 "Memorandum on the Oriel Tuition" (9 July 1830), *LD* ii, 247

the Senior Tutor.[30] For his part (and on the direct advice of Copleston), Hawkins adamantly refused this concession. By 9 June 1830 he began to warn that he would no longer assign any undergraduates to Newman.[31] Newman responded to this ultimatum by refusing to alter his views and so acquiesced to Hawkins's "gradual mode of removing me."[32] On 11 June 1831, Newman confided to his diary, "second day of collections–finished *my* men–and so ends my Tutor's work!"[33]

Newman's pastoral conception of university education expressed itself in a conviction that religion should restrain Oriel's new hegemonic value for intellectual distinction and originality.[34] Writing to his bishop in 1835, Henry Wilberforce summarized the controversy as nothing less than a contest between those who regarded the University as

> "the nursery of the Church of England" and a party who desired to make "knowledge, rather than moral discipline the object of our studies, and to cultivate rather the habit of bold and irreverent Inquiry, often conducted in the most flippant tone and spirit, and sparing no subject, whether human or divine, for that humility and self-distrust which characterizes the true philosopher, whatever be his subject, and which is, above all things, indispensable to the beneficial pursuit of religious truth."[35]

Writing from a much cooler vantage in 1860, Newman conceded that it would have been better to have informed Hawkins of his plans from the

---

30 Newman to Edward Hawkins (5 May 1830), *LD* ii, 216.

31 Edward Hawkins to Newman (15 May 1830), *LD* ii, 232.

32 Newman to Edward Hawkins (15 June 1830), *LD* ii, 242.

33 Newman (11 June 1831), *LD* ii, 334.

34 Peter Nockles refutes the onetime regnant "Gibboneian" caricature of Oxford's "intellectual and moral decay as well as torpor and indolence," arguing instead that the new examination statutes of 1800 and 1807 represented "a genuine tightening up in academic standards and discipline." His essay describes how this new emphasis on academic excellence came into conflict with the "counter-revolutionary" Tractarians. See Peter Nockles, "'An Academic Counter-Revolution': Newman & Tractarian Oxford's Idea of a University," in *History of Universities*, vol. 10, eds. Lawrence Brockliss and Mark Cuthoys (Oxford: Oxford University Press, 1991), 137-39.

35 Henry Wilberforce, *The Foundations of Faith Assailed in Oxford* (London: 1835), 5, 7-9.

beginning. While maintaining his annoyance at the "state of constant bickerings" and Hawkins's typical "coldness, dryness, and donnishness," he admitted to conducting himself with an "insubordination" and "petulance" that was incommensurate with an ethos that championed self-denial, reverence, reserve, and obedience.[36]

Reflecting on his own contemporaneous experiences of Newman shortly before his own death in 1884, Mark Pattison suggested that under the tuition of Newman, Froude, and Wilberforce, Oriel College had been confined to "the narrow and desperate devotees of the clerical interest." He reflected how, "the college must have become a seminary in which the pupils should be trained for church ends, and broken in, like the students of a Jesuit college, to regard the dictates of the confessor and the interests of the clergy as the supreme law of life."[37] Pattison's reflections remain additionally valuable for their connection of Newman's failed tuition reforms with a newfound freedom for patristic research (begun in 1828).[38]

---

[36] "Memorandum on Edwin Hawkins" (15 July 1860), *LD* ii, 202.

[37] Mark Pattison, *Memoirs* (London: Macmillan, 1885), 97. He additionally bemoaned Hawkins's tenure as the beginning of Oriel's decline and derided the "lesser men" appointed to serve after 1830, so Pattison's preferred course remains unclear. H. S. Jones devotes considerable space to Pattison's time at Oriel and to his experience of Tractarianism. In many ways, Newman and Pattison's lives parallel one another in significant ways, with the latter coming to champion the regnant ethos of the Noetics (especially those of the liberal-leaning Hampden) in a way that mirrored Newman's embrace of Keble. See H. S. Jones, *Intellect and Character in Victorian England: Mark Pattison and the Invention of the Don* (Cambridge: Cambridge University Press, 2007), 19-42.

[38] In the *Apologia* Newman speaks of a return to the love of the early church fathers, originally cultivated in him by Joseph Milner. There he dates his beginning a systematic read through their writings during the Long Vacation of 1828, beginning with St. Ignatius of Loyola and St. Justin Martyr. Newman, *Apo*, 87. This research was greatly expanded in October 1831 when he received as a gift from "friends and pupils" thirty-six volumes of the fathers. Among the volumes were the works of "Austin, Athanasius, Cyril Alexandrinus, Epiphanius, Gregory Nyssen, Origen, Basil, Ambrose, and Irenaeus." Of the gift he wrote to his mother, saying, "They are so fine in their outsides as to put my former ones to shame–and the editions are the best. Altogether now I am set up in the Patristical line–should I be blessed with health and ability to make use of them. [My] difficulty now is, where

When Newman studied, it was church history–the Fathers of the fourth century; Athanasius was his hero; he was inspired by the triumph of the church organisation over the wisdom and philosophy of the Hellenic world; that triumph which, to the Humanist, is the saddest moment in history–the ruin of the painfully constructed fabric of civilisation to the profit of the church. Religion was evidently to Newman, in 1830, not only the first but the sole object of all teachings. There was no thought then of ἐν κύκλῳ παιδεία, a genealogical chart of all the sciences; there was not even the lesser conception of education by the classics, as containing the essential elements of humanism. These teachers of the classics had sided with the enemies of humanism. Greek was useful as enabling you to read the Greek Testament and the Fathers. All knowledge was to be subservient to the interests of religion, for which vague idea was afterwards substituted the definite and concrete idea of the Visible Church.[39]

Here the experienced failure of Newman's first efforts to form his school occasioned and influenced his study of early Christianity. Driven by his developing Apostolical ethos, he could not leave off the values he hoped to inculcate at Oriel. His newfound liberty enabled him to think through them in a more systematic fashion. Newman found his needful precedent in the writings of early Christianity that "[arose] up again full before [him]" just days after dispensing with his duties to the tuition.[40]

A SCHOOL OF TRADITIONARY RELIGION: THE CATECHETICAL SCHOOL OF ALEXANDRIA AND *THE ARIANS OF THE FOURTH CENTURY*

In March of 1831 Newman received an invitation from Hugh James Rose, the High Churchman and Rector of Hadleigh in Suffolk, to author a history of the church councils for a new library of theological works that Rose would coedit with William Rowe Lyall. Newman proposed

---

to put my acquisition–they are too *deep* for my study-bookcases–I mean no pun on the word." Newman to Mrs. Newman (24 October 1831), *LD* ii, 369.

39 Pattison, *Memoirs*, 96-97. Although his words here are intentionally critical–this much is obvious in his conclusion: "Religion is a good servant but a poor master."

40 Newman to Mrs. Newman (25 June 1830), *LD* ii, 245.

a study of the Thirty-nine Articles, but the editors suggested that a history of the ecumenical councils would make a useful introduction to that further work. At precisely the same time, the new Whig government had undertaken the work of passing the Act to Amend the Representation of the people in England and Wales (also known as the Reform Bill) in parliament. According to its preamble, the act was designed to "take effectual Measures for correcting divers Abuses that have long prevailed in the Choice of Members to serve in the Commons House of Parliament."[41] The means employed for this correction would be the deliberate transfer of voting privileges from the small rural boroughs controlled by the nobility and gentry to the heavily populated but underrepresented industrial towns. While these reforms in fact proved modest when the bill was finally passed in 1832, the result was a further democratization of power in English society.[42] As with the Test and Corporation and Catholic Emancipation bills, Newman greatly feared for the further erosion of the Church of England's independence from a meddling state. On 13 March 1831 he warned John Bowden of the dire threats posed by the new *vox populi*:

> I am tempted to put it to you whether the persons you meet generally are (I do not say, consistently religious, we can never expect that in this world) but believe in Christianity in any true meaning of the word. No, they are liberals, and in saying this, I conceive I am saying almost as bad of them as can be said of any man. What will be the case if things remain as they are? Shall we not have men placed in the higher stations of the Church who are anything but real Churchmen? . . . I would rather have the Church severed from its temporalities and scattered to the four winds than such a desecration of holy things.[43]

---

[41] Robert Peel, *The Speeches of the Late Right Honourable Sir Robert Peel, Bart. Delivered in the House of Commons*, vol. 2 (London: George Routledge & Co., 1853), 348.

[42] See the discussion of the bill and its implications in Boyd Hilton, *A Mad, Bad, Dangerous People?: England 1783-1846* (Oxford: Oxford University Press, 2008), 420-38.

[43] *LD* ii, 317. Reflecting on this period in the *Apologia*, Newman expressed a remarkably similar sentiment: "While I was engaged in my work upon the Arians, great events were happening at home and abroad, which brought out into form and

On 24 August of the same year, Newman informed Rose that the councils of the Eastern churches alone would require a single volume. He proposed, in turn, to write "a *connected* history of the Councils . . . not taking them as isolated, but introducing so much of Church History as will illustrate and account for them." Here he pleaded for the importance of historical context in the adequate appreciation of theology–something not incidental given Newman's later perspective on the development of doctrine of the early 1840s.[44]

> What light would be thrown on the Nicene Confession *merely* by explaining it article by article? to understand it, it must be prefaced by a sketch of the rise of the Arian heresy, the words introduced by Arius, his perversions of the hitherto orthodox terms, the necessity of newer and clearer tests, etc.[45]

When Newman completed *The Arians of the Fourth Century* in 1832, its contents largely bore out the proposal outlined in his letter to Rose. As Newman noted in the *Apologia*, the introductory matter comprised 117 of its total 422 pages and covered the "Schools and Parties in and About the Ante-Nicene Church, In Their Relation to the Arian Heresy" in five sections: 1) The Church of Antioch, 2) The Schools of the Sophists, 3) The Church of Alexandria, 4) The Eclectic Sect, and 5) Sabellianism. Beyond this, Newman detailed the great Councils of Nicaea and Constantinople, complete with a full history of various persecutions suffered by the Athanasians at the hands of the Arian and semi-Arian heretics. Considered as a whole, Newman developed

---

passionate expression the various beliefs which had so gradually been winning their way into my mind. Shortly before, there had been a Revolution in France; the Bourbons had been dismissed: and I believed that it was unchristian for nations to cast off their governors. . . . Again, the great Reform Agitation was going on around me as I wrote. . . . The vital question was how were we going to keep the Church from being liberalized?" Newman, *Apo.* 93–94.

44 Rowan Williams has helpfully put it with regard to *Arians of the Fourth Century*, "an important step has been taken: doctrine, even if only in its outward expression, does have a *history*." Rowan Williams, "Newman's *Arians* and the Question of Method in Doctrinal History," in *Newman After One Hundred Years*, eds., Ian Ker and Alan G. Hill (Oxford: Clarendon, 1990), 276.

45 Newman to Hugh James Rose (24 August 1831), *LD* ii, 352-53.

a single case in *Arians of the Fourth Century* wherein he contrasted the history and legacy of two great centers of early Christianity: Alexandria and Antioch. In its opening pages, he spent nearly a third of the work examining the role of "schools." Newman understood these to exist in distinction from mere "parties" or "sects" in and about early Christianity "at the time of its rise,"[46] but there is an "marked resemblance"[47] in Newman's exposition to the various schools of his own time and place. Here the various themes in Newman's personal history come very near to the surface, exercising an unmistakable influence on his narration of events in the fourth century. In evidence are Newman's evangelical regard for the contra-mundane nature of holiness and his tendency to invest history with polemic value as did Joseph Milner before him. Present also was Newman's deep distrust of private judgment and unassisted human reason as a sure guide to moral and religious truth.

The establishment of Antioch as the patristic center from which Arianism originally sprang was critical to Newman's case. Here he focused on the figure of Paul of Samosata, a crypto-Sabellian and

> founder of a school rather than a sect, as encouraging in the Church the use of those disputations, and skeptical inquiries, which belonged to the heathen academies, and scattering up and down the seeds of errors, which sprang up and bore fruit in the generation after him.[48]

Appealing to the work of the church historian, Theodosius, Newman also posited a vital connection between the semi-Arian "school" of Lucian, associating him with Arius and other later Arians by name.[49] From these twin points, he then established an essential continuity between Arianism and "the school of Antioch," locating the seeds of its heresies in two "foreign" sources: Judaism and pagan philosophy.

Touching on the former, Newman certainly indulged an unchecked bigotry by associating Judaism with an endemic skepticism, absent any "definite interest in the subject of dispute, but a sort of spontaneous

---

[46] Newman, *Ari*, 2.

[47] See Newman, *Ari*, 393, where he established this link himself.

[48] Newman, *Ari*, 6.

[49] Newman, *Ari*, 7.

feeling, that the side of heresy was their natural position."[50] This conclusion is historically indefensible, of course, as Newman anachronistically attributed post-Nicene features of the latter Antiochene exegetical method to the earlier, ante-Nicene school. Rowan Williams has helpfully demonstrated that Newman's real interlocutor here was the church historian, Johann Mosheim, a faithful Protestant historian who lionized the biblicism and historicism of Antioch.[51] What Williams neglected to incorporate into his analysis, however, were the ways the school of Anglican evangelicals–Newman's brother, Francis, noteworthy among them–and their "wretched Protestant principle about Scripture" stood alongside Mosheim, sharing his values completely. This lent more than a few degrees-worth of existential heat to Newman's rhetoricisation of the ancient Christian past. His "Judaizers" at Antioch were less non-Christian foreigners, representing a corrupting influence on the faithful, than they were pathetically derisible Christians who sold their rightful inheritance for a bowl of lukewarm gruel.[52] Understood in this light, Newman saw the school at Antioch and the evangelical school as being alike in their "Galatian" apostasy, preferring a Judaizing gospel of their own creation. The underlying *anathema* is unmistakable in his narration.

Treating the influence of pagan philosophy at Antioch, Newman then charged the "schools of the sophists" with an undue reliance on Aristotle, giving them a self-assured confidence in "scholastic eloquence."[53] He additionally wrote of their "disputing for the sake of exercise or amusement." These, in turn, inculcated a tendency to assail "received opinions."[54] Viewing these influences together, Newman concluded that "[t]he progress of unbelief naturally led them on to disparage, rather than to appeal to their predecessors; and to trust their cause to their own ingenuity, instead of defending an inconvenient

---

[50] Newman, *Ari*, 23.

[51] Williams, "Newman's *Arians*," 281.

[52] Williams, "Newman's *Arians*," 282.

[53] Newman, *Ari*, 29.

[54] Newman, *Ari*, 31.

fiction concerning the opinions of a former age."[55] Here then were Oriel's Noetics–especially in their liberalizing cast–with a propensity for "calling everything into question" and their "rejection of authority as a judge in matters intellectual."[56] Here too was his brother, Charles, whose unbelief Newman came to regard as the inevitable end of liberal principles. Like Charles, Newman's sophists tended to regard "the ecclesiastical authorities of former times as on a level with the uneducated and unenlightened of their own days."[57] According to Newman's view, these schools pressed Antioch toward a low Christology, wherein Jesus appeared, at best, an inspired prophet or a superhuman mediator between the world and a God who was wholly other.[58]

In the Church of Alexandria, Newman identified both a true church and a true school, describing the former in ideal terms as "the Missionary and Polemical Church of antiquity."[59] He surpassed the limits of his historical sources in a zealous effort to exempt Alexandria from any stain of Arius's heresy. This was no mean feat given that Arius was born and ordained in Alexandria. Newman accomplished this by a creative appeal to the manner in which the Alexandrian Church, through its catechetical school, initiated catechumens in a deliberate process of conversion and initiation. Here, the Alexandrian catechists reserved full disclosure of the deep mysteries of the faith (that is, doctrines of the Trinity, Incarnation, and Atonement) for an appropriate time after the converts had established a capacity for moral discipline and self-restraint. In Newman's analysis, this *disciplina arcani* initially left the church vulnerable to the assaults of the very middle- and neo-Platonic syncretism that he associated with the "eclectic" school. These

---

55 Newman, *Ari*, 40.

56 Pattison, *Memoirs*, 78-79. This passage in Pattison was quoted approvingly by William Gladstone: British Library Add MS 44792 f. 53. It also reflects Pattison's earlier judgment in his "Philosophy at Oxford," *Mind* 1 (1876): 82-97.

57 Newman, *Ari*, 35-36. As Rowan Williams has written, "Newman's 'Antioch' is an ideal type not an historical reality. It is the type of a theology dictated by human wisdom, human desire, the reluctance to be humble before revelation." Rowan Williams, "Introduction," in *Arians*, xxxix.

58 Brian Daley, "The Church Fathers," in *The Cambridge Companion to John Henry Newman* (Cambridge: Cambridge University Press, 2009), 30-31.

59 Newman, *Ari*, 45.

opponents flaunted their errors in open controversy while the early church hesitated before enunciating a public creed.[60] Newman argued that "freedom from symbols and articles, is abstractedly the highest state of Christian communion, and the particular privilege of the primitive Church."[61] When confessions did not exist, he maintained, the mysteries of divine truth were "kept hidden in the bosom of the Church, far more faithfully than is otherwise possible." It was "reserved by a private teaching, through the channel of her ministers, as rewards in due measure and season, for those who are prepared to profit by them; those, i.e. who are diligently passing through the successive stages of faith and obedience."[62]

By his recourse to the Apostolical ethos, inherent in the *disciplina arcana*, Newman evaded the charge that Alexandrian allegory was ultimately rooted in paganism. Rather, he viewed it as evidence of the church adapting itself to the limited capacities of its audience in public dispute. Moreover, Newman detected in the practices of Alexandria a greater reliance on the authority of the church than was the case at Antioch. To his eyes, this illustrated the conviction that he first learned from Edward Hawkins: "Surely the sacred volume was never intended, and is not adapted to *teach* us our creed; however certain it is that we can *prove* our creed from it, when it has once been taught us, and in spite of indivisible produceable exceptions to the general rule."[63]

Newman's treatment of the ante-Nicene schools arose from a twin context, one in late antiquity, the other in the experience of his own context in the early decades of the nineteenth century. As numerous authors have observed, his penchant for rhetoricising history allowed the latter to eclipse the former, but Newman was not interested in presenting a dispassionate, critical history of the fourth century.[64] Like Milner before him, he perceived schools of thought in the early

---

60 Newman, *Ari*, 35.

61 Newman, *Ari*, 37.

62 Newman, *Ari*, 37.

63 Newman, *Ari*, 50.

64 As Rowan Williams puts it, Newman indulged in "brilliant argument, linking all sorts of diverse phenomena . . . built on a foundation of complacent bigotry and historical fantasy." Williams, *Arius*, 4–5.

church as bearing "a marked resemblance" to the "present perils" of his own day. He sought, therefore, to discover resources that were "especially cheering and edifying to Christians of [his] present day."[65] The Judaizing sympathies at Antioch along with their "sophistical" arrogance thus found a counterpoint, both in evangelicalism's erosion of the church's catholic inheritance, and in liberalism's insistence on "the right of Private Judgment." Both affirmed "no existing authority on earth competent to interfere with the liberty of individuals in reasoning and judging for themselves about the Bible and its contents, as they severally please."[66]

In their respective treatments of Newman at this point, Thomas Ferguson and Frank Turner have diverged on the question of which contemporary opponent falls under condemnation in Newman's treatment of Antioch. Turner has relied heavily on Newman's absence of clarity on the meaning of "liberalism" and so insists that modern evangelicals were almost exclusively in view.[67] Ferguson, on the other hand, has been more inclined to take Newman at face value, identifying his opponent at various places with the liberalism described in the *Apologia* and in Newman's much later Biglietto speech.[68] As I have argued, however, Newman understood evangelicalism and liberalism as twin fruits of the same heretical imperative, locatable in their twin rejection of received dogma and reliance on private judgment. According to Newman's view, the same skepticism and arrogance that led his brother Charles to reject Christianity for atheism was present too in his brother Francis when he rejected both the authority and received teaching of the Church of England for his place among the Plymouth Brethren. These "false schools," repeatedly encountered by Newman since his early adolescence, withered under the implied associations in *Arians*. His prescribed remedy for the tendencies in his own time

---

[65] Newman, *Ari*, 393.

[66] Newman, *Apo*, 367.

[67] Frank M. Turner, *John Henry Newman: The Challenge to Evangelical Religion* (New Haven: Yale University Press, 2011), 142–45.

[68] Thomas Ferguson, "The Enthralling Power: History and Heresy in John Henry Newman," *Anglican Theological Review* 85 (2003): 641–62, esp. 646–47.

was a deliberate return to the "divinity of traditionary religion" that he associated with the Alexandrian Church and its *school*.[69]

While Newman spent the latter chapters of *Arians* lauding the prophetic heroism of "Athanasian" theologians through various persecutions at the hands of Arian heretics, he understood them to be tradents in a direct lineage taking them back to the school at Alexandria. Their creative theological endeavors were oriented against heretical innovation and intended to preserve a faith entrusted to the church from its foundation by Christ and his apostles. This narration opened for Newman a powerful vision for his own beleaguered Church of England and supplied him with the ideological warrant necessary to recommit himself to the agenda he had commenced in the reforms of the Oriel Tuition.

Near the end of *Arians*, Newman closed the historical circle between the fourth century and the nineteenth century, writing:

> And so of the present perils, with which our branch of the Church is beset, as they bear a marked resemblance to those of the fourth century, so are the lessons, which we gain from that ancient time, especially cheering and edifying to Christians of the present day. Then as now, there was the prospect, and partly the presence in the Church, of an Heretical Power enthralling it, exerting a varied influence and a usurped claim in the appointment of her functionaries, and interfering with the management of her internal affairs. Now as then, "whosoever shall fall upon this stone shall be broken, but on whomsoever it shall fall, it will grind him to powder." Meanwhile, we may take comfort in reflecting, that, though the present tyranny has more of insult, it has hitherto had less of scandal, than attended the ascendancy of Arianism; we may rejoice in the piety, prudence, and varied graces of our Spiritual Rulers; and may rest in the confidence, that, should the hand of Satan press us sore, our Athanasius and Basil will be given us in their destined season, to break the bonds of the Oppressor, and let the captives go free.[70]

---

[69] Newman, *Ari*, 79. Rowan Williams characterizes Newman's Alexandria as the idyllic "home of true theology . . . characterized by reverence, by the expectation that the Bible will always be deeply mysterious, working through elusive symbolism over a lifetime of contemplation; this is a theology giving priority to God." Rowan Williams, "Introduction," in *Arians*, xxxix.

[70] Newman, *Ari*, 393-94.

Thomas Ferguson has helpfully pointed out a significant flaw in the contextualization of Newman proposed by Rowan Williams in a 2001 introduction to *Arians of the Fourth Century* and more fully explored in his monograph on Arius. In both, Williams convincingly argues that the proper historical lens for *Arians* is the nineteenth rather than the fourth century, but he continually speaks as though it were an *ex post facto* apologetic for the Oxford Movement.[71] Aiming to correct this anachronism in Williams's analysis, Ferguson observed that the *Arians of the Fourth Century* was published in 1833, well prior to Keble's *Assize Sermon* or, as I will argue in the next chapter, any other formal commencement of the Oxford Movement.[72] Thus, *Arians* becomes a prospectus of sorts, wherein Newman assumed a role like that of Athanasius or Basil.[73] The critical missing component of Ferguson's analysis, however, is any recognition that Newman's focus was on Alexandria being a *school of theologians*, working collaboratively with the church in the transmission of traditionary religion. If we are to read *Arians of the Fourth Century* as a prospectus, we should read it as a prospectus for a new "Alexandrian" school that Newman would begin constructing on the ruins of his failed tutorial reforms in 1833.

---

[71] Williams writes, for example, that "*The Arians of the Fourth Century* is, in large part, a tract in defense of what the early Oxford Movement thought of a spiritual religion and spiritual authority." Rowan Williams, *Arius: Heresy and Tradition*, rev. ed. (Grand Rapids: Eerdmans, 2001), 5.

[72] Ferguson, "The Enthralling Power," 643ff. Ferguson's complaint is only further strengthened by observing that the work was actually completed in July of 1832 but rejected by Rose and Lyall on the ground of its being overly friendly to Roman Catholicism. Newman was forced to find another publisher and only then did it appear in 1833.

[73] This connection is independently suggested by Benjamin King for different reasons and for different purposes. See, Benjamin J. King, *Newman and the Alexandrian Fathers: Shaping Doctrine in Nineteenth-Century England* (Oxford: Oxford University Press, 2009), 72n4.

VENTURING OUT ONTO THE TIGHTROPE: A THEOLOGIAN'S VOCATION

Referencing John Henry Newman as a theologian is in our day uncontroversial. Still, it bears mentioning that the man who has been described as "the invisible peritus" of the Second Vatican Council stalwartly refused in his own day to speak of himself as a theologian–and that despite his having been made a Doctor of Divinity as well as a Roman Catholic Priest by Pius IX in May of 1847.[74] While it is possible to treat such disclaimers as an indication of humility or as evidence of a reluctance to claim authoritative judgment on controversial matters, their exclusive appearance in Newman's Roman Catholic letters suggests that he may have simply been stipulating the regnant neo-Scholastic conception of theology, which held sway at the time. It was, after all, a method that Nicholas Lash has rightly spoken of as "alien to his whole mentality."[75] According to the consensus of the Catholic Church in his day, theology was a deductive enterprise, purposed, not for the discovery of new truths, but to apprehend and explain the always-already given truths of revelation.[76] Given his status as a convert,

---

[74] While references to Newman as the "invisible peritus, etc." are ubiquitous and the phrase itself often misattributed, it is the coinage of George Rutler who placed Newman alongside his "anonymous peritus," Monsignor Josemaria Escriva. George Rutler, "The Rise of Opus Dei," *New Oxford Review* 119 (1983): 19-23. Newman repeatedly used the phrase "I am no theologian" in letters to Acton (2 August 1858), *LD* xviii, 433; to Edward Pusey (14 November 1868), *LD* xxiv, 171; and to Richard Holt Hutton (16 February 1870), *LD* xxv, 32. These disclaimers were all made with regard to his being invited by several French bishops to serve as personal theologian during the First Vatican Council. Newman was also offered the opportunity of serving as a Consultor by Pius IX. As late as July 1877, he wrote to an unknown correspondent of how "in spite of the Pope having made me a D D–I am not a theologian." Newman to An Unknown Correspondent (July 1877), *LD* xxviii, 216. On 22 December of 1878, he went still further in a letter to Robert Whitty writing, "If anyone is obliged to say 'I speak under correction' it is I; for I am no theologian and am too old, and ever have been, to become one." *LD* xxviii, 431.

[75] Nicholas Lash, "Was Newman a Theologian?," *Heythrop Journal* 17 (1976): 322.

[76] See for example how he explores theology as a science in his *Idea of a University* where he writes that "no new truth can be gained by deduction; Catholics assent, but add that, as regards religious truth, they have not to seek it at all, for they have it already. Christian Truth is purely of revelation; that revelation we can but explain,

Newman's public loyalty to his church led him to recognize how his strengths as a controversialist, a generalist, and an occasional writer left him ill-suited for the profile of a theologian as Rome understood it.

That being said, there remain a few instances in Newman's Catholic writings wherein he hinted at the possibility of conceiving theology as an *inductive* and *historical* discipline–one that transcended the constraining givens of Rome's neo-Scholastic hegemony and better preserved that "loving inquisitiveness which is the life of the *Schola*."[77] A letter to Maria Giberne on 10 February 1869 would seem to warrant our looking past the *prima facie* disclaimers of the Catholic Newman to better integrate his conceptions of a theology while he was still an Anglican. There he reflected:

> One who has mastered theology–who can say how many opinions there are on every point, what authors have taken which, and which is the best–who can discriminate exactly between proposition and proposition, argument and argument, who can pronounce which are safe, which allowable, which dangerous–who can trace the history of doctrines in successive centuries, and apply the principles of former times to the conditions of the present. This is it to be a theologian– this and a hundred things besides. And this I am not, and never shall be. Like St Gregory Nazianzen I like going on my own way, and having my time my own, living without pomp or state, or pressing engagements. Put me into official garb, and I am worth nothing; leave me to myself, and every now and then I shall do something. Dress me up and you will soon have to make my shroud–leave me alone, and I shall live the appointed time.[78]

Here Newman redescribed the vocation of a theologian in a way that was better suited to his way of practicing theology. From his earliest days as an Anglican priest, and in *Arians of the Fourth Century* in particular, Newman traced the history of doctrine in successive centuries and applied principles gleaned from former times to his present context.

---

we cannot increase, except relatively to our own apprehensions." Newman, *Idea* (London: Basil, Montagu, Pickering, 1873), 223-24.

77 Newman, *Dev*, new ed. (London: Basil, Montagu, & Pickering 1878), 337.

78 Newman to Maria Giberne (10 February 1869), *LD* xxiv, 212-13.

Still more significant is the similitude he named between himself and Gregory Nazianzen, the great Cappadocian father who has ever been invoked as Gregory the *Theologian*.[79]

Five months after completing *The Arians of the Fourth Century*, Newman was persuaded in December 1832 to tour southern Europe with Hurrell Froude and his father, Archdeacon Robert Froude. On board the mail steamship *Hermes*, they visited Gibraltar, Malta, and the Ionian Islands. From there, they made their way to Italy and visited Sicily, Naples, and Rome. While in Naples he read in the papers of the Irish Church Temporalities Bill. Proposed by Lord Charles Grey's Whig government, the bill represented a thorough administrative and financial restructuring of the Church of Ireland. Ten redundant bishoprics would be dissolved, and their endowments dispersed among the remaining sees. In place of the deeply unpopular church rates, imposed as they were on a largely Catholic population, the bill also levied a tax on higher clerical incomes to pay for the upkeep of the remaining churches. Although the Whigs defended the move as an obvious and rational piece of legislation, the fact that it appeared in the immediate wake of the 1828 and 1829 reform acts stoked the fears of churchmen like Newman. In a letter to his mother drafted the same day, he lamented,

> The state of the Church is deplorable. It seems as if Satan were let out of prison to range the whole earth again. As far as our little experience goes, every thing seems to confirm the notion received among

---

[79] In all probability Gregory attracted the moniker "Theologian" because reference to his authorship of the *Five Theological Orations* neatly distinguished him from his friend and fellow Cappadocian Father, Gregory of Nyssa. The earliest historical reference to "Gregory the Theologian" introduces an excerpt from Gregory's first letter Cledonius (Ep. 101), ascribed to "the blessed Gregory the Theologian" (τοῦ μακαρίου Γρηγορίου τοῦ Θεολόγου) in the florilegium of patristic authorities appended to the Address to the Emperor Marcian in the *Acta* of the Council of Chalcedon in 451 CE (*ACO* 2. 1, 3.114 [473].14). The title also appears in a defense of the two wills and operations in Christ from Session 18 of the Third Council of Constantinople, 16 September 681 (*DS* §558). "Gregory the Theologian" also functions as a familiar title in works by such later Greek writers as the Emperor Justinian (*Against Origen*: *ACO* 3.193.2, 26, 35; 194.4; 195.32; *Edict against Origen*: *ACO* 205.37), Maximus the Confessor (e.g., *Dialogue with Pyrrhus*: *PG* 91.316 C) and John of Damascus (*On the Orthodox Faith* 3.15).

ourselves of the infidelity and profligacy of the priesthood–while the Church on the other hand is stripped of its temporalities and reduced to great distress.[80]

Still fuming upon his arrival at Rome, Newman complained to Thomas Mozley that the bill made him "hate the Whigs (of course, as Rowena says, in a Christian way) more bitterly than ever." His thoughts also turned to Oxford and his imagined pathetic reaction of Edward Hawkins (that is, *Magister Praepositstus*) and to "poor Whatley" concerning "the atrocious Irish sacrilege bill."[81] For Newman, there was no hope for England while Oriel remained as it was. While he could describe Italy as a "wonderful place, piercing the heart with a strange painful pleasure!," he found the Catholic Christianity at Rome to be little more than "polytheistic, degrading, idolatrous."[82] In its churches he saw a vision of England's foreboding future, with a "timid and poorspirited" church clinging to "beautiful and rich structures" while lacking any desire to personally appropriate the Christian faith.[83]

Instead of accompanying the Froudes home in April 1833, Newman returned to Sicily alone and there fell dangerously ill with gastric or typhoid fever at Leonforte. Though he entrusted dying requests to a servant, he nevertheless expressed confidence that he "should *not* die" because "God had work" for him in England.[84] In later years, Newman recalled how tearful rumination on the meaning of his recovery endowed him with a profound confidence in his vocation as a priest and scholar.[85] Upon his arrival at home, he would commence with a

---

[80] Newman to Mrs. Newman (28 February 1833), *LD* iii, 224.

[81] Newman to Thomas Mozley (9 March 1833), *LD* i, 372.

[82] Newman to Jemima Newman (19 February 1833), *LD* iii, 219; Newman to Samuel Rickards (14 April 1833), *LD* iii, 289.

[83] Newman to Henry Wilberforce (9 March 1933), *LD* iii, 246.

[84] Newman to Frederic Rogers (5 June 1833), *LD* iii, 314.

[85] Newman, *AW*, 126. In the *Apologia* Newman recalled his visit in early April to "Monsignore" Nicholas Wiseman, who was then the rector of the English College at Rome. Upon their being invited by Wiseman to make a return trip, Newman remembered his response as "We have a work to do in England." Newman, *Apo*, 99. While it is not impossible that Newman expressed similar sentiments to Wiseman,

new attempt to realize his vision for a school at Oxford. Having been left to himself for a time, John Henry Newman was now prepared to do something.

---

the words are better suited to the sentiments of a man who had recovered from a grave illness. Unfortunately, we are wholly dependent on Newman's late autobiographical reflections to establish his disposition at the time.

CHAPTER 3

Commending the Episcopate and Constructing a Popular Church
Oxford's Apostolical Men amid England's Imperiled Ecclesial Structures

We must never forget that the concert of early Tractarian theological commonplaces–the apostolic succession of bishops, the liturgical stability of the Book of Common Prayer, the sacramental powers of the clergy, and the divinely established jurisdiction of the church–were practically consequential. Newman and his fellow "Apostolicals," as Froude dubbed them, established these ramparts under an expectation of the Church of England's impending disestablishment–a development he saw taking place in full view of the public with the passive complicity of its chief shepherds. Newman interpreted this "national apostasy," as Keble famously termed it, by light of similar apostasies in the fourth century. He saw in both an institutional church that was seemingly powerless to mount a concerted defense. As was true of the Alexandrian school in that distant era, Newman conceived his school as an instrument of spiritual suasion, encouraging the church to recoup its flagging cultural sway by restoring the episcopate to a role befitting its status as successor to the apostolic college. Richard Whately had long since persuaded him against any Erastian notions that the Church of England was a constituent creation of the Crown. Bitter experience left him convinced that it could no longer claim a privileged place in hearts of Lord Grey's reform parliament. In Newman's mind this left one option: direct popular appeal. In his mind the church would thrive and survive by being "thrown on the people"–that is, by commending itself *directly* to the faithful in an economic–and more importantly, in a *theological*–sense.[1] But this enterprise would require a distinct *place* to make their stand. "To make the Church more *popular*" as Newman put it, would necessitate an appeal to pre-recognized authority and a name that could command attention and evoke public deference.[2] For this reason, Newman actively and independently sought to associate his school with the august name of Oxford and the university that made its home there.

THE PERSONAL INFLUENCE OF APOSTOLICAL MEN

From the 25th to the 29th of July 1833, Hugh Rose convened a meeting at his rectory in Hadleigh, Suffolk to discuss the "important ecclesiastical questions" posed by the Irish Church Temporalities Bill. The hope was to plot a course of action following its ratification on 14 August of that year.[3] For Newman and his fellow Apostolicals, the bill represented a usurpation of ecclesial prerogative by a parliament that was no longer exclusively composed of members of the Church of England. With the ten Irish bishoprics suppressed and English churchmen largely complicit in the exercise, Newman judged it high time for a more aggressive course of action. He began, as he explained to a friend, by "poking into the Fathers with a hope of rummaging forth passages of history which may prepare the *imaginations* of men for a changed state of things, and also be precedents for our conduct in difficult circumstances."[4]

Newman did not attend the Hadleigh meeting, but he was careful to note that Oxford was represented by those he spoke of as "*our*

---

[1] Newman to John William Bowden (31 August 1833), *LD* iv, 34. Cf., Newman, "Primitive Christianity," *HS* i (New York: Longmans, Green and Co., 1914), 340. In a letter to R. F. Wilson, dated 8 September 1833, Newman similarly wrote that "the *people* were the fulcrum of the Church's power." *LD* iv, 44.

[2] Newman to Charles Portales Golightly (11 August 1833), *LD* iv, 28.

[3] Newman to Charles Portales Golightly (30 July 1833), *LD* iv, 13.

[4] Newman to Charles Thomas Mozley (5 August 1833), *LD* iv, 24.

deputies": William Palmer of Worcester and Hurrell Froude.[5] It was by means of the latter that Newman subsequently ascertained the details, and he wasted no time in conceiving a strategic response. As he wrote to Charles Golightly on 30 July, they would make use of his gathered precedents from early Christian history to organize and raise a popular movement wherein the church would be "thrown on the people" for its temporal support and warrant to minister.[6] Carefully avoiding any impression that the church was sacrificing its *spiritual* authority–something it received by direct commission from Jesus Christ and the charism of the Holy Spirit–their intent was to establish the independent authority of the episcopate without trading subservience to the state for subservience to the *demos*.

While the Roman Catholic Newman of the *Apologia* regarded Keble's 14 July 1833 *Assize Sermon* on "National Apostasy" as "the start of the Oxford Movement," contemporaneous sources suggest that the event was little noticed and of only minor importance at the time.[7] The *Apologia*'s waning historiographic authority in recent studies have served to strengthen Henry Tristram's suggestion that the event should be subordinated to Newman's own *University Sermon* of 22 January 1832 as an inaugurating event.[8] Entitled "Personal Influence, the Means of Propagating the Truth," Newman's primary thesis was that "the influence of Truth in the world at large" arises primarily from "*the Personal Influence*, direct and indirect, of those who are commissioned

---

[5] Newman to Charles Portales Golightly (30 July 1833), *LD* iv, 13. Emphasis mine.

[6] Newman to Charles Portales Golightly (30 July 1833), *LD* iv, 14. "Spoliation" in his letter was Newman's pejorative nickname for the Irish Temporalities Bill.

[7] Sir John Taylor Coleridge considered it too abstruse for a sermon. J. H. Rigg, a Methodist historian of the Oxford Movement, called it a "solemn but feeble threnody." J. H. Rigg, *Oxford High Anglicanism and its Chief Leaders* (London: C. H. Kelly, 1895), 19-20.

[8] In the end, Tristram conceded that these alternative views are "not irreconcilable" and proposed that while Newman's sermon was "an appeal for volunteers in the spiritual combat," Keble's sermon represented "a call to action in the political crisis that seemed to menace the Church of England." Newman, *AW*, 119. Cf., Sheridan Gilley, *Newman and his Age* (London: Darton, Longman and Todd, 2003), 112; Peter Nockles, *A History of Oriel College* (Oxford: Oxford University Press, 2013), 328.

to teach it."[9] This twin emphasis on commissioned teaching and the personal qualities of the commissioned teacher is pivotal for the way that it consolidates Newman's hard-won values for theological orthodoxy and personal holiness. They developed from his evangelical experience, through his attempted reform of Oriel's tutorial system, and through his composition of *The Arians of the Fourth Century*. Here those values took on an embodied shape.

For Newman, the promised Holy Spirit animated the embodied church and echoed the incarnate words and works of Jesus. Thus, the church and Spirit cooperate to become the "Teacher of Truth after Christ's departure" by speaking authoritatively on "a subject-matter far more diversified than that on which our Lord had revealed Himself before Him."[10] Coming to individual teachers of the church, Newman argued that "Truth" has ultimately been upheld in the world, "not as a system, not by books, not by argument, nor by temporal power, but by the personal influence of such men as have already been described, who are at once the teachers and the patterns of it."[11] Borne aloft by this potent combination of deep learning and personal holiness, he concluded that the effect of even "a single individual, trained to practise what he teaches" might prove so morally powerful that the effects on his own circle would be inestimable.[12] Summoning his audience to such an endeavor, Newman then concluded with a promise that "a few highly-endowed men will rescue the world for centuries to come" and that the mode of their ministrations would be *prophetic*:

> Such men, like the Prophet, are placed upon their watch-tower, and light their beacons on the heights. Each receives and transmits the sacred flame, trimming it in rivalry of his predecessor, and fully

---

9 Newman, *US*, 79-80.

10 Newman, *US*, 82-83.

11 Newman, *US*, 91-92.

12 Newman, *US*, 94. While Newman could not yet imagine using the feminine pronoun, it remains important to note that he would eventually locate such an iconic exemplar in the person of the Blessed Virgin Mary. See here his "Sermon XV. The Theory of Developments in Religious Doctrine," first preached on 2 February 1843. *US*, 312-51.

purposed to send it on as bright as it has reached him; and thus the self-same fire, once kindled on Moriah, though seeming at intervals to fail, has at length reached us in safety, and will in like manner, as we trust, be carried forward even to the end.[13]

To be sure, Newman foresaw that virtually any Christian might fill such an exemplary role. He was quite clear, after all, that such persons were likely to be the product of obscurity and imitated only through extreme effort. That said, he also foresaw that such persons could conspire to become "a *school*" to which the educated and eloquent were "almost strangers."[14] Newman thus summoned his congregation to gather with what might become "the humblest and most obscure lot" or "a small circle" occupying "a lower place in the Church."[15] He additionally judged that such persons and places formed an abiding constant in church history, carrying forward the Spirit's work in the world and imitating the apostles of Jesus as "successors to their holiness."[16]

These expressions are especially important for the way Newman would later conceptualize theology as a definite *munus* of the church, existing in vital communion with the Apostolical *munus* of the episcopate while remaining distinct from it. While one cannot say more for Newman at this point than that he was feeling his way forward to a decisive breakthrough that would finally crystallize in his dispute with a Abbé Jean-Nicolas Jager three years on, one notes that all the ingredients for Newman's conception of the "Prophetical Office of the Church" were already preset in this sermon: 1) a conspiracy of learned, holy persons; 2) forming a succession from the church's apostolic foundation distinguishable from the episcopate; 3) functioning in a didactic role as a school; and 4) speaking with a prophetic voice. While Jager would become a provoking catalyst, helping Newman to consolidate thoughts that were still latent at this point, one can readily see how these themes developed in his first Tractarian writings, purposed as

---

[13] Newman, *US*, 97.
[14] Newman, *US*, 93. Emphasis mine.
[15] Newman, *US*, 97-98.
[16] Newman, *US*, 96.

they were both to rouse England's episcopate and to secure its proper role in the popular imagination. The form and function of Newman's school was beginning to take shape even here.

THE VERY MODEL OF AN APOSTOLIC BISHOP: *THE CHURCH OF THE FATHERS*

Newman's earliest published work as a Tractarian was a four-part series of letters on "The Church of the Fathers."[17] These were drafted in early August and submitted to Hugh James Rose, then editor of the *British Magazine*, with the purpose that they might blossom into a regular feature. Rose responded favorably and agreed to commence the series in the 1 October 1833 issue. He added his hopes that Newman would be "able and willing to continue it very long," and these epistolary sketches appeared henceforth at regular intervals until May 1837.[18]

The first four letters "on the principle of popularity as an element of Church power, as exemplified in the history of St. Ambrose," are remarkable for the way they imagine a role for the Apostolical bishop in relation to the state and the lay faithful. Newman's first letter began with the "practical question" facing every churchman and asked a simple question: "by what instruments the authority of religion is to be supported, should the protection and patronage of the government be withdrawn[?]"[19] By "supported" here, it is important to recognize that Newman did not first mean *financial* support. As the preceding chapters have made clear, Newman contemplated far more pressing dangers for the church than a prospective social and monetary impoverishment.[20] Certainly the disestablishment of the Church of England

---

[17] In his 5 August 1833 letter to Thomas Mozley, Newman wrote that his "precedents for our conduct in difficult circumstances" would be submitted to Rose for publication in the *British Magazine. LD* iv, 24.

[18] Hugh James Rose to Newman (20 August 1833), *LD* iv, 30.

[19] Newman, "Primitive Christianity," *HS* i (New York: Longmans, Green and Co., 1914), 339.

[20] Frank Turner, *John Henry Newman: The Challenge to Evangelical Religion* (New Haven: Yale, 2002), 168-89. Turner's portrait of Newman as ever-obsessed with

would necessitate looking to its solvency, but Newman was preoccupied with the existence of the church as "that peculiar institution which Christ set up as a visible home and memorial of Truth."[21] Convinced of the failure of England's "regal and aristocratical" powers to preserve and defend the church, he proposed that faithful churchmen were duty-bound to "*look to the people*" for its temporal maintenance and spiritual reputation.[22] This was not to compromise his conviction of the church's divine origin. Still less did it reduce the church to a mere creation of the people. For Newman, the apostolic succession of the priestly ministerium was a sure defense against the church falling prey to mere populism. "[W]e are an APOSTOLICAL body," he warned,

> we were not made, nor can be unmade by our flocks; and if our influence is to depend on *them*, yet the Sacraments reside with us. We have that with us, which none but ourselves possess, the spirit of the Apostles; and this, properly understood and cherished, will ever keep us from being the creatures of a populace.[23]

Newman's ecclesiological vision lived by the selfsame convictions of the vitality and ultimate invincibility of traditionary religion that drove his narrative in *The Arians of the Fourth Century*. Here he put those convictions to work, arguing for the "undeniable fact that the Church, when purest and when most powerful, *has* depended for its influence on its consideration with the many." This entailed that the clergy might similarly "be 'in favour with all the people' without any subserviency to them."[24] His walking epitome in this case was the fourth century bishop, St. Ambrose of Milan.

In Newman's reckoning, the Church of Milan was an ancient mirror of the nineteenth-century Church of England in that it was a contested venue. The orthodox Ambrose was immediately preceded by the

---

mundane ends of "local social standing" and the protection of temporal "status" is a characteristic flaw.

21 Newman, "Primitive Christianity," 340.
22 Newman, "Primitive Christianity."
23 Newman, "Primitive Christianity," 422.
24 Newman, "Primitive Christianity," 342, 348.

heterodox Arian bishop, Auxentius. The orthodox emperor, Valentinian I, was being pressured to commend the church to a heretical successor. When the Arians began to press Valentinian, he foolishly ignored the advice of his orthodox counselors and determined to have a bishop chosen by popular acclamation. At this, Milan descended into conflict between Orthodox and Arian partisans. Ambrose then intervened in his capacity as civil governor to quell the tempest. Amid the cacophony of voices, a small child was heard to say, "Ambrose is bishop," and the conflicted crowd spontaneously coalesced around the idea as an expression of the divine will. Although he was in that moment only a lay catechumen, and, though he initially fled from the appointment, Ambrose was nevertheless finally made a bishop in the span of eight days under the canonical provision for elections κατὰ θείαν χάριν.[25]

Recounting this story as self-evidently providential, Newman highlighted the ways that Ambrose made use of this popular support at various points throughout his tenure. In a rather long digression, he detailed the ways that Ambrose resisted Valentian's younger son and namesake when he sought to extort from Ambrose one of the Milanese churches for the Arians. In words that adapted well for his own efforts to fortify the Church of England against a similar alliance of enthralling temporal and heretical powers, Newman celebrated Ambrose's defense of the Portian Basilica. As the Arian and Catholic parties shared the opinion that a bishop could not cede what Christ had committed to him in trust, so too was England obliged to defend the divine prerogatives of its bishops. Newman's practical inference from his example is worth quoting at length.

> If there was a body to whom the concerns of religion were intrusted, there could be no doubt it was that over which Ambrose presided. It had been there planted ever since Milan became Christian, its

---

[25] Literally translated as, "According to the grace/gift of God." Newman supplies here his own gloss: "by the immediate suggestion of God." Newman, "Primitive Christianity," 344. In his 14 November 1833 letter to the editor of the *Record*, Newman stated, "It would be invidious to mention names: and there would be much to hope for the future, if the appointment of bishops had some kind of dependence on the will of their people; which may in process of time be effected.'" *LD* iv, 102-103.

ministers were descended from the Apostles, and it was the legitimate trustee of the sacred property. But in our day men have been taught to doubt whether there *is* one Apostolic Church, though it is mentioned in the Creed: nay, it is grievous to say, clergymen have sometimes forgotten, sometimes made light of their own privileges. Accordingly, when a question arises now about the spoliation of the Church, we are obliged to betake ourselves to the rules of *national* law; we appeal to precedents, or we urge the civil consequences of the measure, or we use other arguments, which, good as they may be, are too refined to be very popular. Ambrose rested his resistance on grounds which the people understood at once, and recognized as irrefragable. They felt that he was only refusing to surrender a trust. They rose in a body, and thronged the palace gates. A company of soldiers was sent to disperse them; and a riot was on the point of ensuing, when the ministers of the Court became alarmed, and despatched Ambrose to appease the tumult, with the pledge that no further attempt should be made on the possessions of the Church.[26]

Responding to obvious anxieties among cultured readers that he was entrusting "the cause of religion" to "mobs and outbreaks," Newman again responded that while "the multitude of men is always rude and intemperate, and needs restraint,–religion does not make them so." He pleaded, "better they should be zealous about religion, and repressed by religion, as in this case, than flow and ebb again under the irrational influences of this world." In the end, Newman asked, "Is it not probable that, when religion is thus a popular subject, it may penetrate, soften, or stimulate hearts which otherwise would know nothing of its power?"[27]

These sentiments carried over into Newman's second letter, that subsequently appeared in the 1 November 1833 issue of the *British Magazine*.[28] There, Newman returned to the contest between Valentinian II and Ambrose, with the latter steadfastly refusing to accommodate the heretical emperor in his usurpations of ecclesial power on behalf

---

26 Newman, "Primitive Christianity," 346-47.
27 Newman, "Primitive Christianity," 347-48.
28 Newman, "Primitive Christianity," 335.

of the Arian party. In this letter Newman more deliberately explored the relationship between his popular bishop and the Milanese laity as one characterized by mutual support and edification. In this capacity Ambrose made good use of psalmody and hymnody to promote the Catholic faith, and the laity responded by barricading themselves together with Ambrose in the Portian Basilica. The orthodox assembly was bound together in Newman's narration by the antiphonal singing that, by turns, united them to St. Ignatius, the Catholic disciple of St. Peter and the prelate who had introduced the antiphonal Trinitarian doxology to Antioch.

The limitations of space preclude a detailed treatment here, but one hastens to note that the *Lyra Apostolica* was among the earliest literary productions of Newman and his school. Very near the end of November 1832, Newman had written Rose with plans to "systematize a poetry department" for the *British Magazine* in order to "make a front against the coming danger." By this he hoped "to bring out certain truths and facts, moral, ecclesiastical, and religious, simply and forcibly, with greater freedom, and clearness" than the poetry of John Keble's celebrated *Christian Year*.[29] For each issue, Newman proposed to contribute short verses with "each bringing out forcibly *one* idea." Writing to Frederic Rogers regarding the plan, Newman expressed his hope that the *Lyra Apostolica* would in this way become "an effective quasi-political engine" all its own. As the hymnody of Ambrose had once served to steel the simplest Milanese layperson against a combined imperial and heretical assault, so too would Newman win the hearts of the English laity to their bishops' cause. As he put it to Rogers, "Do not stirring times bring out poets? Do they not give opportunity for the rhetoric of poetry, and the persuasion? And may we not at least produce shadows of high things if not the high things themselves?"[30]

Newman's third letter on the penitence of the emperor Theodosius under the episcopal discipline of Ambrose was the most pointed of his "precedents" for Apostolical resistance to the civil usurpations of

---

[29] Newman to H. J. Rose (26 November 1832), *LD* iii, 119-20.
[30] Newman to Frederic Rogers (1 December 1832), *LD* iii, 119, 121.

ecclesial power in his own day.[31] Published in the 1 December 1833 issue of the *British Magazine*, the letter recounted the "conduct of St. Ambrose" following a massacre of seven thousand inhabitants of Thessalonica by Gothic troops acting under the command of Theodosius.[32] Ambrose rebuked the emperor for ordering the massacre and forbade him entrance to the Basilica at Milan for eight months until he made a public gesture of penance. Most interesting in this letter is the role Newman constructs for Apostolical bishops vis-à-vis the state. There Ambrose transgressed the confining "library of the theologian" and "the precincts of consecrated ground" to "thrust the claims of sacred truth upon the world, which unbelievers would fain have shut up."[33] By this, Newman imagined the popular effect of such audacity among the faithful: "[F]or what sight can be more edifying to the Christian, or more impressive than that of a bishop conscientiously and calmly

---

[31] Newman made this much clearer in a paragraph added to the beginning of his letter in the 1840 edition of *The Church of the Fathers*. There Newman castigated his own Church of England's preference for "prudent conduct; by temporizing and conceding" ecclesial powers to the reigning monarch, and he predicted the consequence of such "courtliness" in both its nineteenth-century liberal and in its sixteenth-century Protestant forms: "The Basilica would have been surrendered to the heretics; yet I fear without that change of heart being wrought in prince or prime minister, by timid policy in the Church to which Valentinian was led by meeting with resistance. Certainly we have not made great men more religious by letting them have their own way." Newman, *The Church of the Fathers* (London: J. G. F. & J Rivingtons, 1840), 43.

[32] Newman, "Letters on the Church of the Fathers, No III," *The British Magazine* 4 (1833): 640. According to the Christian historian, Theodoret, a Gothic *magister militum* named Butheric had a popular charioteer arrested for a homosexual offense wherein the latter attempted to rape a male cupbearer. The populace of Thessalonica demanded the charioteer's release and, upon Butheric's refusal, a general insurrection ensued wherein Butheric and several other Roman authorities were killed. When Theodosius heard of the uprising, he ordered a violent suppression of the insurrection, which was conducted as if the Goths had captured a hostile city. According to Theodoret, "The anger of the Emperor rose to the highest pitch, and he gratified his vindictive desire for vengeance by unsheathing the sword most unjustly and tyrannically against all, slaying the innocent and guilty alike. It is said seven thousand perished without any forms of law, and without even having judicial sentence passed upon them; but that, like ears of wheat in the time of harvest, they were alike cut down." Theodoret, *Ecclesiastical History*, 5.17.

[33] Newman, "Letters on the Church of the Fathers, No III," 643.

rebuking a great warrior, and that warrior and sovereign humbly confessing and repenting of his sin?"[34] Were there any remaining doubt as to his intended message for the ministerium of the Church of England, Newman carefully noted Theodosius's own reflections on the episode: "Of all whom I have met, Ambrose is the only BISHOP."[35]

The final letter on Ambrose–an account of the discovery of the remains of Saints Gervasius and Protasius and their subsequent use to heal a blind man–never saw print in the *British Magazine*. Newman withdrew the article himself in a letter to Rose dated 23 November 1833.[36] The account nevertheless stands out for the way Newman continued to champion Ambrose as an exemplar of theological orthodoxy and popular churchmanship. Early on, he took up the basic question of whether such ancient reports of the miraculous could be trusted, the absence of miracles in the present witnessing against belief that they occurred in ancient times. Drawing on his intimate familiarity with Butler's *Analogy of Religion*, Newman argued in just the opposite direction: "Pretenses to revelation make it probable that there is a true

---

34 Newman, "Letters on the Church of the Fathers, No III," 640.

35 Newman, "Letters on the Church of the Fathers, No III," 644.

36 Newman had intended that it appear fourth in the series but subsequently thought that "it should come (if at all) third not fourth" before finally resolving that "it certainly had better be laid aside." Newman to Hugh James Rose (23 November 1833), *LD* iv, 120. The sentiments here suggest that his retraction was probably rooted in more than the simple anachronism–the discovery of Gervasius and Protasius being found in 386 CE and the massacre at Thessalonica in 390 CE–and it may be that Newman understood the crowning of his own contemporaneous program with the divine warrant of a historical miracle to be more than even a sympathetic public might comfortably digest. Two years after the death of Rose, however, Newman wrote to Edward Pusey to express concerns about correspondence between himself and Rose falling into the custodial care of John Miller, an old High Churchman of Worcester College. There Newman judged Miller to be "the kindest, most amiable of men," but he also mistrusted his intentions when treating Rose's Tractarian sympathies and complained that Miller had "no views" and was "much frightened and would catch at any thing in Rose's letters." Among Rose's papers, Newman named the "paper of mine in[tended] for the Church of the Fathers, sent him and then withdrawn by me, on Gervasius and Protasius." Newman to Edward Pusey (19 January 1840), *LD* vii, 219-20. Newman did subsequently recover the letter and published it in 1840 as the third of the four letters in his *The Church of the Fathers* (London: J. G. F. and J Rivingtons, 1840).

revelation; pretenses to revelation make it probable that there are real ones; false Christs argue a true Christ; a shadow implies substance." Despite his withdrawal of the letter, Newman was personally convinced of the implicit logic, and the fourth letter contributes decisively to his overall portrait of Ambrose as an Apostolical bishop. Having concluded that the miraculous events did in all likelihood transpire as reported, he summarized the entirety of his fourfold portrait concluding that, "a certain measure of authority, more or less, surely must thereby attach to St. Ambrose,–to his doctrine and his life, to his ecclesiastical principles and proceedings, to the Church itself of the fourth century, of which he is one main pillar."[37]

Newman looked to the episcopate in its unbroken succession of the apostles as the primary instrument for the preservation of church authority against erosion by the English state. This explains his subsequent focus on rousing *both* the clergy and the lay faithful to the bishops' cause. The presenting difficulty was that the shape and necessity for such an instrument had gone unrecognized, or at least unappreciated, by *bishops* as well as the laity. To secure the future of "traditionary religion" in the Church of England, such a thing would have to be *constructed* as well as promulgated. This suggested the need for a *schola theologorum*–a school of theologians, laboring on behalf of the bishops, but in a manner that was independent of their direct control. In service to this end, Newman led the drive to locate their work at the University of Oxford, conscripting its name and marshaling popular regard for its intellectual authority in service to their cause.

AN APOSTOLICAL SCHOOL FOR AN APOSTOLICAL CHURCH: CULTIVATING POPULARITY BY PLACE

Writing at a comfortable distance from the events in 1868, Newman recalled that the initial constituency of the "Oxford Movement" was of two minds regarding the best way to respond to the political and religious crisis facing them. One faction, represented by William Palmer of Worcester, Arthur Perceval, and somewhat less stridently by Hugh

---

[37] Newman, "Primitive Christianity," 374.

Rose, proposed that they function as "a Committee, an Association"–something Newman later ridiculed as "a board of safe, sound, sensible men . . . with rules and meetings, to protect the interests of the Church in its existing peril."[38] Alternatively, Newman described his faction as one constantly urging that they work less formally, agitating the public discourse with an unrefined, potent set of ideas, set forth by individual scholars and churchmen. His preferred name for this was the "Society" and he envisioned that its members would be bound together by a loose set of commonplaces. According to Newman's scheme, they would promulgate the expressions of their individual minds in the inexpensive popular form of individual tracts.

Although little regarded among readers of the *Apologia*, Newman also mentioned his desire that the work of his Society originate from, and be associated with, Oxford. Of the Hadleigh group, only he and Palmer were finally resident at Oxford. Rose was in Suffolk to the east; Perceval was based in Surrey, southwest of London; and Keble's parish was in Gloucestershire to the west. Due to his failing health, Hurrell Froude was forced to depart Oxford in late October of 1833 and so lived in Barbados, returning just prior to his death of tuberculosis in 1836. Oxford being central to them all, it became the obvious practical location for them to meet, but Newman additionally believed that a university was the proper center for an intellectual movement.[39]

While later recollections function well enough as a thin summation of Newman's practical endeavors over their first year, one should keep in mind that he composed the *Apologia Pro Vita Sua* as a defense against Charles Kingsley's charges of willful deceit. Any report of complicating textures and calculation on his part would sit rather uncomfortably with that intended purpose. The texture and personal calculation nevertheless remain, and they yield some insight into Newman's fuller conceptualization of their school and his discrete vision for its role in the Church of England. Here Newman was carrying forward the vision established for him by the fourth-century Alexandrine school by constructing a role for Apostolical bishops. This, in turn, explains why he

---

[38] Newman, *Apo*, 109.

[39] Newman, *Apo*, 166.

made use of popular respect for the University of Oxford to promote this theological construct throughout the country and to secure the loyal consent of the faithful.

Immediately following the July 1833 meeting at Hadleigh, Newman wrote John Keble to discuss next steps. He first expressed his desire for a "society" over a "committee" and urged that they publicly support the Archbishop of Canterbury, William Howley, in his objections to the Irish Church Temporalities Bill with "tracts, pamphlets, etc."[40] Newman then turned to the role of Oxford, suggesting to Keble that they petition against the bill under the head of "We the Undersigned Members of the University of Oxford." The invocation of the university was premised on his personal calculation that Oxford's name and reputation lent gravity to their actions and would thereby enhance popular appeal. As he wrote,

> I do not think we have yet made as much as we ought of our situation in Oxford and the deference paid it through the Country. Are not many eyes looking towards us every where, not as 'Masters and Scholars,' but as residents–so that our acts as coming from the University might have the authority of a vote of Convocation almost, in such cases as [when] Convocation cannot be expected to speak out. Now no party is likely to be *active* in Oxford but ourselves; so the field is before us.[41]

While the precise circumstances are unclear from available evidence, it was John Keble who, at some time prior to the end of August, suggested that members of the Hadleigh group proceed down a twin course of action. They formed an "Association"–formally titled the "Friends of the Church in Oxford"–with Newman and Palmer serving as its secretaries. They would simultaneously convene a distinct "Society," centered on the publication of tracts promoting and supporting their bishops in their "Apostolical succession"–that is, their divinely ordained succession from the Apostles of Jesus and their independent authority, understood as distinct from the powers of the civil magistrate. On this dual course they would also defend the liturgical orthodoxy of the

---

40 This speech subsequently appeared in the *British Magazine* 4 (1833): 457-63.
41 Newman to John Keble (5 August 1833), *LD* iv, 21.

Book of Common Prayer and its immunity from any diluting revision by Parliament.[42]

Viewed in light of Newman's characteristically open and informal correspondence with Froude, it seems clear that Newman warmed to Keble's plan after gaining consent to their holding any meetings of the association at Oxford. As to the association's membership, Newman conceded that others might join, but as secretary he only made efforts to include "Oriel men."[43] In this way Newman "stacked the deck," and this much is obvious from his resistance to Froude's proposal that they include Edward Marshall-Hacker. Marshall-Hacker matriculated at Oriel but subsequently departed for a scholarship at Corpus Christi College.[44] Of him, Newman begrudgingly wrote, "I could slur over his being an Oriel man."[45]

Judging from the crisscross of publication, promotion, and correspondence trading back and forth among the Hadleigh group, the present fissures among them in July gradually deepened. Newman, Keble, and Froude continually pressed for a fuller sacramental

---

[42] Newman's original draft charter of the Association appears with a letter he wrote to Perceval on 6 September, while the first official version appears in a letter from Newman to Froude on 9 September. *LD* iv, 48-49. Of Keble's being the originator of the plan, Froude wrote to Newman on 2 November 1833 saying, "I told K[Keble] all about the association stoppages and how you were sorry that his original plan had been deviated from. He on his part had only given way so easily under the notion that you were desirous for the change, so he comes back most cordially to his own plan and means for the future only [to] recommend local associations whether Palmer and Hook say yea or nay. I hope we shall not all be at cross purposes." *LD* iv, 81-82. On the approximate date of Keble's proposal, Palmer wrote to Newman on 31 August about "principles of the Association," addressing him as "Mr Secretary" and advising him of Perceval's desire to join them. Curiously, however, Palmer also spoke of the "Society" and expressed his willingness to "enter warmly into your plan." *LD* iv, 36-37.

[43] Newman to Richard Hurrell Froude (9 September 1833), *LD* iv, 47.

[44] The *Letters and Diaries* do not supply information regarding Edward Marshall-Hacker or the details of his career. While there are no print sources, the circumstances of his transfer from Oriel to Corpus Christi and his later career as a Fellow at Corpus are available by consulting the brief online record of his life provided by his place of burial, St. Sepulchre's Cemetery, Oxford. See, www.stsepulchres.org.uk.

[45] Newman to Richard Hurrell Froude (9 September 1833), *LD* iv, 47.

treatment of apostolic succession in the *Tracts*, while Palmer, Perceval, and Rose persisted in cautioning that they not draw boundaries so tightly as to imperil a broad and politically advantageous diversity of opinion among them. On 1 September 1833, Newman published the first of the *Tracts for the Times*. It was an apocalyptic warning to Presbyters and Deacons of the Church of England, urging that they support the "SUCCESSORS OF THE APOSTLES" in their struggle to deliver "Holy Mother" from the perils of an apostate English state.[46] Their warrant for taking up the Church of England's cause, so Newman argued, was their unique "APOSTOLICAL DESCENT" received at ordination from the bishop who "gave us the Holy Ghost, gave us the power to bind and loose, to administer the Sacraments, and to preach." Upon reading the work, Rose admonished Newman to omit these latter clauses or explain his intended sense fully, distinguishing what it was "supposed to mean" from what it did not. Newman complied with the request by softening the agency of the bishop, so that it became "*through* the Bishop who ordained us, [that] we received the Holy Ghost, [etc.]"[47]

A similar occurrence happened in *Tract 10*. There Newman sought to instill regard among the laity for bishops as "standing in the place of the Apostles" and incarnating the "office of Christ" by their witness and sufferings. On the subject of the parish priesthood and their role in extending the bishop's ministry, Newman raised the specter of the Church of England's possible disestablishment while assuring that its unique sacramental authority would nevertheless remain due to the graces of ordination. "Then you will honor us with a purer honor than you do now," Newman wrote, "as those who are intrusted with the keys of heaven and hell, as the heralds of mercy, as the denouncers of woe to wicked men, as intrusted with the awful and mysterious gift of making the bread and wine CHRIST'S body and blood, as far greater than the most powerful and the wealthiest of men, in our unseen strength and our heavenly riches." Interestingly enough, the precise wording in his

---

[46] *Tracts* i, 1.

[47] Rune Imberg, *Tracts for the Times: A Complete Survey of All the Editions* (Lund: Lund University Press, 1987), 144. Imberg's work is essential for noting important and unacknowledged differences between various editions of the *Tracts*.

penultimate "making the bread and wine CHRIST'S body and blood" had been urged on Newman by Froude less than two months prior as something to be introduced into the founding prospectus of the "Friends of the Church." Replying at the time, Newman rebuffed the suggestion writing,

> I cannot but hope on the whole, that this Society will be a first step towards bringing men of like minds together. We must not be impatient–Never mind, tho' our creed is not stamped on the body; we may single out from them those who agree with us, and form a second society out of the first. As to your correction for 'the continuance and due application of the Sacrament,' I differ from you in toto. I am rash enough, but you are furious. If my tract marches beyond the age, what does your phrase![48]

Samuel Rickards, who by Newman's own account was "connected" with the Society, upbraided Newman for including the words in the November *Tract*, warning that the "errors of the Church of Rome" would be attributable to the Association.[49] Newman responded contemptuously, defending the autonomy of the *Tracts* as being "connected with no Association" and "answerable to no one except God and His Church, committing no one, bearing the blame, doing the work." As though implications of the Association's indolence were not enough, Newman added that the *Tracts* were "the work of Oxford men" and that they alone were answerable for them.[50] Such inflammatory prose did not

---

[48] Newman to Richard Hurrell Froude (18 September 1833), *LD* iv, 52. On 15 September 1833 Froude had written to Newman, "I don't quite see the good of talking about 'the continuance and due application' of the Sacrament of the Lords Supper, instead [of], 'the making of the Body and Blood of Christ.' But the criticism will come too late so it is no use saying more." *LD* iv, 50.

[49] Samuel Rickards to Newman (20 November 1833), *LD* iv, 115. On Rickards's connection to the society, Newman lists him alongside John Davison, Charles Atmore Ogilvie, John Miller, Hugh Rose, and John Keble. See Newman to John William Bowden (23 September 1833), *LD* iv, 54.

[50] Newman to Samuel Rickards (22 November 1833), *LD* iv, 116-17. Emphasis mine. On the manuscript of the letter, Newman later recorded the result of the exchange: "Rickards would have liked Tracts written in the style of Richard Hooker or Izaac Walton. They would have been classical, but would have failed of their Purpose." He also added in 1860, "Thus ended an intimate friendship, which, while

fail to alienate. Rickards had also matriculated at Oriel and served as a fellow there from 1819 to 1822. Newman's increasingly strident hard line could not help but damage the friendship irreparably. While he did go on to amend the offending phrase for a time to "mysterious privilege of dispensing CHRIST'S body and blood," Newman ultimately reintroduced the former phrase in the final editions.[51]

While there are many clear indicators of an oncoming cleavage among the various "Friends of the Church," the most telling measure of Newman's disposition is the clear contrast between his concern that they not offend the bishops by appearing to configure their association as a rival power and his willingness to cast the Association aside in preference for seeing the *Tracts* continue with their implied association with the university intact. As early as 16 July 1833, Newman expressed his desire that they secure episcopal sanction for their collective endeavors.[52] By mid-October Newman began to worry over the "awkwardness" of forming an association "without the sanction of the Bishops."[53] These precise sentiments–and nearly the precise wording each time–continued through the first month of the following year when the Association was all but defunct. Contrariwise, Newman's initial suspicions of the Association developed into strong objections

---

it lasted, viz for seven years <(1826-1833)>, had been very affectionate and sympathetic. It never recovered the blow which the first Tracts gave to it. There was no heart in it afterwards. I seldom met Rickards henceforth; once on my sister H's marriage in 1836 at Derby–once when he and his wife called on me at Littlemore–doubtless some other times. He had no sort of drawing to Catholicism, and, when I became a Catholic, he called me a weathercock. From what I know, he is hard and unforgiving to this day." *LD* iv, 116n1.

51 *Tracts* x, 4. Cf., Imberg, *Tracts for the Times*, 148-49.

52 Newman to Henry Wilberforce (16 July 1833), *LD* iv, 9. These concerns were expressed again in letters from 11 August (Newman to Charles Golightly), 31 August (Newman to John Bowden), and 2 September (Newman to Richard Froude). Cf., *LD* iv, 29, 33, 39.

53 Newman to William Palmer (of Worcester College) (24 October 1833), *LD* iv, 67. This theme appears again in a Memorandum containing Instructions to Propagandists dated to the Autumn of 1833 (*LD* iv, 78-79) and in letters from 1 November (Newman to Charles Girdlestone), 13 November (Newman to John Bowden), 1 January (Newman to Hugh James Rose), and 3 January (Newman to Thomas Mozley). *LD* iv, 80, 97, 159, 161.

by mid-September. There Palmer pressured him to suspend production of the *Tracts* for six weeks out of a desire that they be controlled by a committee.⁵⁴ When Newman resumed publication on 18 October with John Bowden's *Tract 5*, it appeared with a concluding statement that "Anyone is at liberty to reprint these *Tracts*, with such alterations as approve themselves to his judgment."⁵⁵ Eight days later, Newman began to express firm wishes that the *Tracts* be "immediately disowned as far as the responsibility of any Association is concerned."⁵⁶ Although he flirted briefly with a conceit that the strident tone of the *Tracts* might be of some service to the Association in its desire to appear broad and moderate, the separation was all but complete. By mid-November he urged correspondents to speak of them only as "the Oxford Tracts" and announced his plan to explicitly advertise them as "Tracts for the Times by Residents in Oxford."⁵⁷ When in November of 1834, the *Tracts* began to appear together in bound volumes, the title page read "Tracts for the Times by Members of the University of Oxford."⁵⁸

---

54 On 24 September 1833, Newman wrote to Keble, "We are getting on very well—but are anxious on the subject of Tracts. Those hitherto published are not yet acknowledged as 'the Society's'—for myself I doubt whether the Society ought to pledge itself to more than a *general approval* of the principles of *any* tracts. One thing strikes one reader, another another. If you correct according to the wishes of a board, you will have nothing but tame dull compositions, which will take no one—there will be no rhetoric in them, which is necessarily πρὸς τίνα. But it is a subject of much difficulty." *LD* iv, 55.

55 Keble later expressed his opposition to this in a letter dated 5 November 1833 and the permission to reprint with alterations was withdrawn. *LD* iv, 86. The last *Tract* to appear with this permission was *Tract 15*. Rune Imberg, *In Quest of Authority: The "Tracts for the Times" and the Development of the Tractarian Leaders, 1833-1841* (Lund: Lund University Press, 1987), 24.

56 Newman to John William Bowden (13 November 1833), *LD* iv, 97.

57 Newman to John William Bowden (17 November 1833), *LD* iv, 109.

58 Rune Imberg has written of the "haphazard history" of the bound volumes and notes how a person who owned some *Tracts* or most of them could purchase the only missing numbers and the title page for binding. While this makes identification of a "first edition" impossible, the date of the title page represents a *terminus ad quem* of the volume. Rune Imberg, *In Quest of Authority* (Lund: Lund University Press, 1987). My bound copy of the first volume lists 1834 as the date of publication, and Newman's advertisement was composed on "The Feast of All Saints, 1834."

In addition to their being promulgated by "Members of the University," the *Tracts for the Times* were often addressed to their intended recipients under a Latin superscript–to the people (*Ad Populum*), to the clergy (*Ad Clerum*), or to other schools (*Ad Scholas*). This practice commenced with Newman's *Tract 6*, addressed "Ad Populum" and treating "The Present Obligation of Primitive Practice." In all, 45 of the 90 *Tracts* were addressed in this manner. Sixteen were authored by Newman directly. Twelve were reprinted writings from Bishop Thomas Wilson (1663-1755), a member of the English episcopate that Newman once described as a "burning and shining light . . . like [John] the Baptist, in an evil time" who "seemed as if a beacon lighted on his small island."[59] Another was a reprinted writing on ancient liturgy by George Bull, a venerable English bishop and theologian. John Keble and Richard Hurrell Froude each had two such *Tracts*, and five were authored by Edward Pusey once he joined their number formally. While a case might be made that the superscripts were simple indicators of the intended audience or subject of the given *Tract*, the use of Latin and the *Ad Populum*, *Ad Clerum*, and *Ad Scholas* nomenclature strongly suggests that they were meant to convey the impression that they were authoritative, ecclesial pronouncements. Their concentrated use in *Tracts* authored by Newman or in reprinted episcopal documents edited by Newman lends weight to this hypothesis.

As was true in his sermon on personal influence, Newman's emergent conception of his school at Oxford as an instrument for promoting the Apostolical powers of the English episcopate opened to a corresponding need for genuine distinction from it. Rather than conceiving its role as a chorus of would-be ecclesiastical salesmen, proffering an apostolic Christianity that the bishops already recognized and embraced, Newman came to recognize how the bishops also wanted for education and exhortation. In the sure footing of Oxford, then, Newman believed that he had found an Archimedean place to stand so as to move the church as well as the world. His zealous use of Oxford's name and corresponding desire to protect his claim for the sake of his

---

[59] Newman, "Preface," in *Sacra Privata: The Private Meditations, Devotions and Prayers of the Right Rev. T. Wilson, D.D.* (Oxford: J. H. Parker, 1838), v.

school was a primary factor in the separation of the Tractarians from one-time-sympathetic High Churchmen. This distinct motif in Newman's thought additionally helps to explain his activities in two subsequent controversies.

AN IMPERILED EPISCOPATE: MISS JUBBER AND BISHOP RICHARD BAGOT

In early July of 1834, certain parties at Oxford were beginning to reflect the liberalizing trends at work in English politics, and efforts to include dissenting Protestants among the students was gaining momentum. Newman's personal resistance to this trend first took the unusual form of a refusal to preside at the wedding of a Miss Jubber because she was unbaptized. That this request was imposed on Newman was no small irritant given that both he and his curate, Isaac Williams, spent considerable time attempting to convince the prospective bride's mother to present her children for the sacrament. Although he would have probably preferred to consult his bishop about the matter beforehand, Newman was caught off guard, learning of the betrothed couple's identity on the eve of their prospective wedding. His description of the account in his diary indicates only that "*a row followed*" upon his refusal to preside, but Newman additionally made a transcript of his subsequent conversation with the bride's father:

Newman:	I have had a note from Mr Plowman. Is it one of your daughters who is going to be married.
Mr. Jubber:	Yes.
Newman:	Has she been baptized?
Mr. Juber:	No.
Newman:	Indeed! (in a lower tone of voice) really, I cannot marry her.
Mr. Jubber:	Well, that *is* superstition–that is superstition indeed.
Newman:	Why, how can I, (give Christian marriage,) to one who is still an outcast?
Mr. Jubber:	That *is* superstition.

COMMENDING THE EPISCOPATE 121

Newman: Mr Jubber, I did not come here that you might teach me, but to tell you my feelings of duty.

Jubber: Sir, I do not wish you of course to act against your sense of duty–There are several clergymen quite desirous to <of> marrying them.

Newman: Why did you not let me know sooner–I have only just got intelligence who the parties were–

Jubber: Mr Pl.[Plowman] has called on you three or four times and could not find you.

Newman: Why could not he have left a note. I had a message brought me in College yesterday between 4 and 5–but no names were mentioned. I have just walked into Oxford and found this note sent since that time. However I beg you will convey to your daughter my great regret that I should seem to do any thing harsh or unkind to her, but I cannot help it. Pray say so to her. I am much distressed at it. (And I repeated this.)[60]

This might have ended the matter but for the fact that news of the affair also found its way into the newspaper on the following Saturday. The story read:

> *Intolerance.*–The Vicar of St Mary the Virgin parish Oxford, in his hyper-anxiety to signalize his zeal against dissent and in favour of 'orthodoxy' refused on Tuesday last to marry a young couple of very respectable connexions in that City solely because the blooming to be Bride had not been christened, and was in the rev: bigot's phraseology an *outcast*, the matrimonial knot was however tied directly afterwards by the more tolerant and less pharisaical minister of a neighbouring parish church, and the happy pair were very properly relieved from the cruel disappointment which threatened them.[61]

In his response to the paper, Newman clarified his intended sense of "outcast" in the conversation with Mr. Jubber. He had intended to say that the unbaptized were "outcast from Christian privileges and

---

60 "Memorandum, The Jubber Affair" (July 1834), *LD* iv, 288–89.
61 *Weekly Dispatch* (6 July), *LD* iv, 290n2.

blessings."[62] Although friends supported his taking a firm line, the response of his bishop, Richard Bagot of Oxford, was much more tepid. On 16 July 1834, Newman received word from Bagot's archdeacon, Charles Carr Clerke, that a Baptist minister at Oxford had written the bishop to inquire if there existed some statute or canon prohibiting the marriage. Bagot's reply had been that there was no such law. While it is impossible to say for sure whether he was speaking diplomatically on behalf of Bagot or merely expressing his opinion in the matter, Clerke's read of the bishop's disposition was clear: Newman ought to have performed the wedding.[63]

While he held his peace publicly, Newman's subsequent private correspondence clearly indicated a breach of confidence in Bagot. He had spent innumerable months, developing, promulgating, and conducting himself with an exalted view of his bishop's authority as a successor to the apostles. Newman later remembered his sentiments this way:

> I loved to act in the sight of my Bishop, as if I was, as it were, in the sight of God . . . I could not go very wrong while I had reason to believe that I was in no respect displeasing him . . . My own Bishop was my Pope; I knew no other; the successor of the Apostles, the Vicar of Christ.[64]

It is striking, then, that when he received Clerke's communiqué, Newman chaffed at Bagot's implied wishes. In his response, he all but demanded confirmation that his bishop was *directing* him to marry unbaptized persons should another such occasion present itself.[65] Clerke's answer could not have been clearer: "It certainly is the Bishop's

---

[62] Newman to The Editor of the *Oxford Conservative Journal* (10 July 1834), *LD* iv, 299.

[63] Archdeacon Charles Clerke to Newman (16 July 1834), *LD* iv, 298n1.

[64] Newman, *Apo*, 122-23.

[65] However politely worded, Newman's request was firm: "I understand you to mean that I have the Bishop's direction to marry unbaptized persons–therefore certainly I will do so, should the case occur again, stating that I do it *by direction* from the Bishop. However, will you, if you please, send me a line, to tell me if I am correct in thus understanding you." Newman to Archdeacon Clerke (18 July 1834), *LD* iv, 305.

wish that parties should be married if they offer themselves under circumstances similar to those of Miss Jubber's case . . . I can assure you that such is his wish."[66] But Newman would not hear it unless Bagot communicated his wishes directly. Writing to Arthur Perceval the same day, Newman lamented the "wretched unchurch-like conservative spirit among" High Churchmen like Bagot and judged it unlikely that the bishop would "*commit himself* to an express command."[67] Seven days later, Newman's complaint gave way to still harsher words:

> O that we had one Bishop for us! what a net we are in–this is what Satan has been toiling at this 300 years, gradually bringing it about– and now his day is coming. All I can say is that under such circumstances it is pleasant and soothing to think of such texts as Is lix, 19.[68]

In his King James translation of the Bible, Isaiah 59:19 read, "So shall they fear the name of the LORD from the west, and his glory from the rising of the sun. When the enemy shall come in like a flood, the Spirit of the LORD shall lift up a standard against him." As was true in the case of his sermon on personal influence, Newman was clearly convinced that his Oxford school could be that prophetic standard, summoning England's impotent bishops to a true sense of themselves. But his "Apostolical" banner would first have to fly securely in the contested fields of Oxford before it could claim the allegiance of the church and its faithful–and Oxford was proving far more difficult to hold than he had first imagined.

AN IMPERILED OXFORD: RENN DICKSON HAMPDEN AND THE SUBSCRIPTION CONTROVERSY

Newman's complicated relationship with Renn Dickson Hampden began with the latter receiving Newman's students after he left the Oriel Tuition. When the Moral Philosophy Chair became vacant in early

---

[66] Archdeacon Clerke to Newman (20 July 1834), *LD* iv, 305n1.

[67] Newman to Arthur Perceval (20 July 1834), *LD* iv, 307-308.

[68] Newman to Henry Wilberforce (27 July 1834), *LD* iv, 312.

1834, the two were again set on a collision course, with Newman being passed over in preference for Hampden. His words in a letter to Henry Wilberforce four days after the announcement expressed his profound disappointment and a growing sense of rivalry with Hampden: "I give you without delay intelligence of an important event, viz my having been floored as regards the Professorship." He ended with a quote in Greek from Aeschylus, "I have met my conqueror and departed."[69]

Longstanding agitation to remove religious tests at Oxford and Cambridge suddenly crested in March 1834 with a bill to admit Dissenters. On 17 March 1834, Newman wrote a long letter to the *British Magazine*, giving his reasons for rejecting the move, and he continued to play a critical role in the months that followed by rallying members of the university to sign an Oxford Declaration against the Admission of Dissenters.[70] While the conservative line prevailed in Parliament–the bill coming to defeat in the House of Lords on 1 August 1834–this was only an initial skirmish in a longer conflict that began immediately after the vote.

Whatever reservations Hampden may have initially had with the Oxford Declaration, the generalized wording of the final document left him free to join the 1,900 members of convocation and over 1,050 undergraduates–Newman's Apostolicals most prominent among them–in adding his name. Before the month's end, however, Hampden reversed his position and published his *Observations on Religious Dissent with Particular Reference to the Use of Religious Tests in the University*. There he openly advocated the admission of dissenters and the abolition of all doctrinal tests by making recourse to a distinction between "religion," that Hampden understood to be divinely revealed, and "theological opinion." He argued that Christians sufficiently agreed on the former and suggested that fallible human interpretations of the divine word alone led Christians to differ over the latter.[71]

---

[69] Newman to R. H. Froude (14 June 1834), *LD* iv, 201.

[70] The text of Newman's "Letter to Hugh James Rose (II) Editor of the British Magazine" appears in *LD* iv, 208-12.

[71] Renn Dickson Hampden, *Observations on Religious Dissent* (S. Collingwood: Oxford, 1834), 18.

Upon reviewing the work, Newman warned Hugh Rose that "Hampden . . . has just published a pamphlet which, I fear, destroys our glory. Hitherto Oxford was all on one side, as far as print goes, in this late dispute with the Commons and Co."[72] His report was not completely accurate. In fact, the Oriel College Noetics were much divided on the subject of subscription. Baden Powell had even published his *Reasons for Not Joining in the Declaration* the previous April.[73] Newman's sentiments are of critical importance, however, for the way he cast the implications of the subscription controversy, not just for Oxford, but also for the Church of England and for his school's status in relation to both. Newman understood that any relaxation of subscription to the Anglican formularies–the Thirty-nine Articles principally among them–would represent a clear threat to the Anglican identity of the university and a proxy attack on the integrity of the established church. Oxford was, after all, a place for theological as well as vocational formation. Aside from the diploma, a standard "Certificate of having attended the Lectures of the Regius Professor of Divinity, and of one, at least, of the other Divinity Professors if the Candidate be a Graduate of the University of Oxford or Cambridge" was required of postulants to holy orders in every English diocese.[74] So the status of his Apostolical school at Oxford was vital, not only for the credibility of Newman's agitprop in the popular mind, but also for his ability to personally influence future deacons, priests, and bishops. In what must have felt like a bitter return to his days as a tutor, Hampden was now on record, siding with Newman's old masters in a belief that the university was "not the Church" but "a literary society" and only "accidentally a

---

[72] Newman to Hugh James Rose (20 August 1834), *LD* iv, 323.

[73] Powell self-published three pages of his *Reasons for not Joining in [the] Declaration*. An undated leaflet of the three pages addressed to "Christian Parents" was also printed in London with testimonies from the universities of Oxford, Cambridge, and London, along with a form of petition to the king. This was also printed in the *British Magazine* 5 (1834): 592-95.

[74] On this requirement see T. W. Wood, *A Guide to Ordination in the Church of England with Instructions to Candidates for Holy Orders* (London: Bremrose and Sons, 1878), 119-22.

society of church members."[75] Newman's words to Rose–that Hampden's work "destroys our glory"–well indicate his panic at losing the ground he had been fighting to establish. Hampden's anti-dogmatic ethos now competed directly with the apostolical ethos he had been advancing under the Oxford moniker.

A new effort to admit dissenters to Oxford appeared in March 1835, with the Earl of Radnor reopening the question of subscription to the Thirty-nine Articles in Parliament. Oxford again brought the matter before Convocation that met in the Sheldonian Theatre on 20 May 1835. There the Hebdomadal Board of the university heads of houses drafted a proposal that substituted a weakened "Declaration of Conformity to the Church of England" for compulsory subscription to the Thirty-nine Articles. Although as Provost, Edward Hawkins insisted that no relaxation of principles was involved in the measure but only a change of form, so as "to clear our system from objections," his claim was immediately dismissed by Newman and Pusey.[76] Although the measure was overwhelmingly defeated, with the statutes on subscription ultimately going unchanged until 1852, the conflict between what were obviously *two competing schools* would harden and intensify for almost another decade. Nowhere was the row more intense than when Regius Professor of Divinity, Edward Burton, fell ill and died on 19 January 1836. While Newman briefly entertained hopes that Keble, Pusey, or even he himself might win the appointment, his greatest fears were realized when on 8 February, Prime Minister Lord Melbourne named Renn Dickson Hampden as Burton's successor.

Newman had begun the previous year with hopes that their efforts at Oxford would prove so popular and influential that their *"school of theology"* would grow to become a hegemonic *"theological law,"* established in the "ecclesiastical law" of the Church of England.[77] Where Newman saw "Nestorianism preached in every other pulpit, etc. etc.," he nurtured hope for the return of church courts, strong to combat such

---

[75] Hampden, *Observations on Religious Dissent*, 38-39.

[76] [E. Hawkins and Edward Pusey], *Subscription to the Thirty-nine Articles* (Baxter: Oxford, 1835), 23.

[77] Newman to Richard Hurrell Froude (18 January 1835), *LD* v, 10.

"heresy and false doctrine." In his mind's eye, he even foresaw that the "Divinity Professors in the Universities" would serve as the gatekeepers of the system, guaranteeing a learned discernment of what was genuinely heretical while maintaining a necessary freedom for theological exploration.[78] It was, as he confided to Froude, "a fine scheme," but now Hampden would be the prospective gatekeeper. The *Observations on Religious Dissent* represented an alternative, even anti-theological law. For Newman, Hampden's work heralded the ascendancy of a very different school. It was a school tainted with the laxity and "doctrinal error" of Thomas Arnold, the "Sabellianism and Nestorianism" of Samuel Hinds and Richard Whately, and the variegated apostasies of Blanco White. In his panicked imagination, these were but the "*advanced guard* of a black host" that would surely follow.[79]

Newman and his fellows acted quickly, launching a petition to the king against Hampden's final appointment. As Keble wrote,

> I should think a sort of respectful memorial to the Archbishops and Bishops might be got up, stating *facts* merely, as to what Hampden has taught, and as to what influence he would have, and leaving them to judge whether something should not be done to remove candidates for Orders out of his reach.[80]

On 10 February 1836 Newman responded to Keble's challenge by publishing the anonymous pamphlet, *Elucidations of Dr Hampden's Theological Statements*.[81] In its brief 47 pages, he cited Hampden's writings as witness to his heterodoxy regarding the doctrines of the Trinity, the Incarnation, the atonement, the sacraments, original sin, the nature of the soul, and moral theology. In Newman's summation, the refusal to "identify his own opinion on any point, however sacred in itself, with the facts of the revealed history, or to assume that a belief in it is necessary for the salvation of another, or to impose it as a condition

---

[78] Newman to Richard Hurrell Froude (18 January 1835), *LD* v, 10.
[79] Newman to Henry Wilberforce (23 March 1835), *LD* v, 51.
[80] John Keble to Newman (10 February 1836), *LD* v, 228.
[81] Newman, *Elucidations of Dr Hampden's Theological Statements* (W. Baxter: Oxford, 1836).

of union with another" left Hampden unable to pronounce judgment on opinions that stood opposed to the creedal orthodoxy of the Church of England. The prospective gatekeeper being incapable of performing his sacred duty, Newman warned that "ten years hence, those who are in no way protesting against his appointment now, would, if then alive, feel they had upon them a responsibility greater than has been incurred by Members of this University for many centuries."[82]

When the Hebdomadal Board met to consider the appointment, Hampden made an appearance to defend himself. As Newman recounted the events, the Dean of Christ Church, Thomas Gaisford, addressed Hampden inquiring if he wished to remain, because "We are going to talk about you."[83] Hampden answered in the affirmative, but when questioned as to whether he intended to cast a vote, he replied that "he should be guided by circumstances."[84] In the end he did vote for himself and thereby tipped the scales in his favor, but the matter was still not settled. A remedial measure was first launched against Hampden in Convocation, but the Oxford proctors vetoed the effort on 22 March 1836. A new requisition was then drawn up–principally by Newman and Pusey–to clear the university from any implication in the doctrines taught by Hampden. This effort was successful by a vote of 474 to 94. On the second attempt, following another veto by the proctors, Convocation then deprived Hampden of his powers to appoint and select preachers, to exclusively lecture postulants for holy orders, or to sit among the judges of heresy cases. The gatekeeper had been at least temporarily deprived of his keys.

Newman had won a victory for his school, but it would prove to be a Pyrrhic victory. Before a decade would pass, Newman's fine scheme of his school's orthodox theological law finding form in the ecclesiastical law of a popular Church of England would lay in shambles. He himself would be dispossessed by the University of Oxford in a manner far more decisive and permanent than the momentary privations suffered by Hampden. The remains of his school–at least the portion he

---

82 Newman, *Elucidations of Dr Hampden's Theological Statements*, 47.
83 Newman to J. W. Bowden (17 February 1836), *LD* v, 237.
84 Newman to J. W. Bowden (17 February 1836), *LD* v, 237.

recognized as his own—would be forced into exile by the very episcopate he had fought to establish.

THROWN AGAIN ON THE PEOPLE

A clear understanding that Newman's initial Tractarian efforts were an experiment in ecclesiastical populism is especially helpful for the way it illumines a similar conflicted period in Newman's later journey as a Roman Catholic. John Moore Capes, a man like himself, founded *The Rambler* in 1848 with the purpose of rehabilitating Catholic thought in non-Catholic England. Unfortunately, however, the periodical had fallen into ecclesiastical disfavor in view of its perceived confrontational posture toward church authority. By the beginning of 1859, it became clear that unless special measures were taken, the *Rambler* would be censured in the forthcoming Pastorals of the English Catholic Bishops. Newman, who had retired in November of 1858 from his duties as rector of the Catholic University in Dublin, intended to devote himself fully to the work of theology. Faced with the periodical's imminent demise, he reluctantly agreed to edit the *Rambler* in Lord John Acton's and Richard Simpson's stead.[85]

Although he intended to steer the *Rambler* away from theological topics and "back to its own literary line," critics of the periodical seized on two items in the *Rambler*'s new series for May 1859.[86] The second and more serious of these appeared amid commentary on "Contemporary Events: Home Affairs," wherein Newman expressed his anonymous editorial opinion regarding the judgment of the English Catholic Bishops on a proposed Royal Newcastle Commission to evaluate the quality of Catholic elementary education.[87] Although Newman was unaware that the bishops had previously communicated their

---

[85] John Coulson, "Introduction," in John Henry Newman, *On Consulting the Faithful in Matters of Doctrine*, ed. John Coulson (New York: Sheed & Ward, 1961), 2-3.

[86] Newman to Sir John Acton (31 December 1858), LD xviii, 562.

[87] The first issue was minor and regarded the decision to publish a letter bearing only the author's initials, "H. I.," which concluded with the question "How far is it allowable, or desirable, for laymen to study theology?" Newman, "Questions and Answers," *The Rambler* 1, new series (May 1859): 109.

opposition to the Royal Inspection of Catholic Schools, he urged them to consider the disposition of the English Catholic faithful, writing how

> even in the preparation of a dogmatic definition the faithful are consulted, as lately in the instance of the Immaculate Conception, it is at least as natural to anticipate such an act of kind feeling and sympathy in great practical questions, out of the condescension that belongs to those who are *forma facti gregis ex animo*.[88]

This passage, particularly the final Latin quote of Saint Peter, urging in context that pastors lead the faithful by good example rather than by "lording authority over those assigned to their care," aroused the suspicions of John Gillow, Professor of Dogmatic Theology at Ushaw. Gillow sent a letter on 13 May 1859 advising Newman that any suggestion of *consultation* in matters of doctrine was essentially Protestant:

> that the infallibility of the Church resides in the Communitate fidelium, and not exclusively in the Ecclesia docente. Else the infallible portion would consult the fallible with a view to guiding itself to an infallible decision. But the above principle would be characterized as at least *haeresi proxima*.[89]

Newman quickly dispatched a retort advising Gillow of his failure to understand his meaning: "To the unlearned reader the idea conveyed by 'consulting' is not necessarily that of asking an opinion. For instance, we speak of consulting a barometer about the weather. The barometer does not give us its opinion, but ascertains for us a fact."[90] Newman additionally reported Gillow's objection to his bishop, William Bernard Ullathorne, and thereafter printed news of the bishops' judgment in the May issue of the *Rambler* with an editorial apology confessing that "we did not know that the Bishops had spoken formally" when his editorial remark was printed. Newman also defended his motivating sentiments adding, "surely we are not disrespectful in thinking, and having thought, that the Bishops would like to know the sentiments

---

[88] "Be examples to the flock." *The Rambler* 1 (May 1859): 122.
[89] "Proximate to heresy," John Gillow to Newman (15 May 1859), *LD* xix, 134n3.
[90] Newman to John Gillow (16 May 1859), *LD* xix, 135.

of an influential portion of the laity before they took any step which perhaps they could not recall."[91] He additionally cautioned against "the misery of any division between the rulers of the Church and the educated laity."[92] This latter remark did little to stifle the matter and so, in a difficult meeting on 22 May, Ullathorne expressed regrets that there appeared to him "remains of the old spirit" in the *Rambler*.[93] Newman reported Ullathorne's general opinion: "It was irritating. Our laity were a *peaceable* set, the church was *peace*. They had a deep faith–they did not like to hear that any one doubted."[94] When Newman reported of his experience of the laity in Ireland as indeed "docile" but also "unsettled," Ullathorne, Newman reported his reply as being something like "Who are the laity?"[95]

Newman seized upon the place of the laity in church affairs in the final issue of *The Rambler* on July 1859. Newman's essay, *On Consulting the Faithful in Matters of Doctrine*, revisited the issue at stake, not only in his May reply to Gillow, but also in his early Tractarian effort "throw the church on the people." For Newman, the laity did indeed possess a right to be consulted given that "the body of the faithful is one of the witnesses to the fact of the tradition of revealed doctrine, and because their *consensus* through Christendom is the voice of the Infallible

---

[91] Newman, "Contemporary Events-Home Affairs," *The Rambler* 1, new series (1859): 122.

[92] Newman, "Contemporary Events-Home Affairs," 123.

[93] Newman, Memorandum (22 May 1859), *LD* xix, 140.

[94] Newman, Memorandum (22 May 1859), *LD* xix, 140.

[95] Newman, Memorandum (22 May 1859), *LD* xix, 141. The Irish laity were particularly unsettled at this point because Archbishop Paul Cullen of Dublin was actively uprooting the Irish Gallican tradition and seeking to replace it with a strident ultramontanism. Cullen, who had spent nearly thirty years in Rome prior to his coming to Ireland, nursed a bitter memory of Italian nationalism and its effect on the church in Rome. He had constantly opposed Newman's efforts to make the Irish laity a substantive power in the University of Dublin. See here Desmond Brown, *Paul Cardinal Cullen and the Shaping of Modern Irish Catholicism* (Dublin: Gill and Macmillan, 1983), 30-84, 151-52 and Colin Barr, *Paul Cullen, John Henry Newman, and the Catholic University of Ireland, 1845-1864* (Notre Dame, IN: University of Notre Dame Press, 2003).

Church."[96] Put differently, Newman affirmed that while infallibility was not, strictly speaking, "*in* the consensus fidelium," consensus yet remained "an *indicium* or *instrumentum* to us of the judgment of that Church which *is* infallible."[97] He was thereby convicted that

> the tradition of the Apostles, committed to the whole Church in its various constituents and functions *per modum unius*, manifests itself variously and at various times: sometimes by the mouth of the episcopacy, sometimes by the doctors, sometimes by the people, sometimes by liturgies, rites, ceremonies, and customs, by events, disputes, movements, and all those other phenomena which are comprised under the name of history.[98]

It followed, then, that "none of these channels of tradition may be treated with disrespect; granting at the same time fully, that the gift of discerning, discriminating, defining, promulgating, and enforcing any portion of that tradition resides solely in the *Ecclesia docens*."[99]

Most important in his contemplation of this latter point was Newman's stated confidence in the discernment of the faithful and in their resilience when rejecting false doctrine. Alluding to remarks made in the second of his *Lecture on Anglican Difficulties*, he thus wrote,

> We know that it is the property of life to be impatient of any foreign substance in a body to which it belongs. It will be sovereign in its own domain, and it conflicts with what it cannot assimilate into itself, and *is irritated and disordered* till it has expelled it.[100]

This insight led him to return to those early studies of the fourth-century Arian crisis and to a critical historical insight that Newman defended in multiple examples drawn from sources across the fourth-century world:

---

[96] *The Rambler* 1 (1859): 205.
[97] *The Rambler* 1 (1859): 208.
[98] *The Rambler* 1 (1859): 205.
[99] *The Rambler* 1 (1859): 205.
[100] *The Rambler* 1 (1959): 212.

I mean still, that in that time of immense confusion the divine dogma of our Lord's divinity was proclaimed, enforced, maintained, and (humanly speaking) preserved, far more by the "Ecclesia docta" than by the "Ecclesia docens;" that the body of the episcopate was unfaithful to its commission, while the body of the laity was faithful to its baptism; that at one time the Pope, at other times the patriarchal, metropolitan, and other great sees, at other times general councils, said what they should not have said, or did what obscured and compromised revealed truth; while, on the other hand, it was the Christian people who, under Providence, were the ecclesiastical strength of Athanasius, Hilary, Eusebius of Vercellae, and other great solitary confessors, who would have failed without them.[101]

These latter sentiments, borne aloft by the same historical traces that first gave birth to *The Arians of the Fourth Century*, are instructive for the reader who wishes to properly understand Newman's early Tractarian period. They make good sense of Newman's words and works from the Summer of 1833 to the early months of 1836. While *The Arians of the Fourth Century* was not written with the purpose of highlighting failures of faith in the episcopate, there are nevertheless several instances of such failure reported in the work. These play a disproportionate and recurring role in Newman's narrative.

Chronicling the history of Antioch after the death of Arius, he briefly touched on the story of Leontius, who had been promoted to the see of Antioch by the Arian party in 348. Although Leontius remained an Arian until his death in 357, Newman notes that Catholic orthodoxy did not fail. Despite Leontius's attempts to weaken Trinitarianism among the clergy by his ordination of an Arian successor in Aetius, Newman noted how the Nicene faith remained "strong in the city, particularly among the laity"–so strong, it seems, that it became "dangerous to avow the plain blasphemies of the first founder of their creed [Arius]."[102] Returning to these years at Antioch nearly a hundred pages on, Newman wrote again of how members of the Catholic party in Antioch–clergy and laity acting in tandem–successfully resisted

---

[101] *The Rambler* 1 (1859): 213.

[102] Newman, *Ari*, 297-98.

Arianism in successive heterodox bishops by refusing communion with them. When Athanasius passed through Antioch on return from his second exile in 348, Newman noted both Athanasius's praise for their fidelity and his advocacy of the rights of clergy and laity to elect a Catholic bishop.[103] One notes here that Athanasius had no episcopal jurisdiction at Antioch, so his words were delivered in his capacity as a theologian. At this, Newman stressed how "[t]wo laymen, Flavian and Diodorus, protested with spirit against the heterodoxy of the crafty Leontius, and kept alive an orthodox party in the midst of the Eusebian communion."[104]

A bit further on in the *Arians of the Fourth Century*, Newman devoted significant space to the orthodox bishop, Meletius of Antioch who had been elected to the see with Arian support in light of his perceived indifference to doctrine. Newman highlighted Meletius's clear orthodox teaching against the Arian bishop, Acacius of Caesarea, noting how the latter's "ambiguity of language" was "characteristic of his [Arian] school."[105] Significantly, when Meletius defended the Trinitarian faith, he was embraced by the assembled congregation of laypeople at Antioch. As Newman recorded it, they responded "with shouts of joy," causing the Arian archdeacon to clap his hand over the patriarch's mouth in order to prevent his further speaking. Undeterred, Meletius raised three fingers signifying the truth he wished to communicate.

---

103 As bishop of Alexandria, Athanasius had no canonical jurisdiction in Antioch. His use of Athanasius here is like the later uses Newman made of his patristic hero in the 1845 *Essay on the Development of Doctrine* and in his two translations of the *Select Treatises of S. Athanasius* in 1842-1844 and in 1881. As Benjamin King has noted, Newman's rhetoricisation of history could often supersede the limits of his subject, leading to situations where he was clearly "less interested in the historical Athanasius than in Catholic theology." This propensity could sometimes manifest itself in Newman supplanting Athanasius's words with his own. Benjamin King, "'In Whose Name I Write': Newman's Two Translations of Athanasius," *Zeitschrift für Neuere Theologiegeschichte* 53 (2008): 55. Cf., Benjamin King, *Newman and the Alexandrian Fathers* (Oxford: Oxford University Press, 2009), 247. Here it is enough to note that Athanasius was, for Newman, less a man than a symbol of orthodox theology's stubborn durability and ultimate triumph. Athanasius the theologian functions in just this way here.

104 Newman, *Ari*, 384.

105 Newman, *Ari*, 386.

The Anglican Newman of the early 1830s and the Roman Catholic Newman of the 1850s are in close accord as regards the importance of the laity in bearing witness to the revealed truths of the Christian faith. Newman would raise the subject again when speaking of the "illative sense" or "judgment in ratiocination" in the *Grammar of Assent* of 1870, but here it remains to note the way that Newman consistently imagined the theologian as an essential tether, mediating the teachings of the church to the faithful and mediating the responsive faith of the faithful to the episcopate.[106] To accomplish both functions, Newman believed that the office of theology required recognition as something distinct–something very much like the theological school he attempted to construct at Oxford. While Newman could never have entertained a theological office as something separate from the church or severed from full implication in its life, he nevertheless recognized that theology is a distinct charism, requiring a distinct ecclesial space and the church's respect as a distinct authority. Beginning in the early months of 1835, Newman would find a proper name and pedigree for this office under the sharp interrogations of Abbé Jean-Nicolas Jager.

---

[106] Works treating Newman's thought on the laity are too numerous to mention. One of the more recent and helpful works on Newman's thoughts vis-à-vis the laity is that of Frederick D. Aquino, *Communities of Informed Judgment: Newman's Illative Sense and Accounts of Rationality* (Washington, DC: Catholic University of America, 2004). See also John Guitton, *The Church and the Laity: From Newman to Vatican II* (New York: Alba House, 1964) and Samuel Femiano, *Infallibility of the Laity: The Legacy of Newman* (New York: Herder, 1967).

CHAPTER 4

Imagining and Inhabiting The Prophetical Office of the Church

By midsummer 1834, accusations of Roman Catholic sympathy were commonplace for Newman and his emergent school of "Apostolicals." As early as 5 December 1833, the *Tracts for the Times* provoked this line of critique in the evangelical newspaper, *The Record* (later to become *The Church of England Newspaper*). The editorial read in part,

> We must confess the surprise was extreme and the sorrow poignant with which we read the tracts of the Apostolical Society at Oxford, extracts from which appeared in our last number. Had we not read them with our own eyes it would have been difficult to persuade us that such effusions could have escaped, at any time, from the pens of Protestant clergymen . . . In time of need to go for spiritual weapons to the armoury of the "Man of Sin"–to lay a foundation which, in fact, will not give solid support to that lapsed body, the *heretical* Church of England, but on which the only true Apostolical Church of Rome has ever rested in imaginary security and triumph, alike in prosperity and adversity–deliberately, learnedly, zealously to pursue such a course as this would, if persevered in, be ominous of nothing less than destruction.[1]

---

[1] The text of the 5 December editorial has been helpfully reproduced by Peter Toon, *Evangelical Theology 1833-1856: A Response to Tractarianism* (Louisville, KY: Westminster John Knox, 1980), 18. In a letter dated 4 December 1833, the *Record*'s editor wrote Newman directly to refuse a piece attacking Temperance Societies. This letter prefigured the editorial of the following day, expressing "extreme regret at the character of the Tracts countenanced by the New Society at Oxford. He must confess that soberly viewing them on the one hand in the light of God's word, and

Samuel Charles Wilks, evangelical editor of *The Christian Observer*, likewise wrote to complain of "a Society formed at Oxford, the members of which, professing themselves to be the most orthodox upholders of the Church, have begun to scatter throughout the land publications which, for bigotry, Popery, and intolerance, surpass the writings even of Laud and Sacheverell."[2]

Evangelical churchmen might have been expected to react in this fashion. Stalwart defenses of apostolic succession and sacramental efficacy such as appeared in the early *Tracts for the Times* would stoke the outrage of the gentlest Calvinist. But close collaborators too had written Newman with worries that, however much his works had been received with "great satisfaction" and "much interest," they also provoked complaints for their "papistical" and "more than semi-popish" tendencies.[3] It was in this context that Newman's longtime friend, John William Bowden, wrote to warn Newman that the "Oxford Tracts" would soon be charged with "rank Popery" among potential allies. As a suggested remedy, he proposed that it would be *"worldly wise* to put out in the Series one number containing a few sweeping assertions obviously inconsistent with the truth of such a charge." Bowden concluded, "I can fancy a state of things, in which reference to [such a number] would be invaluable, not only for your own justification, but for the ultimate promotion of your views."[4] This rising tide of politically injurious association with Roman Catholicism eventually led Newman to

---

estimating them on the other by their measure of adaptation to reach and affect the minds of men in the present day, he considers them as the fruit of something nearly akin to Infatuation. May God in mercy preserve us for we are shewing to all the world that we cannot preserve ourselves." *LD* iv, 136. Owing to this disappointing response, Keble wrote Newman on 6 December encouraging him to "Go on and prosper–and let the Record dry its own ink." *LD* iv, 136.

2 [Samuel Charles Wilks], *The Christian Observer Conducted by Members of the Established Church for the Year 1833* (London: J. Hatchard and Son, 1833), iii. In a published letter dated 11 January, Newman upbraided Wilks, writing that "the tone of that challenge, I must own, or rather the general conduct of your Magazine towards the Tracts, since their first appearance, has been an exception to its usual mildness and urbanity." Newman, *Tracts* iv (London: J. G. & F. Rivington, 1838), ix.

3 James Dean to Newman (16 December 1833) *LD* iv, 144.

4 John William Bowden to Newman (14 July 1834) *LD* iv, 304.

fulfill Bowden's plea for new *Tracts* to exculpate their Apostolical school from charges that they were emulating the "Popish system" of Rome.[5] In July and August of 1834, Newman published *Tracts 38* and *41*.

Appearing under the titles "Via Media I" and "Via Media II," both works addressed what for Newman were the central points of divergence between Anglican and Roman Catholic thought: the relation of the creed to the Thirty-nine Articles, the development of doctrine, and the place of the Church of England as a distinct *via media*. Anglicanism was not a *via media* between Roman Catholicism and Puritanism, as was popularly held, but between Roman Catholicism and Protestantism as such.

A few weeks later, Newman also ventured into a controversy over Roman Catholicism with a French Catholic priest.[6] The dispute suited the need of the hour, but it also occasioned their mutual interaction with a short *Tract* that had appeared two decades earlier under name of the Anglican Bishop, John Jebb of Limerick. The work bore the title *The Peculiar Character of the Church of England; as distinguished, both from other branches of the Reformation, and from the modern Church of Rome*. Its author argued that Anglicanism had "adopted a middle course" between Protestantism's superficial regard for antiquity and Rome's pretentions to be an authority superseding antiquity. Anglicanism alone had adopted "the same delightful path, and treading in the same hallowed footsteps, with Vincentius, and the Catholic bishops, and the

---

5 Newman, *VM* ii (New York: Longmans, Green and Co., 1923), 21.

6 Newman's pretense at being caught unawares by the row is belied by the clear political advantage of a public debate with a Roman Catholic, and there is evidence that Newman volunteered to engage Jager for this very reason. In a 25 October 1834 letter to Archdeacon Froude, Newman wrote, "I have got entangled (as it seems) in controversy with a French Abbé on the question of Romanism–from the way matters have gone hitherto, I do not expect any thing will come of it–but at least I shall get some experience in the controversy and the Romanist mode of arguing." *LD* iv, 347. In a letter to John Bowden dated 5 February 1835, Newman wryly commented that while he found Jager to be "weak" and "no fun," the real object of the controversy was making the anti-Roman opinions of the Tractarians known. *LD* v, 25. Similarly, in a 16 July letter to Hurrell Froude, Newman described Jager as "the most ignorant of men and the most inconsequent of reasoners." "Yet," he wrote, "with these sets-off–first it obliges me to get up the controversy–next it shows I am not a Papist." *LD* v, 100.

ancient Fathers; proceeding as far as they proceeded; and stopping where they stopped."[7]

The importance of this historical intersection between Newman, Jebb, and the fifth-century theologian, Vincent of Lérins, cannot be overestimated, for it occasioned the critical consolidation of Newman's thought on the ecclesial vocation of the theologian. In his hands, theology became a "prophetical" office and theologians the successors of Elijah, Jeremiah, and John the Baptist. This crucial turn in Newman's thought established a storied precedent for his Apostolical school and would ultimately warrant his attempted reconstruction of Anglicanism. This advance would then run like a scarlet thread, linking Newman's life as an

---

[7] This *Tract* had been reprinted several times, but its origin and authorship have represented a puzzling question over the years. Although Jebb acknowledged in the brief preface to the work that it had "grown unexpectedly" under his own hands, John Overton proposed in 1889 that Jebb's friend, the lay theologian Alexander Knox (1757-1831), was "virtually the author." John Overton, *The Anglican Revival* (Chicago/New York: Herbert S. Stone & Co., 1889), 18-21. Indeed, while Jebb did not credit Knox by name, he anonymously acknowledged Knox's contribution "with equal gratitude and pleasure" for the "authorities" and "arguments" of the work. In a letter dated 31 May 1815, Jebb acknowledged receiving the work from Knox as a "valuable paper" and thereupon expressed his reluctance "to abridge or injure it," instead proposing that "the whole must be employed." Charles Forster, ed., *Thirty Years' Correspondence Between John Jebb, D.D., F.R.S., Bishop of Limerick, Adfert, and Aghadoe and Alexander Knox, Esq., M.R.I.A.*, vol. 1 (Philadelphia: Carey, Lea, and Blanchard, 1835), 150. Jebb also explained there that his acknowledgment of his debt to Knox by name would be "impolitic (for the debt would inevitably be detected) and wanting in integrity not to." Forster, *Thirty Year's Correspondence*, 150. From the available evidence, then, it seems clear that Jebb altogether abandoned his own initial draft and substituted Knox's work in its place, transcribing the paper directly in a span of over eighteen quarto pages, "smally and closely written." Forster, *Thirty Year's Correspondence*, 150. Alan Acheson has detailed the close friendship and collaboration between Knox and Jebb and has uncovered additional unpublished correspondence in the archives at Trinity College Dublin, wherein Jebb wrote in 1824 that he was "not ashamed" of the work under his own name but that the work was "much more Mr Knox's production than mine; and, as such, I don't mean to meddle with it any further." See the discussion in Alan Acheson, *Bishop John Jebb and the Nineteenth-Century Anglican Revival* (Toronto: Clements Academic, 2013), 35-37. Given that the arguments and supporting texts of the 1824 edition are identical to the original published work of 1815, whatever growth there had been under Jebb's hand was demonstrative and ornamental. While I will continue to refer to the work as that of Jebb, it is important that the reader understand the work as the work of both men, and of Knox preeminently.

Anglican with his life as a Roman Catholic convert, and would remain a central and pivotal component in his thought to the end of his life.

Here I will chart the contours of Newman's journey with Jebb and Vincent as he engaged in a vastly underestimated epistolary debate with a then-unknown French Catholic priest, Abbé Jean-Nicolas Jager. Central in the discussion is Newman's innovation of the particular terminology "prophetical office" while defending the borrowed premise of Irish Anglicans, using an improvised defense, culled from a fifth-century Gallic theologian. Isolating these rather intricately woven strands, I describe how Newman wove them together to form the critical tether between his Apostolical school at Oxford and his much broader, more durable conception of theologians functioning together as to form the prophetical office of the church.

L'AFFAIR JAGER: A SERENDIPITOUS CONTROVERSY

The controversy with Abbé Jean-Nicolas Jager resulted from a chance meeting between Jager and Benjamin Harrison while the latter was traveling in France during September of 1834. Harrison was a brilliant young student who was matriculated at Christ Church, Oxford in 1826 and elected in 1828.[8] He was also an early adherent to Tractarianism, having been recognized by Newman as an influential "friend" of the movement in 1833.[9] When the initial rift between Newman's Apostolical school and the High Churchmen of Oxford occasioned the choosing of sides, Harrison remained loyal to Newman and encouraged him

---

8 Harrison's academic prowess was no secret at the time. He took a first *in Literis Humanioribus* and a second *in Disciplinis Mathematicis et Physicis* and won the Ellerton Theological Essay Prize and the Kennicott Hebrew Scholarship the next year. In 1832 he had additionally won the Pusey and Ellerton Hebrew Scholarship and the English Essay Prize. Henry Tristram, "In the Lists with the Abbé Jager," in *Newman Centenary Essays* (London: Burns, Oates, and Washbourne, 1945), 203.

9 Newman to Richard Hurrell Froude (7 November 1833), *LD* iv, 90.

to fulfill his "promise of disclaiming an Association" to produce the Oxford *Tracts*.[10]

Jean-Nicolas Jager was born on 17 June 1790 in France at Grening, a hamlet of 400 inhabitants in the new department of Mosell, near Insming. Always a prodigious student, he took his Baccalauréat-ès-Lettres and received the tonsure and minor orders in 1809. Upon completion of studies at the diocesan seminary, Jager was then ordained, first to the diaconate in 1812 and then to the priesthood in 1813. Aside from his literary dispute with Newman, Jager is best remembered for translations of the major speeches of Demosthenes while stationed as chaplain of the ninth regiment of infantry at Phalsbourg. His ability to accomplish this work without the aid of grammar, dictionary, or commentary bears witness to his scholarly capacities. Upon his release from army service, Jager accepted a chaplaincy at L'Hôtel national des Invalides. There, libraries at Paris gave him greater leave to study Greek. With the help of quotations culled from the Greek Fathers, he worked to revise the Sixtine edition of the Septuagint and thereby established the fidelity of the Vulgate.[11]

Having been seated next to one another by the hostess of a dinner engagement, Harrison and Jager quickly initiated a discussion of the controversies separating the Churches of England and Rome. At the conclusion of their initial encounter, they arranged further meetings, but when Harrison proved unable to prolong his stay, they agreed to continue the amicable dispute by mail. The two additionally committed to publish their letters for public consumption in the Parisian publication, *L'Univers*. Each letter would be numbered and duly acknowledged. Replies would strictly follow the order in which the questions were raised, and no reply would commence until the preceding letter appeared in full. Principles mutually accepted in the course of the

---

[10] Henry Parry Liddon, *Life of Edward Bouverie Pusey*, vol. 1 (London: Longmans, 1894), 335, 342.

[11] Henry Tristram, "In the Lists with the Abbé Jager," in *John Henry Newman: Centenary Essays* (London: Burns, Oates, and Washburn), 205-206.

discussion could not be subsequently altered, and Harrison would remain anonymous save for his initials.[12]

Jager was acquainted with some of the *Tracts for the Times*, and he was familiar with the classic presentation of the Roman-Anglican controversy from the Roman side.[13] Quotes and allusions from his side of the controversy also demonstrate his familiarity with Milner's *End of Religious Controversy* (1818) and Samuel Wix's *Reflections concerning the Expediency of a Council of the Church of England and the Church of Rome* (1818). Harrison had also left a cache of published resources for Jager's consideration prior to his departure for England. Among these was the copy of John Jebb's *Pastoral Instructions: On the Character and Principles of the Church of England*, wherein the work, "On the Peculiar Character of the Church of England" appeared as an appendix.[14] This short piece immediately became the center of the debate between Jager and Harrison. Newman likewise defended Jebb's use of Saint Vincent's *Commonitorium* when he substituted in for Harrison in the Autumn of 1834.

In the essay itself, Bishop Jebb intended to establish the truth of Johann Mosheim's thesis that the Church of England was separated "equally from the Roman Catholics, and from the other communities who have renounced the domination of the Pope."[15] This theory of

---

12 Tristram, "In the Lists with the Abbé Jager," 207. Louis Allen, "Introduction," in *John Henry Newman and the Abbé Jager* (London: Oxford University Press, 1975), 6.

13 Allen, "Introduction," 5.

14 The full title is "On Peculiar Character of the Church of England; As Distinguished, both from Other Branches of the Reformation, and from the Modern Church of Rome." See, John Jebb, *Pastoral Instructions on the Character and Principles of the Church of England* (London: Duncan, 1831), 261-318. This work had been compiled from previous volumes of Jebb's sermons and discourses and was republished in 1824. Quotes from Jebb's *Tract* here are from John Jebb, "Appendix: The Character of the Church of England," in *Sermons on Subjects Chiefly Practical*, 3rd ed. (London: T. Cadell, 1824).

15 Jebb, "Appendix: The Character of the Church of England," 357. Jebb translates here Mosheim's original Latin, suggesting that the English translation of Maclaine was inadequate and at once perceptible. Mosheim's original reads, "Illa quidem religionis veteris correctio, quæ Britannos æque a pontificiis, atque a reliquis familiis, quæ pontificis dominationi renuntiarunt, seungit." See Johann Lorenz von Mosheim, *Institutiones Historiae Ecclesiasticae* (Helmstad, 1764), 676. Maclaine's translation read, "Thus was that form of religion established in *Britain*, which

an English *via media* between Roman Catholicism and Protestantism was ultimately rooted in how each communion handled the Bible. Making recourse to the *Commonitorium*, Jebb argued that the Church of England alone maintained fidelity to that faith "believed in all places, at all times, by all the faithful" because it alone had followed St. Vincent's prescribed methodology.[16] "The Church of Rome," wrote Jebb, "maintains not only that there are two rules of belief, but that these two rules are co-ordinate; that there is an unwritten, no less than a written word of God, and that the authority of the former is alike definitive with the authority of the latter."[17] He thus summarized the Protestant approach as "sending each individual to the Bible alone; thence to collect, as it may happen, truth or falsehood, by his own interpretation, or misinterpretation; and there to measure the most weighty and mysterious truths by the least peculiar and appropriate passages of sacred Scripture."[18] Alternatively, Jebb described Roman Catholics as persons sent, neither to sacred tradition, nor to the Bible alone, but to "an infallible living expositor" that "sometimes limits, and sometimes extends, and sometimes contradicts, both the written word and the language of Christian antiquity."[19] Finally, Jebb celebrated the Church of

---

separated the *English* equally from the church of *Rome* on the one hand, and from the other churches which had renounced popery, on the other." John Lawrence Mosheim [Johann Lorenz Mosheim], *An Ecclesiastical History, Ancient and Modern, from the Birth of Christ to the Beginning of the Eighteenth Century*, trans. Archibald Maclaine, vol. 4 (London: Vernor & Hood, 1803), 391. While Yngve Brilioth was in all likelihood correct to argue that the description of Anglicanism as a *via media* between Roman Catholicism and Protestantism first appeared in the quoted 1813 letter from Knox to Jebb, the *concept* was directly anticipated by Mosheim. See the discussion in Yngve Brilioth, *The Anglican Revival: Studies in the Oxford Movement* (London: Longmans, Green, and Co., 1933), 45-49. See also his "Appendix I–Note on the Question of the Dependence of the Oxford Movement on Knox and Jebb." Brilioth, *The Anglican Revival*, 331-33.

16 Vincent's famous appeal to "Quod ubique, quod semper, quod ab omnibus creditum est." See Vincentius Lerinensis, *Commonitorium* 2.5 (CCSL 64, 149). The English translations of the *Commonitorium* that follow here are my own.

17 Jebb, "The Character of the Church of England," 370-71.

18 Jebb, "The Character of the Church of England," 396.

19 Jebb, "The Character of the Church of England," 396-97.

England as a "middle course," combining reverence for scriptures as the supreme authority; respect of tradition as an authority subordinate to the scriptures; and the commendation of inquiry, assisting private judgment without superseding it. In favor of the Church of England he concluded that,

> Where the Scripture clearly and freely speaks, she receives its dictates as the voice of God. When Scripture is either not clear or explicit; or when it may demand expansion and illustration, she refers her sons to an authoritative standard of interpretation; but a standard, which it is their privilege to apply for themselves. And when Scripture is altogether silent, she provides a supplemental guidance: but a guidance, neither fluctuating nor arbitrary; the same in all times, and under all circumstances; which no private interest can warp, and no temporary prejudice can lead astray.[20]

Jager's opening letter appeared in *L'Univers* on 30 August 1834. There he lauded Jebb's view as one that rightly avoided the "absurd and fatal end" of private interpretation. This was important given that such a view required the individual interpreter to be exhaustively familiar with virtually everything that came before.[21] Jager agreed that scripture was not clear on all points and concurred that were one to solely cling to that which was clear, the result would be a "truncated and incomplete religion."[22] He likewise praised Jebb's reliance on Vincent of Lérins and the methodology commended by the *Commonitorium*.

Harrison's reply, published in *L'Univers* on 18 September 1834, stressed more the differences between the two communions. Referring to the *Churchman's Manual* that he had lent Jager, Harrison argued

---

20 Jebb, "The Character of the Church of England," 397.

21 "L'Eglise anglicane a évité, selon lui, cette extrémité absurde et funeste L'auteur s'attache ensuite à démontrer successivement tous les inconvéniens du principe de l'interprétation privée." Jean-Nicolas Jager and John Henry Newman, *Le Protestantisme aux prises avec la Doctrine catholique, ou Controverses avec plusieurs Ministres Anglicains, Membres de l'Université d'Oxford* (Paris: Debécourt, 1836), 9.

22 "Si donc on prend l'Ecriture pour unique guide, et qu'on s'arrête aux verities clairement énoncés, croyant qu'elles sont l'explication de ce qui est obscure. On n'aura bientôt plus qu'une religion tronquée et incomplete." Jager and Newman, *Le Protestantisme*, 10.

that Rome had presumptuously superseded the scriptures and antiquity in promoting: 1) the adoration of images, 2) the invocation of the Virgin Mary and other saints, 3) the doctrine of Transubstantiation, 4) communion under one kind, 5) the celibacy of the clergy, 6) the doctrine of Purgatory, 7) the authority of Rome over all other churches, 8) obedience due the Pope, and 9) the seven sacraments. He also argued that the Churches of Rome and of England were alike true churches, possessing as they did an uninterrupted apostolic succession. The issue of the controversy, then, was which of the two churches had been more faithful to the Vincentian standard. "We claim," wrote Harrison, "that our Church has faithfully observed, while yours, despite professing to revere and follow this maxim [i.e., *Quod ubique, quod semper, quod ab omnibus*] has really neglected it to follow a very different rule."[23]

Jager's rejoinder appeared the following day. In it he challenged Jebb's points directly, arguing that, where the Church of England accused the Church of Rome of maintaining two co-ordinate rules of belief, one unwritten and one written, Rome had actually recognized only one authority, the word of God, transmitted through the "two channels" of scripture and tradition.[24] Regarding Jebb's charge that the Church of Rome superseded private judgment by imposing its own summary decision, Jager questioned whether it was practicable to require every individual to study collections of the fathers in order to discover sacred truth. To demand such a thing was "absurd" (*l'absurdité*) on its face: "Saint Vincent wanted to help the human mind, but he did not want to overwhelm and despair."[25] Finally, answering Jebb's

---

[23] "Quant à la dissertation de M. Jebb, vous devez avoir vu qu'il est question de savoir entre nous laquelle des deux Eglises a été la plus fidèle à la maxime de Vincent. Nous prétendons que notre Eglise l'a fidèlement observée; tandis que la vôtre, tout en protestant de révérer et de suivre cette maxime, l'a réellement négligée pour suivre une règle toute différente." Jager and Newman, *Le Protestantisme*, 23.

[24] As Jager wrote, "En effet, l'Eglise de Rome admet deux voies par lesquelles la volonté de Dieu nous est transmise; elle reconnaît une parole écrite et une autre non écrite, et en cela elle se trouve d'accord avec l'Ecriture et avec la doctrine des Pères." Jager and Newman, *Le Protestantisme*, 28.

[25] "Saint Vincent a voulu aider l'esprit humain, mais il n'a pas voulu l'accabler et le désespérer." Jager and Newman, *Le Protestantisme*, 28.

charge that the Church of Rome wrongfully suppressed an appeal to antiquity against innovation, Jager argued that the pastors of the church serve to ascertain and proclaim the ancient faith, guiding the faithful into its proper use.[26] One might summarize the argument up to that point by saying that where Harrison read Vincent's canon (via Jebb) as recommending a method for evaluating a given tradition, Jager regarded it as a warrant, demanding obedience to an infallible magisterial authority.[27]

Following Jager's second letter, Harrison hoped that Newman would take over the debate in his stead, but Harrison's "ami d'Oxford" was visiting friends and would not return to Oxford until after the Long Vacation. He thus penned a second reply that subsequently appeared in *L'Univers* on 14 October 1834. Although Jager lauded it as being "full of verve," giving "a great impetus to the discussion," it is unclear how Harrison advanced the conversation. In the end, he simply restated his belief that Rome had failed to adhere to the Vincentian Canon. For Anglicans, scripture contained all things necessary to salvation and those things that were not in scripture could not be imposed as an article of faith.[28]

Jager published his third letter in two consecutive issues of *L'Univers* on 23 and 24 October. There he dismissed Harrison's argument, stating that for three centuries of controversy with Protestants, the Roman Catholic Church denied that scripture alone was sufficient to reveal the whole of the Christian religion. To understand the full sense

---

[26] "Ces pasteurs examinent, soit par eux-mêmes, soit par le secours d'autres savans, la vraie doctrine de Jésus-Christ, cette foi ancienne crue dans tous les lieux, dans tous les temps, et par tous les chrétiens." Jager and Newman, *Le Protestantisme*, 28.

[27] Stephen Thomas draws something close to this conclusion when he writes, "For Harrison, the Vincentian Canon is an invitation to make a judgment about what Tradition is, on the evidence. Jager, on the other hand, argued that, when new heresies arose, *if* they had not been condemned by the Church then one could have recourse to the *quod ubique, quod semper, quod ab omnibus* as a rule of thumb by which to gauge Tradition–but if the Church *had* defined, then obedience was all that was required." Stephen Thomas, *Newman and Heresy: The Anglican Years* (New York: Cambridge University Press, 1991), 186.

[28] Allen, *John Henry Newman and the Abbé Jager*, 24.

of scripture, he argued, one must have recourse to the authority of the church. It alone preserved the antiquity, uniformity, and universality of its teaching against the arbitrary and multiple interpretations of private judgment. Jager further argued that Vincent himself had never argued that scripture contains everything necessary for salvation and protested that it was inconsistent for Anglicans to receive rites and ceremonies from tradition while at the same time rejecting doctrines from the same sources.[29]

INVOKING OXFORD AND ITS DIVINES: THE GRAVITY OF AN UNSENT GREETING

The controversy took a strange turn when Newman finally determined to enter the discussion. Jager believed that he had effectively answered both Harrison and Jebb's charges of Roman infidelity to the Vincentian Canon and so turned to the question of images. This became Jager's fourth letter, published in successive issues of *L'Univers* on 7 and 8 November 1834. The action put him in breach of the initial agreement that replies would follow the order in which questions were raised. This is important to note because it would not be the last such occurrence.

For his part, Newman spent the entire first term of the academic year 1834-1835 composing his first letter. Prior to commencing the public portion of their debate, he drafted an unsent private note to Jager, introducing himself and staking out the ground of his forthcoming contributions. Despite its diffident tone and assurances to the contrary, the letter clearly signals Newman's intention to contend as a theologian of "Oxford" and "a member," as he put it, "of one of the Colleges."[30] There Newman worried aloud that if he did not engage Jager's critique on the university's behalf, "no one else would." He wrote,

---

[29] Allen, *John Henry Newman and the Abbé Jager*, 25.

[30] The sentence reads, "I have no office or station in the University which might give weight to my words. I am but an individual member of one of the Colleges; and have no claim to represent anyone but myself." Newman to the Abbé Jager (end of October, 1834), *LD* iv, 350. Henry Tristram was as inclined to take these words at face value as he was with Newman's vacuous protestations that he was "no theologian." This does not account for Newman's rhetorical style. That the letter mentions

Almost all of us, excepting our Theological Professors and other high organs of our religious opinions have laid aside their arms; which were formally wielded by an Andrewes, a Laud, and a Barrow. I considered with myself that I probably had thought as much on the subject as most of us, tho' I had never practiced myself in polemical exercises[;] that if the controversy between the Churches was to be renewed, there must be a beginning; and that on our side that beginning must be attended with some mistakes in detail in the mode of conducting the argument; that the Romans once had no model for a ship of war but a chance vessel of the enemy's flung upon the beach, yet at last they became lords of sea as well as land. For these reasons I consider I ought not to decline the challenge, believing as I do that the truth is on my side.[31]

That Newman began the dispute by invoking a list of venerable Caroline Divines from Oxford is significant for the way it underpinned, at least temporarily, his larger program. Here Newman was snatching at ballast to endow his school with a gravity borrowed from the reputation and authority of venerated Divines to whom he appealed for normative Anglican divinity.

The limits of space here preclude a fuller discussion of Newman's broader use of the Caroline Divines as witnesses to his theory of the *via media*. Kenneth Parker has explored the complexities of Newman's "integral system," combining appeals to scripture, primitive Christian tradition, and the Caroline Divines in a study of Newman's

---

Oxford by name and gestures to his role at Oriel must not be overlooked. In this context he mentions William Laud, Isaac Barrow, and Lancelot Andrewes who were all deeply connected with Oxford in the seventeenth century–Andrewes being both a fellow of Pembroke College, Cambridge, and incorporated MA at Oxford in 1581. Jager understood both the status of his interlocutors and the stakes of the controversy. Upon being informed by the Monsignor Louis de Quélen, Archbishop of Paris, that Jager was "at grips with the most eminent champions of the Anglican Church" and urged him to "enlist the help of a board of Catholic Theologians." Jager answered, "Why any priest, with the help of God, can confound the combined scholars of Oxford and Cambridge." Tristram, "In the Lists with the Abbé Jager," 208-209.

31 Newman to the Abbé Jager (end of October 1834), *LD* iv, 350.

"individualistic use" of the latter.[32] Parker traces a quarter century's inquiry into how well Newman knew the Caroline Divines and when and whether he had studied them closely. Alternatively, H. D. Weidner has posited Newman's access to Richard Mant's edition of *The Book of Common Prayer* in 1824, with its large catena of Anglican divinity, as a primary source. Weidner also appealed to Newman's reading of works by the Caroline patristic scholars, James Ussher and John Pearson, while in his twenties as an early access point.[33] Philip Rule has likewise suggested that Newman was reading the Caroline Divines in his twenties and cites a letter to Edward Pusey, dated 4 October 1829, where Newman referenced a large number of Caroline authors.[34] Rule's larger theory is subverted, however, by a diary entry dated 4 October 1829, which suggests that Newman spent a good portion of the previous Sunday, intensively researching the writings he cited. This letter functions as something of a window on the ways Newman used sources that eluded or exceeded his special expertise.

Benjamin King has recently confirmed this supposition with a decisive case for the ways that Newman encountered patristic sources in the preparation of sermons.[35] So, like Parker, I am persuaded that Newman was something of a dilettante when using the Caroline Divines. Although he could muster a rough summation of authors that he came to know by general reputation in English church history, Newman's appeals were characteristically cobbled together in the heat of controversial writing with little regard for real contextual depth. It was for this reason that High Church Anglicans proved so successful when

---

[32] See Kenneth Parker, "Newman's Individualistic Use of the Caroline Divines," in *Discourse and Context: An Interdisciplinary Study of John Henry Newman*, ed. Gerard Magill (Edwardsville, IL: Southern Illinois University Press, 1993), 33-42.

[33] H. D. Weidner, "Editor's Introduction," in Newman, *VM*, ed. H. D. Weidner (Oxford: Oxford University Press, 1990), xiii-xxxii. Cf., H. D. Weidner, "Newman's Idea of the *Via Media*: An Introduction to the Lectures on the Prophetical Office of the Church" (D.Phil. diss., University of Oxford, 1984).

[34] Cf., *LD* ii, 169. Philip Rule, "Newman and the English Theologians," *Faith and Reason* 15 (1990): 65-90.

[35] See Benjamin King, *Newman and the Alexandrian Fathers: Shaping Doctrine in Nineteenth-Century England* (Oxford: Oxford University Press, 2009), 127-80.

impeaching Newman's appropriation of the Caroline Divines. While the records of the Oriel College Library demonstrate that Newman read feverishly in the writings of Lancelot Andrewes, Henry Hammond, Thomas Ken, William Beveridge, Henry Thorndike, Edward Stillingfleet, and John Bramhall during the fall of 1836, demonstrated here is how controversy was again the impetus for his quest. Newman's primary interest was in patristics, so he was never able to realize his intuited "Consensus Doctorum" as a secure foundation for his school.[36] Peter Nockles rightly observes that "the *protean* quality of the texts of seventeenth-century Anglican divinity ultimately eluded Tractarian efforts to appropriate them definitively in support of all the Movement's doctrines and practices and to pass them off as the Church of England's 'official' teaching."[37] However much Newman tried to buttress his *via media* by appeals to the Carolines' "stable and uniform Anglicanism," it was ultimately a project of his own imagination and construction. As I presently argue, Newman quickly jettisoned this approach in the course of dispute with Jager and under the insistent critique of Froude and Harrison.

AN OBJECT TO MAKE KNOWN OUR OPINIONS: NEWMAN'S FIRST LETTER TO JAGER

Newman's first public contribution to the debate appeared over three issues of *L'Univers* on 25 December 1834 and on 28 and 29 January 1835. There he first took pains to clarify some points of misunderstanding in the previous exchange with Harrison, noting that the period of "Apostolic purity" he wished to defend was the period of "the first four [ecumenical] Councils, i.e. down to the middle of the fifth century," as opposed to the first seven councils progressing into the eighth century. In this matter Newman followed the Anglican standard set by Joseph Hall in his *Peace-Maker* (1645) and by John Jewel in the

---

[36] Cf., Newman to James Bliss (16 August 1836), *LD* iv, 339-40.

[37] Peter Nockles, "'Survivals or New Arrivals?': The Oxford Movement and the Nineteenth-Century Historical Construction of Anglicanism," in *Anglicanism and the Western Christian Tradition: Continuity, Change, and the Search for Communion*, ed. Stephen Platten (Norwich: Canterbury Press), 190-91.

Apologia Pro Ecclesia Anglicana (1562).[38] Newman then turned to defend Jebb in his use of Vincent, maintaining that for Anglicanism "Scripture is the ultimate basis of proof, the place of final appeal, in respect to all fundamental doctrine."[39] To this, Newman admitted the qualified use of church tradition in much the same way as did Edward Hawkins before him;

> We do not deny that ceremonies and practices may lawfully be made to rest upon tradition, but that doctrines may so rest; nay not simply all doctrines, but fundamental doctrines. Nor do we say that the proof of even fundamental doctrines must rest immediately on Scripture, but ultimately. These three words, *ultimate appeal*, *doctrines*, and *fundamentals* must be clearly understood. E.g. we should be ready to receive the three orders of the Ministry even on *tradition*, as being a point of *discipline*; we receive the validity of heretical baptism on *tradition*, as being a *doctrine not fundamental*; we receive the doctrine of the Trinity, *a fundamental*, *immediately* from tradition, *ultimately from Scripture*. If we are asked what we mean by fundamentals, we answer that we mean such doctrines as are necessary for Church Communion; if we are asked which these are, we answer briefly the articles of the Creed. Further, if we are asked what we consider to be the obligation of receiving doctrines *not* fundamental, or of matters of discipline, (such as come to us on the voucher of tradition), we answer we consider it *pious* to receive them, but not *necessary* for Church communion. Thus we make a distinction between a praeceptum and a consilium of the Church. The reception of pure tradition is pious,

---

38 Joseph Hall, "The Peace-Maker: Laying Forth the Right Way of Peace in Matters of Religion," in *The Works of Joseph Hall*, vol. 7 (Oxford: D.A. Talboys, 1837), 45-108; and John Jewell, "Apologia pro Ecclesia Anglicana (1562)," in *The Works of John Jewell*, vol. 3 (Cambridge: Cambridge University Press,1848), 51-112. By doing this, Newman could sidestep the problematic Second Council of Nicaea, with its commendation of icons as a necessary development of the Christology defined by the Council of Chalcedon. The Catholic nature of Nicaea II has always presented difficulties for Anglicanism, given the explicit iconoclasm of the Thirty-nine Articles (esp. Article 22).

39 Allen, *John Henry Newman and the Abbé Jager*, 35.

of doctrines conveyed to us by Tradition but proved by Scripture is imperative.[40]

Newman then distinguished his Anglican approach to tradition from what he understood to be the Roman Catholic view: "You on the other hand, allowing us our three uses of Tradition, add a fourth, which we deny. You consider Tradition per se the sufficient authority for the Church's considering a doctrine fundamental."[41] For Newman, both the validity of the Anglican view, and his own justification for denying the Roman Catholic view, lay in a broader ecclesiology. At this point, the Anglican and Roman communions were equally part of the one, holy, catholic, and apostolic church.[42] If the one church was to be exclusively identified with the Roman communion, its claim on the consciences of the baptized might have some purchase. Granting that the Church of England was, in its full integrity, a portion of the one church, however,

---

[40] Allen, *John Henry Newman and the Abbé Jager*, 36. Stephen Thomas here complains of Newman's "grotesquely elaborate precision" and judges that it functions to obscure, a "rather confusing" and structurally incoherent argument. I am not so persuaded by Thomas's critique. Much of the divergence and miscommunication between Newman and Jager were due to Newman's diachronic–that is, "historical"–approach, while Jager's arguments remained persistently synchronic. See his *Newman and Heresy*, 185-91.

[41] Allen, *John Henry Newman and the Abbé Jager*, 37.

[42] Christopher Dawson sharply distinguished Newman's *via media* theory of the church from William Palmer's "branch theory" as set forth about the same time in his *Treatise on the Church of Christ* (1838). The branch theory understands Catholic dogma to be "the common denominator or highest common factor of the various branches of the Church that retain episcopal orders," but fails, both to grapple with the "one church" teaching different things in different places, and thus to supply a true warrant to reject communion with Roman Catholicism. Alternatively, Newman's *via media* view warranted the Reformation and allowed the Church of England to take a definite stand against union with Rome, but this risked the collapse of Newman's Anglican defense against private judgment and the manifold expressions of Protestantism. Christopher Dawson, *The Spirit of the Oxford Movement* (1933; repr., London: St. Austin Press, 2001), 103-105. Dawson rightly recognized the similitude between Palmer's branch theory and Newman's *via media*, but he pressed the implications of the difference too far. While Newman could write things like "Popery must be destroyed; it cannot be reformed," etc., this only counted as warrant for England's continued separation from Rome. Newman did *not* believe that Rome was outside the visible church.

she possessed a distinct authority to "develop its fundamental Creed into Articles of religion, according to times and circumstances, not however as necessary to be believed for communion, but useful for all her people as necessary for holding rule or influence."[43] This humbler configuration of local church authority was necessary given the church's subordination to the scriptures. Individual members of the church were exempt from receiving them *de fide* as a basis for communion in either the universal church or in a given local branch of it. While belief in nonessential doctrines–that is, doctrines promulgated by tradition but lacking scriptural warrant–might be licit and even "pious," they could not be made necessary for inclusion. According to Newman's view, and in full keeping with Jebb's thesis, the Roman Church superseded its rightful authority as a local branch of the church by identifying the two. He then summarized his case–as did Jebb–by making recourse to Vincent's *Commonitorium*, defending propositionally that 1) "tradition is secondary to Scripture,"[44] 2) "that [tradition] is interpretive of Scripture,"[45] 3) that "the fundamentals of the faith are ever one and the same,"[46] that 4) "the Church may explain,

---

[43] Allen, *John Henry Newman and the Abbé Jager*, 40.

[44] Newman quotes the *Commonitorium* 2.1: "Quod, siue ego siue quis uellet exsurgentium haereticorum fraudes deprehendere laqueosque uitare et in fide sana san us atque integer permanere, duplici modo munire fidem suam Domino adiuuante deberet, primum scilicet diuinae legis auctoritate, tum deinde Ecclesiae Catholicae traditione." In English, the passage reads, "Should I or any other person wish to unmask the frauds of heretics as they arise, and avoid their snares, and in healthy faith to remain sound and whole, we would, with the Lord's help, doubly fortify our own faith, first, of course, by the authority of the divine law, and, second, by the tradition of the catholic church." The idea here is that scripture is "first" (*premium*) in authority while tradition comes "second" or "after" (*tum deinde*).

[45] Newman quotes the *Commonitorium* 2.2: "[propheticae et apostolicae interpretationis linea secundum] secundum ecclesiastici et catholici sensus normam dirigatur." In English, the passage reads, "[the line used in the exposition of the prophets and apostles] be made straight in accordance with the standard of ecclesiastical and catholic interpretation."

[46] Newman quotes the *Commonitorium* 22.4: "Depositum, inquit, custodi. Quid est 'depositum'? Id est, quod tibi creditum est, non quod a te inuentum; quod accepisti, non quod excogitasti; rem non ingenii sed doctrinae, non usurpationis priuatae sed publicae tradi tionis; rem ad te perductam, non a te prolatam; in qua non

and develop the fundamentals, though it cannot make new ones,"[47] and that 5) "these developments are from tradition, or are the work of the existing Church."[48] Newman then issued a parting challenge to Jager, asking him to locate in the *Commonitorium* any support for the notion "that pure Tradition is a sufficient basis on which the Church may rest in declaring a doctrine necessary to salvation" or "that the Church may impose consent to any article of faith as a condition of communion over and above the original fundamentals."[49]

Jager's response to Newman's first salvo came in the form of three letters published in *L'Univers* between 25 December 1834 and 30 January 1835. This reply appeared prior to the published second

---

auctor debes esse sed custos, non institutor sed sectator, non ducens sed sequens." In English, the passage reads, "[Saint Paul says], 'Guard the deposit.' What does 'deposit' mean? It is what has been entrusted to you, not what has been found by you; what you have received, not what you have thought up yourself; a matter, not of genius, but of teaching; not of personal adoption, but of public tradition; a matter brought to you, not brought out by you, in which you ought to be not the author but the guardian, not the initiator but the adherent, not leading, but following."

47 Newman quotes the *Commonitorium* 23.3: "Crescat igitur oportet et multum uehementerque proficiat tam singulorum quam omnium, tam unius hominis quam totius ecclesiae, aetatum ac saeculorum gradibus, intellegentia, scientia, sapientia, sed in suo dum taxat genere, in eodem scilicet dogmate, eodem sensu eademque sentential." In English, the passage reads, "Therefore, there should be a great increase and a vigorous progress, in individuals and in the whole group, in the single man as well as in the entire church, as the ages and the centuries march on, of understanding, knowledge, wisdom, but, at least, in its own kind, in the same doctrine, that is, in the same sense, in the same meaning."

48 Newman quotes a portion of the *Commonitorium* 23.18-19 that Jager had himself had used in his third letter: "Denique quid unquam aliud conciliorum decretis enisa est, nisi ut, quod antea simpliciter credebatur, hoc idem postea diligentius crederetur... Hoc, inquam, semper neque quicquam praeterea haereticorum nouitatibus excitata, conciliorum suorum decretis catholica perfecit ecclesia, nisi ut, quod prius a maioribus sola traditione susceperat, hoc deinde posteris etiam per scripturae chirographum consignaret." In English, the passage reads, "Finally, what else have the councils ever striven to accomplish by their decrees but that what was formerly believed with simplicity, that afterward should be believed more diligently... This, and nothing else, I say, is what the catholic church, roused by the innovations of the heretics, has brought to fruition by the decrees of its councils. What she had earlier received from the oral tradition of her forefathers."

49 Allen, *John Henry Newman and the Abbé Jager*, 45.

and third portions of Newman's letter and again violated the original agreement between Jager and Harrison.[50] Jager paid compliment to his new interlocutor for producing what he judged to be the "ultimatum" of the Anglican Reformation.[51] This did not, however, dissuade Jager from making a quick work of Newman where he believed the latter had sought novel defenses for an untenable middle way between Rome and Protestantism. Indeed, Jager complained that Newman left unanswered the question of how Jebb (not to mention, Harrison) could grant Christians the right of dissent from aspects of church without conceding, *contra* Vincent, the Protestant right of private judgment and therein throwing "on each individual the onerous obligation to seek his faith in Scripture and in the voluminous writings of the Fathers."[52] He also recognized how Newman's innovative distinction between fundamental and non-fundamental doctrines gave him refuge from the charge that he ultimately rejected the indefectibility of the church, but Jager questioned whether Newman truly had warrant for such a distinction between the commands that must be believed for communion, and negligible council rooted in the exigencies of time and circumstance. Put simply, Jager could not see in the *Commonitorium* any justification for the hard distinction between scripture and tradition. This left Newman without warrant for praising the Church of England's retention of Catholic faith while rejecting certain Roman Catholic teachings.

---

50 In a letter to Newman on 3 January 1835, Harrison thus complained, "Here is the Abbé again at his former tricks. I have written to him at once telling him that it would never do to take your letter piecemeal; and begging him to insert your letters as a whole, in numbers as closely consecutive as possible, and then give us his reply as a whole. I have argued fairly out with him the endless confusion into which the controversy will be brought, if we are to have half a dozen answers awaiting a reply, while there is one long letter lying by him which is to be taken bit by bit, to the utter ruin of its meaning as a complete argument. I hope this may produce some effect; if not, I shall be sorry for my friend and ashamed of the 'Univers's' tactics." *Letters and Correspondence of John Henry Newman*, vol. II, 81–82.

51 Jager, *Le Protestantisme aux prises avec la Doctrine catholique*, 122.

52 "D'imposer à chaque particulier l'onéreuse obligation de chercher sa foi dans l'Écriture et dans les volumineux écrits des Pères." Jager, *Le Protestantisme aux prises avec la Doctrine catholique*, 129.

"In a word," Jager wrote, "it must be all or nothing."[53] Jebb's imagined "via media" (*juste-milieu*) between scripture and tradition was, on Jager's reckoning, more akin to a cul-de-sac. Scripture was rooted in, and validated by, tradition. If Newman could reject tradition in the points that divided Anglicans from Roman Catholics, then there was nothing to prevent his rejection of scripture as well.[54] Clearly Newman's instinctive sense that there was a "hierarchy of truths," with certain doctrines exercising more authority on the conscience than others, required surer foundation.[55]

APOSTLES RULE, PROPHETS EXPOUND: NEWMAN'S SECOND LETTER TO JAGER

Given that rejection of private judgment and its attendant infidelities was a core principle animating his school, Newman could not allow Jager to subvert the key premise on which that rejection was based. But neither could he abide Jager's "all or nothing" approach to Roman Catholic claims. Newman's second letter, the first half of which was sent to Jager in July 1835, thus introduced several critical distinctions for the purpose of holding his theory together.[56] He first reminded Jager of the

[53] "En un mot, il faut être tout ou rien." Jager, *Le Protestantisme aux prises avec la Doctrine catholique*, 225.

[54] "Si vous rejetez donc la tradition sur les points qui nous divisent, il faut la rejeter aussi sur le canon de l'Ecriture." Jager, *Le Protestantisme aux prises avec la Doctrine catholique*, 225.

[55] The phrase "hierarchy of truths" is of recent coinage and entered officially into Roman Catholic teaching during the Second Vatican Council. See *Unitatis Redintegratio* 3, §11: "In Catholic doctrine there exists an order or hierarchy of truths, since they vary in their relation to the foundation of the Christian faith." Cf., Richard R. Gaillardetz, *By What Authority?: Foundations for Understanding Authority in the Church* (Collegeville, MN: Liturgical, 2018), 97-102; Francis A. Sullivan, *Creative Fidelity: Weighing and Interpreting Documents of the Magisterium* (Eugene OR: Wipf and Stock, 2003), 93-108.

[56] The controversy was transferred from *L'Univers* to the pages of *Le Moniteur religieux* in the spring of 1835 with the final section of his sixth letter appearing there on 27 March. Jager inserted a note in the 1 April issue explaining that it was inconvenient to continue the controversy in *L'Univers* given that it was a daily newspaper, printed at night and edited by men who were unfamiliar with theological language.

difference between an individual's eternal salvation and his communion in the church. Newman admitted that such conflation could claim support from the Thirty-nine Articles' statement that, "Holy Scripture containeth all things necessary to salvation." He argued, though, that this was to misunderstand the meaning of Article 6 and to undervalue the way an individual encountered the life of faith diachronically–that is, by admission to the church at baptism with further catechetical instruction following. Jager demanded from converts the affirmation of an implicit faith as a synchronic *fiat*–that is, a belief in anything and everything that would ever be taught by the church regardless of whether the contents were known or understood. For Jager, this obligation was simply implicit in one's baptismal confession of belief in the "holy catholic church." For Newman, however, this obscured the natural interpersonal agency of discipleship and thereby reduced the baptized individual to a passive automaton. Additionally, Jager's viewpoint confused authorized teachers with laity and obstinate heretics with doubting dissenters.

At this point Newman proposed a more generous model for the church's dealings with her children–one that honored mutuality in the relationship and genuine contribution of the church's maturing progeny:

> The Church is our mother . . . A child comes to his mother for instruction; she gives it. She does not assume infallibility, nor is she infallible; yet it would argue a very unpleasant temper in the child to doubt her word, to require proof, to go needlessly to other sources of information. Sometimes, perhaps, she makes mistakes in lesser matters, and is set right by her child; yet neither diminishes her prerogative of teaching, nor his privilege of receiving dutifully. Now this is what the Church does towards her children according to the primitive design. She puts before them, first of all, as the elements of her teaching, nothing but the original Creed; her teaching will follow in due time, as a privilege to children necessarily ignorant, not as a condition of communion; as a privilege which will be welcomed by them, and accepted

---

On 9 May 1835, *Le Moniteur religieux* became *Le Moniteur de la religion* and continued in print until 15 October 1836. Allen, *John Henry Newman and the Abbé Jager*, 184-85.

joyfully, or they would be wanting in that temper of faith which the very coming for Baptism presupposes.[57]

This image presupposed a distinction that Jager had denied–namely that there was a genuine difference between fundamental and non-fundamental doctrine. On one hand, there was apostolic doctrine, provable by the scriptures and requiring explicit assent as a basis for admission to the church's communion. This Newman equated with the Apostles' Creed–a creed affirmed immediately prior to the reception of baptism.[58] On the other hand, there existed a broader body of ecclesial teaching, one that contained all the historical developments and explications of fundamental doctrine. Accordingly, Newman coined new terminology, calling this the "prophetical tradition."

As he explained it, this prophetical tradition differed from the apostolical tradition by the manner in which it was commended to the church. Whereas the apostolical tradition came as "a collection of definite articles, passing from hand to hand, rehearsed and confessed at baptism, committed and received from Bishop to Bishop," the prophetic tradition was more expansive and less definite. Borrowing from the language of the epistle to the Ephesians (2:20, 3:5, and 4:11), Newman contrasted the two:

> God placed in his Church first Apostles, secondarily Prophets. Apostles rule, Prophets expound. Prophets are the interpreters of the divine law, they unfold and define its mysteries, they illuminate its documents, they harmonize its contents, they apply its promises. Their teaching is a vast system not to be comprised in a few sentences, not to be embodied in one code or treatise, but consisting of a certain body of truth permeating the Church like an atmosphere, irregular in its shape, from its very profusion and exuberance. That body of Truth is part written, and part unwritten, partly the interpretation, partly

---

[57] Allen, *John Henry Newman and the Abbé Jager*, 90.

[58] While Stephen Thomas is partially correct regarding the Nicene Creed, and certainly correct concerning the Athanasian Creed, his argument that "Newman does not clarify its relation to the various Creeds which came into existence in the Early Church–the Nicene, Athanasian and Apostles'" is incautious and ultimately leads to a misrepresentation of Newman's argument. Thomas, *Newman and Heresy*, 187.

the supplement of Scripture; partly preserved in intellectual expressions, partly latent in the spirit and temper of Christians; poured to and fro in closets and upon housetops, in liturgies, in controversial works, in obscure fragments, in sermons.[59]

Because the apostolical and prophetical traditions were of a different province, they were to be accorded different authority as well. Though Newman admitted that the church had sometimes "fixed and perpetuated that Prophetical Tradition, in the shape of formal articles or doctrines, as the rise of errors or other causes gave occasion," the size and indefinite nature of the prophetical tradition also exposed it to corruption.[60] Additionally, in circumstances of "love waxing cold and schisms abounding," the various branches of the church found it necessary to develop the prophetical tradition discretely, "according to the accidental influences which prevailed at the time, the work was done well or ill, rudely or accurately."[61] While these developments always called for an attentive, humble respect–what has in our day been codified as religious "deference" or "submission"[62]–they were also "entitled to very

---

[59] Allen, *John Henry Newman and the Abbé Jager*, 95.

[60] Allen, *John Henry Newman and the Abbé Jager*.

[61] Allen, *John Henry Newman and the Abbé Jager*.

[62] By "religious deference" or "submission," I intend what *Lumen Gentium* §25 and the 1983 Code of Canon Law both speak of as "religiosum tamen intellectus et voluntatis obsequium." This refers to the special deference of all the faithful to the teachings of the authentic magisterium of the Roman Pontiff and the college of bishops in communion with him. This "religious assent" is carefully distinguished in Canon 752 of the 1983 Roman Code of Canon Law from the "fidei assensus" or the "assent of faith" owed to infallibly defined teachings. This additionally entails some notion of a "hierarchy of truths" in Christian faith with some theological truths being more essentially linked to the mystery of Christ and others less so. As Benedict XVI's instruction, *Donum Veritatis*, puts it, "When the Magisterium of the Church makes an infallible pronouncement and solemnly declares that a teaching is found in Revelation, the assent called for is that of theological faith." When, however, the magisterium "teaches a doctrine to aid a better understanding of Revelation and make explicit its contents, or to recall how some teaching is in conformity with the truths of faith, or finally to guard against ideas that are incompatible with these truths, the response called for is that of the religious submission of will and intellect." Additionally, this "kind of response cannot be simply exterior or disciplinary but must be understood within the logic of faith and under the impulse of

different degrees of credit."[63] As examples, Newman gestured to the Anglican *Articles of Religion* and the decrees and canons of the Council of Trent.

APOSTLES, PROPHETS, AND *TRACTATORS*: VINCENT OF LÉRINS

Jager's seventh response was published in *Le Moniteur religieux* almost immediately before Newman sent the second half of his letter. In doing so, Jager once again broke the agreed-upon terms of September 1834 for a third and final time. He finally embraced Newman's evolving distinction between the apostolical and prophetical traditions of the church, recognizing as he did that "The prophets or doctors of the Church are obliged to define, to comment, to develop the mysteries of religion, and to put them within the people's reach."[64] But, Jager did not explain the reason for his agreement. In fact, despite the prolix nature of their dispute, neither man clearly acknowledged the source for Newman's distinction as it appears in the *Commonitorium*'s twenty-eighth chapter in which Vincent instructed his readers on the means by which they might detect a heretical innovation and developed the divergent roles of the church's variegated offices as set forth in 1 Corinthians 12:28:

> Lest anyone should possibly suppose that the holy and catholic agreement of these blessed fathers should have little value set upon them, the apostle says in First Corinthians: "And certain men, indeed, God has placed in the church, first, apostles," of whom he was one; "second, prophets": such was Agabus of whom we read in The Acts of Apostles "third, doctors," who are now called "tractators," [*tractatores*]

---

obedience to the faith." (§23). As a Roman Catholic, of course, Newman would concede that the decrees and canons of the Council of Trent were infallibly defined, thus requiring from him the "fidei assensus."

63 Allen, *John Henry Newman and the Abbé Jager*, 96.

64 "Sans doute, il y a une différence entre la tradition apostolique et l'exposition prophétique. Les prophètes ou les docteurs de l'Eglise sont obligés de définir, de commenter, de développer les mystères de la religion, et de les mettre à la portée du peuple." Jager, *Le Protestantisme aux prises avec la Doctrine catholique*, 424.

whom this same apostle at times calls "prophets," because through them the mysteries of the prophets are revealed to the peoples. Whoever, therefore, sets little value on these men when they are in agreement in Christ in their interpretation of some one point of catholic doctrine, established, as they were in the church of God in different times and places, "disregards, not man, but God."[65]

Inherent in Vincent's words are all the moving parts of Newman's prophetic tradition in relation to the apostolic tradition. The apostles are preeminent authorities. Prophets, spoken of by Vincent as interchangeable with doctors or *tractators*, disclose the mysteries of the faith to the people of God. Their agreement with Christ does not result in a simple uniformity. Rather, the prophets maintained a creative fidelity with what came before in accordance with different times and places. While recognizing that the prophetic tradition was fallible and subject to evaluation, Newman also argued that it could not be disregarded if the church were to remain fruitful and faithful. This requires some special emphasis because it has been wholly disregarded in studies of the prophetical office in Newman's thought. Newman's distinction between the apostolical office of the church (that is, the episcopate) and the prophetical office of theology is a distinction first pioneered by Vincent of Lérins.

All through the *Commonitorium*, Vincent warned against the possibility that prophets may in fact be false prophets. A critical point in favor of Newman's diachronic reading of Vincent over Jager's synchronic approach was that the discernment of truth and falsehood was now, as he would later put it his letter to the Duke of Norfolk, "a work of time."[66] Newman was prepared to bear the yoke that this entailed.

---

[65] "Quorum beatorum patrum sanctum catholicumque consensum ne quis sibi temere contemnendum forte arbitretur, ait in prima ad Corinthios apostolus: Et quosdam quidem posuit Deus in ecclesta primum apostolos,–quorum ipse unus erat–secunda prophetas,–qualem in Actibus Apostolorum legimus Agabum tertio doctores,–qui tractatores nunc appellantur, quos hie idem apostolus etiam prophetas interdum nuncupat, eo quod per eos prophetarum mysteria populis aperiantur." *Commonitorium*, 28.9.

[66] Newman, *Duke*, in *Diff* ii, (London: Longmans, Green and Co., 1892), 176. Emphasis mine.

Near the end of his second letter, he explored the details of the Donatist controversy as it afflicted Latin North Africa during the fourth and fifth centuries. The Church of England admitted the validity of baptism administered by heretics in Article 26, but Jager was nonplussed by Newman's declaration that St. Cyprian's denial of said validity was a non-fundamental doctrine. Although Newman admitted that "to maintain an opinion against the voice of the whole Church stubbornly and publicly" was "of itself without any doubt a mortal sin" in the days of the Donatists, he was unwilling to impose that sentence on Cyprian in the third century.[67] At that time, "the question was not sufficiently clarified," so Cyprian "could still doubt the universality of the ecclesiastical teaching, since many shared his views." Thus, Newman argued that the charge of "heresy"–that is, false prophesying–was inapplicable in Cyprian's case.[68] Turning to the implications of this for his own church regarding the doctrine of transubstantiation, Newman concluded, "I beg your pardon, my dear sir, that is precisely the situation in which we find ourselves in England. We believe that your particular points of doctrine are not yet sufficiently clarified. We are, like St. Cyprian, in that state of doubt on the *Universality of the teaching,* and *many bishops share our views.*"[69]

One is left here with the question of what would happen when Newman's "many bishops" finally achieved concord on the subject and imposed their collective discernment of true prophesy as a developed creedal formulary. It seems at this point that Newman either failed to recognize, or declined to consider, the possibility of apostolically defined development in Christian doctrine. This question would reassert itself in his subsequent reconsideration of the Donatist controversy following in the wake of Nicholas Wiseman's article on Anglican claims to apostolical succession in August 1839. At this point, however, it remains important to appreciate Newman's distinction between the prophetic tradition and the apostolic tradition as a critical breakthrough, having important implications for Newman's school at

---

[67] Allen, *John Henry Newman and the Abbé Jager*, 103.
[68] Allen, *John Henry Newman and the Abbé Jager*, 104.
[69] Allen, *John Henry Newman and the Abbé Jager*, 204.

Oxford. Up to this point he had intuitively grasped the necessity for a close solidarity with the English episcopate and a clear distinction from it. The bishops possessed a clear institutional and doctrinal authority that could not be sacrificed without forfeiting the great contest against private judgment. At the same time, "traditionary religion" lay in an underdeveloped, unnamed, and unpopular mess that required a learned winnowing. In the *Commonitorium* Newman found the proper ecclesiological place for his school of theologians among the biblical and early Christian prophets. Their *Tracts for the Times* would now become the product of St. Vincent's *tractatores*.

In the end, Jager's repeated breaches and Newman's increasing sense that the controversy was losing coherence brought the exchange to an end. Newman never completed the remaining portion of his second letter and, though he briefly entertained inserting a notice in the *British Magazine* to the effect that "the correspondence between the Abbé Jager and an English clergyman has come to an end in consequence of the former having continued to decline inserting his own replies to them respectively," this too was simply dropped.[70] A final note was sounded by Newman, expressing, via Harrison, both his appreciation and his consent to having their letters published in book form.[71]

FAITHFUL THE WOUNDS OF A FRIEND: FROUDE'S CRITIQUE

Mention should be made here that Newman's second reply to Jager was not his first invocation of the "prophetical tradition." Neither was it the first time he distinguished between the prophetical tradition and the "Apostolical or Episcopal" tradition. Pride of place here is reserved for a private letter Newman wrote to Richard Hurrell Froude on 20 July 1835, less than a week before he sent the second public letter to

---

[70] Tristram, "In the Lists with the Abbé Jager," 205-206.

[71] The volume, *Le Protestantisme aux prises avec la Doctrine catholique*, is where I have derived Jager's part in the exchange throughout this chapter.

Jager.[72] Newman and Froude had been in constant contact throughout the latter's struggles to find relief from what would be a fatal case of tuberculosis. Their correspondence continued until well after his final journey from Oxford to Dartington in early June of 1834. From his sickbed on the English Channel, Froude had been assisting Newman in the preparation of responses to Jager by assuming the Abbé's perspective in the dialogue. Froude's view of the "Latin Church" was, after all, a perspective that was often quite amenable to that of Jager. The correspondence that passed between the two men during this period is important for the way that Froude forced Newman to follow the logic of his innovations to their eventual destination beyond the *via media*.

Upon reading the first letter to Jager–and more particularly, Newman's assertions that scripture was the "sole rule of faith in *fundamentals*"–Froude denounced Newman's thinking as a "mutilated edition" of "Bible-Christianity" that lacked "the breadth and axiomatic character of the original."[73] Froude denied the present-day infallibility of the church as readily as Newman, but he also held that an infallible tradition did exist at one time. From this, Froude reasoned that where it had been faithfully transmitted, tradition was as "binding on men's consciences as the written word itself."[74] For Froude, this obligation held true with the present-day church as much as it did with the ancient church. Newman, however, denied this, arguing that scripture was an "authoritative depositary, i.e., speaking by inspiration," while traditions "over and above the Apostles' Creed" were not.[75] For him, this was simply recognizing tradition for what it was: "the voice of the body of the Church, the received system of the Church, the spirit circulating through it and poured out through the channels of its doctors and writers." Such "Prophetical Tradition" was delivered as "an *instruction*

---

[72] In his diary entry for Saturday, 25 July, Newman wrote that he had been "at the Abbé *Jager*–(my 2ⁿᵈ letter)," since the previous Wednesday, 22 July, and finished it that evening. *LD* v, 107.

[73] Richard Hurrell Froude to Newman (2 July 1835), *LD* v, 98.

[74] Richard Hurrell Froude, *The Remains of the Late Reverend Richard Hurrell Froude*, vol. 3 (Derby: Henry Mozley & Sons, 1839), 348-49.

[75] Newman to Richard Hurrell Froude (20 July 1835), *LD* v, 102-103.

not a *command*," so Newman found himself "*driven* to Scripture as a denier [sic] resource, to find there, *if anywhere*, fundamentals."[76]

Newman experienced greater difficulty when meeting Froude's observation that the Nicene and Athanasian Creeds were, like his admittedly fundamental Apostles' Creed, authoritative interpretations of scripture carrying "the assertion of its fundamentality."[77] When treating the Nicene Creed and other successive doctrinal formularies, Newman spoke of them as ecclesial developments, drafted by "separate branches" of the church "according to times and circumstances, not however as necessary to be believed for communion, but useful for her people as necessary for holding rule or influence."[78] Of these, Newman commented that,

> The object of these additions is either to secure the fundamentals, as was effected at Nicea but the Homoousion, or to fortify the Church itself, as our article denying the jurisdiction of the Roman See in England. And in this respect it is the Church [that] has "authority in controversies of faith" viz. first to oblige her Ministers to take her view and exposition of the fundamentals, next to hinder individuals from openly professing or teaching any other exposition.[79]

Newman was developing an idea that he first explored in *The Arians of the Fourth Century*. The great Athanasius himself had once (in *De Synodis*) embraced the semi-Arian Christians as brothers. From this,

---

[76] Newman to Richard Hurrell Froude (20 July 1835), *LD* v, 103-104. By "denier" here, Newman probably intended "dernière"–i.e., "last" or "final."

[77] Richard Hurrell Froude to Newman (3 September 1835), *LD* v, 128. Newman's first letter to Jager had argued, "These three words, *ultimate appeal*, *doctrines*, and *fundamentals* must be clearly understood. E.g., we should be ready to receive the three orders of the Ministry even on *tradition*, as being a point of discipline; we receive the validity of heretical baptism on *tradition*, as being a *doctrine not fundamental*; we receive the doctrine of the Trinity, *a fundamental*, *immediately* from tradition, *ultimately from Scripture*. If we are asked what we mean by fundamentals, we answer that we mean such doctrines as are necessary for Church Communion; if we are asked which these are, we answer briefly the articles of the [Apostles'] Creed." Allen, *John Henry Newman and the Abbé Jager*, 36.

[78] Allen, *John Henry Newman and the Abbé Jager*, 40.

[79] Allen, *John Henry Newman and the Abbé Jager*.

Newman deduced that, when dealing with lay Christians as opposed to clergy, the well-being of the church sometimes required that the privileges of "private Christian fellowship" be extended to those who "stumbled at the use of [homoousion]."[80] In the second letter to Jager, this led Newman to posit a careful distinction between the word "homoousion" and the meaning of the doctrine set forth by the Council of Nicea. Without compromising on the "celebrated expression" of the council, Newman pointed out that the semi-Arians who repudiated the term nevertheless agreed fully with the "general doctrine" of Nicea. On this basis they were received as "brothers with brothers" in full communion.[81] This warranted, then, Newman's recognition that tradition was of a lesser authority than scripture. Where the latter was inspired, thus demanding a *de fide* assent to its *ipsissima verba*, tradition was uninspired and whatever truth it held could be honored apart from an explicit assent to the verbiage. Such unauthoritative tradition was, therefore, a "subordinate guide as explaining, illustrating, [and] reconciling the Scriptures."[82] At this, Froude demurred, responding,

> If you allow tradition an interpretative authority I cannot see what is gained—For surely the doctrines of the Priesthood and the Eucharist may be proved from Scripture interpreted by tradition; and if so what is to hinder our insisting on them as terms of communion? I don't mean of course that this will bear out the Romanists, which is perhaps your only point; but it certainly would bear out our party in excommunicating Protestants. Also, you lug in the Apostles' Creed and talk about expansions—What is to be the end of expansions? will not the Romanists say that their whole system is an expansion of the 'H.C.C. [Holy Catholic Church] and the Communion of Saints?' Also

---

[80] Newman, *Ari* (London: J. G. and F. Rivington, 1833), 321, Cf., 165. The text of *De Synodis* reads, "Those, however, who accept everything else that was defined at Nicæa, and doubt only about the [*homoousion*], must not be treated as enemies; nor do we here attack them as [Arians], nor as opponents of the Fathers, but we discuss the matter with them as brothers with brothers, who mean what we mean, and dispute only about the word." Athanasius, *On the Councils of Ariminum and Seleucia* 41 (*NPNF*, vol. 4, 472).

[81] Allen, *John Henry Newman and the Abbé Jager*, 86, 92.

[82] Allen, *John Henry Newman and the Abbé Jager*, 132.

what are the Nicene and Athanasian Creeds but expansions? Also to which class of tradition do you refer the Athanasian Creed? for I suppose you will admit that it carries in its form the assertion of its fundamentality.[83]

As Sheridan Gilley has helpfully pointed out, Newman's response to Jager had been "a kind of obverse" to the argument he had been pressing against Hampden at nearly the same moment.[84] Whereas Newman advocated a strict subscription to the Thirty-nine Articles over against the Hebdomadal Board's more relaxed "Declaration of Conformity to the Church of England," with Jager he relaxed his approach to the authority of formularies produced by the prophetic tradition. Froude perceived the aporia in Newman's thought and thus questioned:

> Why treat a subject of great perplexity and deep and general interest on a narrow and insufficient ground which may avail in one or two controversies with the Romanists (supposing i.e. that you can prove what you think you can from the fathers) but which in no way serves to meet the general question, or to guide our own practice? I cannot see what we owe to our Protestant predecessors that should make us so very anxious to skrew [sic] a sense out of all their dogmata.[85]

The point, as Froude well understood, was that once Newman granted to the apostolical or episcopal office a right to discern and judge the truth or falsehood of developments proposed by the prophetical office, he was thereby committed to grant it something more than mere local and provisional authority. Froude's example of the Athanasian Creed is a particularly good exemplar given its clear insistence that "Whosoever will be saved" must keep its doctrines "whole and undefiled" or "perish everlastingly."[86] If such assertions of fundamentality are to be regarded as nothing more than the development and expansion of the Apostles

---

83 Richard Hurrell Froude to Newman (3 September 1835), *LD* v, 128.

84 Sheridan Gilley, *Newman and His Age* (London: Darton, Longman and Todd, 1990), 138.

85 Richard Hurrell Froude to Newman (3 September 1835), *LD* v, 128.

86 "Sed necessarium est ad aeternam salutem, ut incarnationm quoque Domini nostri Iesu Christi fideliter credat."

Creed–that is, merely another expression of the prophetical office of the church–it becomes difficult to see how the apostolic office ever achieves its own integrity. Rather, it collapses entirely into the prophetical office. Here again, Newman would eventually be forced by the constraining logic to consider the notion that Christian doctrine develops over time. While Newman still proved unwilling to explore this matter further, Froude was forcing Newman onto the horns of Jager's dilemma and preparing the ground for Newman's deeper exploration of what it meant for a school of prophets to function prophetically in a church whose doctrine develops.

THE THEOLOGICAL SOCIETY, THE UNSENT LETTER ON TRADITION, AND HARRISON'S RETORT

Since at least the summer of 1835, members of Newman's school had been contemplating the formation of a theological society at Oxford.[87] By the end of October, they commenced the project formally, and a first meeting was held at Pusey's residence on 12 November. The objects of the society were threefold. First, it would serve as a vehicle for promoting "knowledge of several branches of theology and to further full, clear, and definite views by reference to original sources." Second, the society would encourage theological study "according to the peculiar character" of the Church of England "by combining the study of Christian antiquity with that of Holy Scripture." Third, the society would not be confined to older men or experts but would "afford students facilities of hearing subjects discussed, or difficult texts of Scripture explained fully and in detail."[88]

As the original rules and bylaws attest, everything relating to the Theological Society would be regulated by a committee consisting, at least ordinarily, of the Lady Margaret and Regius Professors of Divinity,

---

[87] In a letter to John Bowden dated 7 July 1835, Newman briefly mentioned that "Our plan for a Theological Society has progressed slowly, owing to the necessity of consulting Burton etc., who decline. However, we have done the civil thing, and rid ourselves of the imputation of schismatical proceedings." He concluded, "We are to commence at once after the Long Vacation." *LD* v, 94–95.

[88] Liddon, *Life of Edward Bouverie Pusey*, vol. 1, 332–33.

the Regius Professor of Hebrew, the Archdeacon of Oxford, and three other members, whose places were to be filled by the whole body when there were vacancies. The first committee consisted of only five members by necessity. Pusey was the Regius Professor of Hebrew, and Archdeacon Charles Carr Clerke of Oxford was numbered among them. Regius Professor of Divinity Edward Burton refused the offer to join the society.[89] Lady Margaret Professor of Divinity Godfrey Faussett, a traditional High Churchman, likewise proved unwilling to join them.[90] This left John Keble and Frederick Oakeley to join Newman in filling the remaining initial vacancies.

The presentation of papers would be the primary work of the Theological Society. They held regular meetings every Friday in Michaelmas and Lent term, every second Friday in Easter and Act Term, and on the first Friday of each month in full term. In keeping with the gravity of their subjects, comments were deferred to the following meeting in order "to prevent the possibility of unadvised and random observations on sacred subjects."[91] This ethos, an extension of the principle of reserve first identified by Newman in *The Arians of the Fourth Century*, carried over to the restriction of eligible presenters to "those with standing to preach before the University (i.e. has passed his M.A. degree two years,) and in Orders." They kept a book with subjects on which members would write, with the committee retaining power to approve and restrict papers on inexpedient topics. Finally, in keeping with the third aim of the society, they welcomed students who had "passed the degree of B.A.," and any member of the society was permitted to invite friends provided they were not undergraduates. The substance of each paper was to be briefly summarized at the subsequent meeting with a view to further discussion when there had been an interval for thought and reading. In the words of Pusey's biographer, Edward Liddon, there was

---

[89] Shortly thereafter Burton fell ill and died on 19 January 1836.

[90] Of Faussett, Newman wrote at the time that he was "by nature sharp," but complained that he had "been made cautious by age." As Newman put it, "I believe, [he] is afraid of us" and, therefore "unwilling to get into hot water at Oxford." Newman to Hugh James Rose (3 January 1836), *LD* v, 194.

[91] "Theological Society Rules and Bye Laws," *Pusey Papers*, Pusey House.

no question of the influence of this Society on the Oxford movement. It stimulated theological thought and work more than any other agency in Oxford at the time; it gave a point to study, and prevented desultoriness and a one-sided interest in the controversies of the day. Above all, it fed both the *British Magazine* and the "Tracts for the Times," especially the latter, with a series of essays upon subjects of which little was known or thought in those days.[92]

The Theological Society is important as a window into inner workings of the Oxford school. Papers read at their meetings resulted directly in the lengthening of the *Tracts for the Times*. Prior to this, they consisted of the short pamphlets one sees in numbers 1 through 66. Afterwards, they appeared as the full-length treatises one sees in numbers 67 through 90. Keble delivered eight papers total to the Theological Society, with "No. 89 On the Mysticism Attributed to the Fathers of the Church" being the primary result. *Tracts 80* and *87* by Isaac Williams, "On Reserve in Communicating Religious Knowledge" began as two papers read before the society. Pusey's paper, "An Historical Account of the Doctrine of the Eucharistic Sacrifice in the Anglican Church," likewise grew into "No 81 Testimony of Writers in the later English Church to the doctrine of the Eucharistic Sacrifice."[93] The Society was also the first venue wherein Newman vetted his developing insights on the history of the Apollinarian and Monophysite heresies. The importance is not limited to these general influences, however. Indeed, the inner workings of the Theological Society are, perhaps, most important for their occasioning another critical development in Newman's conception of the prophetical office as he attempted to secure his already-crumbling Anglican *via media*.

As the intermediary responsible for passing correspondence between Newman and Jager, Benjamin Harrison had naturally read Newman's second letter. His enthusiasm for the controversy could be somewhat heavy-handed at times–so much so that Newman once

---

[92] Liddon, *Life of Edward Bouverie Pusey*, vol. 1, 334-35.
[93] Liddon, *Life of Edward Bouverie Pusey*, vol. 1, 335.

described him to Froude as "agitatorum facile princeps"[94]–and on the occasion of its being dispatched, he expressed his relish at the thought of Jager "looking out the words in the English dictionary, in order to do full justice to the stings which you have been so pitilessly planting in his sides."[95] At some point thereafter, Harrison wrote Newman to express something close to the same concern that Froude raised over Newman's refusal to grant the fundamental nature of new developments of the Apostles' Creed. In Harrison's case, however, the concerns were driven by his Protestant desire to establish the doctrine of justification by faith alone–imposed by Article 11 of the Thirty-nine– as likewise fundamental. To this, Newman responded that while an "invented" phrase might be introduced into the creed by "a general Council (when the Holy Ghost is present)," or a "hereditary" phrase introduced by "the testimony of those among whom it is hereditary," neither the Nicene "homoousion" nor the Protestant "sola fides" were so imposed.[96]

Responding four days later, Harrison pleaded with Newman over the potential "ultra-Protestant"–that is, sola scriptura–implications of his position:

> Has the Ch[urch] the right to enlarge its own foundation? to call its own tradition the "Catholic faith" which must be believed on pain of perfecting everlasting salvation? Has it the right to require implicit faith in itself, instead of in Christ? Of these truly Catholic fundamentals may we not say that they are proved to be such by Scripture as well as tradition and history? . . . Might it not be well to guard against the impression that the Church of England, in her principles as well

---

[94] "Chief among simplistic agitators." Newman to Richard Hurrell Froude (18 May 1835), *LD* v, 73.

[95] Allen, *John Henry Newman and the Abbé Jager*, 150-51. This letter was not included in the *LD*.

[96] Newman to Benjamin Harrison (24 November 1835), *LD* v, 168. In addition to this, Newman seems to have later sent Harrison a document, "nineteen quarto pages inscribed" on the expression "Justification by Faith only." LD v, 169n1.

IMAGINING AND INHABITING THE PROPHETICAL OFFICE 173

as in her modern practice, is not strict enough against diversities of opinion within her pale?[97]

Harrison concluded with a request that Newman share a copy of his paper on "The Rule of Faith" as delivered on 20 November 1835 at the second meeting of the Theological Society.[98] It was the paper Newman intended to submit as the second half of his second letter to Jager.

This last letter was never sent to Jager, and it survives only in the hand of an amanuensis with a later note by Newman reading, "part of a controversy with the Abbé Jager." There Newman sought to further clarify the sense of his words to evade the charge of "pure" or "ultra-Protestantism." He did this by first distinguishing the rule of faith from the "Prophetical Tradition" and more particularly from "the Creed with its developments and supplements." This made scripture the singular "court of ultimate appeal."[99] Lest this be taken as a simple identification of the *regula fidei* with a *regula scripturae*, however, Newman also insisted that "Tradition is as much necessary to explain Scripture as Scripture to verify and circumscribe Tradition; so that, where possible, neither should be used by itself."[100] Newman then contrasted his own "theory of the Anglican church" with what he understood to be the Roman Catholic view, writing of how it "opposes your notion that the Gospel is in part unwritten; and consequently, that certain doctrines may be rested and enforced on Tradition only, though Scripture is silent concerning them."[101] In coming to the practical implications of his difference with ultra-Protestantism, Newman argued that

> Scripture has one and but one sense, however men may differ in their views about it. That one sense is not unknown or obscure; it is

---

[97] Allen, *John Henry Newman and the Abbé Jager*, 155-56. This letter was not included in the *LD*.

[98] See Newman's diary for 20 November 1835, *LD* v, 165. An unpublished, unsent version of this has been published in Allen, *John Henry Newman and the Abbé Jager*, 117-44.

[99] Allen, *John Henry Newman and the Abbé Jager*, 117.

[100] Allen, *John Henry Newman and the Abbé Jager*.

[101] Allen, *John Henry Newman and the Abbé Jager*, 118.

> the Sense in which the Church Catholic has even that sense which the whole Christian world from the beginning or for many centuries maintained. . . . Every individual, who does not take it in that one sense, will have to give account for his not so taking it, and will be excused only on the ground of unavoidable ignorance, whether from the want of instruction, from prejudice etc. as aforesaid.[102]

Here it seems that Newman was either withdrawing or, more probably, neglecting what he had previously conceded to Harrison about the potential situation of an "invented" phrase being introduced into the creed by a general council. This would effectively add to the fundamental doctrines of the church. Such an admission in this context would require Newman to concede the possibility of true development in Christian doctrine. This is to say that, by fixing and establishing a particular reading of scripture, a given product of the prophetical tradition was now assimilated into the apostolic tradition. Newman was far from prepared to make such a concession, but he did venture, albeit unwittingly, something quite similar.

Near the end of his letter, Newman traced out his understanding of the relationship between the New Testament Gospels and the New Testament Epistles. He started with the words of Jesus himself, words he described as the "Prophetical character of our Lord's teaching," though without restricting such teaching to the Gospels exclusively.[103] Regarding the Epistles, Newman argued that they were "a comment on our Lord's teaching to bring out and fix His sacred sense, that we might not miss it."[104] Thus, the "office of the Holy Spirit" consisted of "imparting prophetical inspiration" and "especially in illuminating the Son, in throwing lustre upon and drawing lustre from all which belonged to His person."[105] Commenting on the promise of Jesus to send the Holy Spirit in John 14:25-26, Newman additionally suggested that such illumination would be both progressive and adapted to the capacities of those on whom the Spirit inspired: "Such passages of the Gospels,"

---

102 Allen, *John Henry Newman and the Abbé Jager*, 121.
103 Allen, *John Henry Newman and the Abbé Jager*, 129.
104 Allen, *John Henry Newman and the Abbé Jager*.
105 Allen, *John Henry Newman and the Abbé Jager*, 130.

he wrote, "show clearly that during our Lord's ministry the Apostles were laying up in their minds stores of doctrine which they were not intended to understand or at least to reveal till after the Holy Spirit came."[106] Thus did Christ–the "chief Prophet of the Church"–inspire "his Apostles' writings" as part of the "Rule of Faith as expounders of His divine maxims."[107]

Newman took great pains in his last letter to disallow any notion that the church might continue to interpret the doctrine of Christ as did the Apostles. He did this, however, by employing an argument that was ill-suited to his assertion. Insisting on the unique nature of scriptural revelation and the absolute closure of the biblical canon, Newman sought to establish a *terminus ad quem* on further additions to fundamental doctrine, but he had already granted the fundamentality of the Apostles' Creed. While it did not make a claim to inspiration or present itself as an addition to the biblical canon, the creed was still the church's authoritative comment on the scriptures and thereby functioned to establish fundamental doctrine. This is to say that, however the creed evolved as a product of the prophetical tradition–that is, as comment on scripture in liturgies, controversial works, obscure fragments, and sermons, etc.–the apostolic office of the church had determinately crowned it as an expression of the tradition that was binding on the conscience. The creed thus established a true reading of the scriptures amid the sea of contesting false readings and served as a hermeneutical plumb line to settle controversy and foreclose dissent. It added to fundamental doctrine, not by coining a novel truth, but by denying contrary claimants to the truth.

Harrison wasted no time pointing out the damning flaw in Newman's reasoning. Quoting Newman's words extensively, he concluded that Newman's "theory" was "essentially Ultra-Protestant" and threatened to "sweep away the teaching of the Church altogether, & bring in utter liberalism, skepticism, & infidelity, or else to give us over to enthusiasm, to Popery, or Socinian blasphemy."[108] While Newman

---

106 Allen, *John Henry Newman and the Abbé Jager*.
107 Allen, *John Henry Newman and the Abbé Jager*, 131.
108 Allen, *John Henry Newman and the Abbé Jager*, 158.

insisted that scripture had "but one sense," Harrison believed that he buried that singular sense under a bushel of qualifications about "natural defects of mind," "prejudices," and "supernatural and private assurance[s] that the Catholic sense is false." As Harrison framed it, this represented a "goodly field, surely for private judgment and the inward light! . . . and where is the end to be?"[109] Coming to a particular historical example, he wrote of the Council of Constantinople pronouncing in favor of the divinity of the Holy Spirit but observed how "Gregory of Nazianzen himself tells us that the doctrine was not clearly revealed till after the Ascension but reserved for later times than those of the New Testament."[110] At the time, Gregory admitted the divinity of the Spirit was at best a "pious notion" but declared that he received the doctrine under the guidance of the self-same spirit, that he would hold it to the end of his life, and that he would endeavor to convince others of its truth. "Doubtless," Harrison satirized, "'a supernatural & private assurance' of the truth of a certain doctrine (for Gregory does not pretend that it was a tradition) would make it canonical to the individual: but shall a Council therefore impose it upon all Christians to the end of the world?" With bitter scorn, he concluded, "And thus we are left desolate, among the blasphemies of Unitarianism."[111]

At the end, Newman mounted no real defense against Harrison's critique and only answered to assure him of his intentions to study it. On 5 December 1835 he ridiculed the "mad" impudence of Harrison's barrage as "a formal and violent charge urged without previous conversation or inquiry of me, or appeal to Pusey who had approved the paper, and on a man's own private judgment in most serious matters."[112] Clearly agitated by the exchange, he wrote again on 9 December to upbraid Harrison for his rhetorical excesses and breach of good manners:

> I give myself to the judgment of anyone whom we both respect whether or not as you state "candidly and unreservedly," I have put

---

109 Allen, *John Henry Newman and the Abbé Jager*.
110 Allen, *John Henry Newman and the Abbé Jager*, 161.
111 Allen, *John Henry Newman and the Abbé Jager*.
112 Allen, *John Henry Newman and the Abbé Jager*, 162. Cf., *LD* v, 170n1.

forward "a theory of my own," "essentially ultra-Protestant," "and the tendency of which, followed to its sequences would be to sweep away the teaching of the Church altogether and bring in utter liberalism, scepticism, infidelity, or else give us over to Popery or Socinian blasphemy." You have not offended me at all personally–I think not. But I am alarmed for your own usefulness hereafter, if you have not more judgment or self-command or faith in your friends.[113]

Newman's dumbfounded conclusion is arresting, coming as it did from a man who could brandish his keenest thinking and sharpest rhetoric in controversy. Although Newman had taken a critical step by rooting his school's theological work in the prophetical tradition, the trenchant critique of Jager, Froude, and now Harrison exposed a disquieting weakness in his thought that would nag at him even as he moved to publish the fruits of his discovery.[114]

CONSTRUCTING NEW MEMORIALS OF OXFORD: THE PROPHETICAL OFFICE OF THE CHURCH

Having been denied a professorial chair from which to lecture, Newman created his own forum in the Adam de Brome Chapel of St. Mary's in the spring of 1834.[115] Nearly two years later he began a series of "lectures on Romanism," commencing on 16 May 1836 and

---

[113] Newman to Benjamin Harrison (9 December 1835), *LD* v, 174.

[114] Froude and Harrison were not the only persons to consider the possibility of doctrinal development as a genuine lacuna in Newman's thought at this point. James Pereiro recently published a batch of letters from Samuel Wood to Newman and to Henry Manning. Critical in Wood's 1 January 1835 letter especially was his insistence that Newman grapple with the question of development by reference to the "profectus religionis" in chapter 23 of St. Vincent's *Commonitorium*. Newman did not respond to Wood that we know of, but the correspondence shows how the question of development becomes a necessary development of Newman's thought. See James Pereiro, *'Ethos' and the Oxford Movement: At the Heart of Tractarianism* (Oxford: Oxford University Press, 2008), 239-51. Cf., Kenneth Parker, "Coming to Terms with the Past: The Role of History in the Spirituality of John Henry Newman," in *Newman and Life in the Spirit: Theological Reflections on Spirituality for Today*, eds. John Connolly and Brian Hughes (Minneapolis: Fortress, 2014).

[115] See Newman's diary for 23 April 1834, *LD* iv, 238.

continuing until 11 July.[116] These lectures were edited and published later that same year and finally appeared in March of 1837 under the title, *Lectures on the Prophetical Office of the Church*. In these lectures, Newman drew heavily–often verbatim–on his correspondence with Jager, but his defense of the Anglican *via media* also witnesses to some careful revision in light of the resolute criticisms of Froude and Harrison.[117]

Where Newman began his debate with Jager by restricting the fundamentals of faith to the Apostles' Creed and identifying the rule of faith with the scriptures, he now adjusted his lectures to address Harrison's charge of ultra-Protestantism. He spoke of them as the "foundation of the fundamentals." Newman then treated the rule of faith as the "Bible and Catholic Tradition taken together." Now, tradition "gives form to the doctrine" and Scripture "gives life."[118] From this Newman was able to more clearly differentiate his conception of the *via media* from the Protestant and Catholic alternatives. Thus, where Protestantism insisted on the Bible as the sole source of Christian doctrine, with each individual dependent on private judgment to formulate the faith according to his or her own capacities, Catholicism assumed the right to expand the church's fundamental doctrines by an infallible appeal to tradition alone. Protestantism failed to regard how "the Bible does not carry with it its own interpretation" and so risked a lapse into the "Latitudinarian . . . recognition of [even] Socinians and Pelagians as Christians."[119] Catholicism alternatively "[imposed a] yoke" on the church's

---

116 As late as 17 July 1836, Newman consistently spoke of them as "Lectures on Romanism"–even when discussing their publication. Newman to John Keble (17 July 1836), *LD* v, 328. Cf., Newman to John Frederic Christie (26 June 1836), *LD* v, 313.

117 As Newman himself put it in the 1837 Advertisement of his volume, "Great portions of a correspondence which the writer commenced with a learned and zealous member of the Gallican Church are also incorporated in it." Newman, *Pro*, in *VM* (Basil Montagu Pickering, 1877), xi. Louis Allen has helpfully outlined the explicit parallels linking Newman's letters to Jager with the 1837 first edition and the 1877 third edition of the *Lectures on the Prophetical Office of the Church*. Allen, *John Henry Newman and the Abbé Jager*, 186-88.

118 Newman, *Pro*, 241, 274.

119 Newman, *Pro*, 245.

children, "repressing the elastic or creative force of their minds."[120] In so doing, the Church of Rome had traded out its proper role as a "keeper" and "witness" to revelation and became instead a "judge" with a direct power over revelation.[121] In Newman's reckoning, Anglicanism stood alone in maintaining the proper relationship between scripture and tradition, with the church and its tradition subordinated and subject to scripture's *norma normans* as a *norma normata*.

The *Lectures on the Prophetical Office of the Church* are likewise important for the way Newman's newly conceived "Episcopal"–or "Apostolical"–and "Prophetical" offices function in the church as offices rather than simply as traditions. Adding this differentiation to his hinted-at "Sacerdotal" office in the volume's 1837 advertisement, it is as clear as it is undeniable that Newman conceived his analogy between the three ecclesiastical offices and the classical *triplex munus Christi* as an Anglican. As Christ perfectly realized the ancient Hebrew offices of prophet, priest, and king, so too did his Spirit-filled ecclesial body continue their incarnate expression.[122]

While he certainly intended to cast himself against Protestantism in the course of his treatment, Newman's primary focus in the *Lectures on the Prophetical Office* was ever focused on Rome's tendency to smother the local theological creativity of the prophetical tradition under the heavy blanket of episcopal authoritarianism.[123] Had the church remained a unified whole rather than being rent asunder by schism, Newman believed that it would have enjoyed the full predicted privileges of a "Continual infallibility" in its teaching.[124] The prophetical

---

[120] Newman, *Pro*, 258.

[121] Newman, *Pro*, 268–69.

[122] *Contra* Misner, *Papacy and Development*, and Boyle, *Church Teaching Authority*, et. al. Cf., the discussion on 8ff. In the 1837 Advertisement Newman wrote, "had its limits admitted," the lectures "would have embraced the Sacerdotal as well as the Prophetical office of the Church." Newman, *Pro*, xi.

[123] *Pace* Frank Turner who has argued, "Despite powerfully critical remarks against Romanism in these lectures, which Newman thought would prove he was not a Papist, his fundamental target remained evangelical religion and its proponents." *John Henry Newman*, 258.

[124] Newman, *Pro*, 202.

office would then function in perfect accord with the sacerdotal and apostolical offices with the latter expressing the fullness of the former. In the present circumstance of pervasive schism, however, "purity of doctrine" was "one of the privileges . . . infringed" and this led inexorably to "the separate branches of the Church . . . disagree[ing] with each other in the details of faith" and "discordance . . . among witnesses of the truth" being the result.[125] While the church managed to retain an indefectible core of fundamental apostolical truth in its baptismal creed, the rest of its teaching lay in a scattered admixture of traditional truth and distorting error.

That said, things were not utterly hopeless. While Newman believed that Christian unity "admits of fuller or scantier fulfilment," he did not think that the privileges of unity were forever lost.[126] Rather, "higher measures of truth" might accompany greater ecclesial accord and consensus. Granting for argument's sake that God intended humans in this age to enjoy the highest of all unity and the grace of a "continual Infallibility," such a thing would surely "require the presence of a superhuman charity and peace, such as has never been witnessed since the time when the disciples 'continued steadfastly in the Apostles' doctrine and fellowship, and in breaking of bread, and in prayers,'" etc.[127] Because corruption of the truth was the inevitable consequence of schism, the church could repair to the indefectible truth of the apostolic age wherein the three offices of the church existed in a purer communion and collaboration. From there, it might find a way forward. Here, his conception of theology as a prophetical office served a productive as well as a preservative role. Borrowing from a more recent conception of things, Newman imagined that the theological office might prophetically express itself in *aggiornamento* as well as in *ressourcement*.[128]

---

[125] Newman, *Pro*, 199, 201-202.

[126] Newman, *Pro*, 202.

[127] Newman, *Pro*, 202. Newman was quoting from Acts 2:42-47.

[128] *Aggiornamento* ("bringing up to date") and *ressourcement* ("returning to the sources") are famously part of the terminological furniture of the Second Vatican Council. Rooted in the speech delivered by Pope John XXIII at the opening of the council on 11 October 1962, the terms well express his intention that the council would re-source the church, "in the sacred heritage of truth which she has received

For Newman, the prophetical office was not simply a repository of historical theological information–the "vast system . . . not to be embodied in one code or treatise, but consisting of a certain body of Truth, permeating the Church like an atmosphere, etc."[129] This was certainly the product, but he understood the production as an ever-present vocation of theologians within the church. "Apostles rule and preach," but "Prophets expound"–present tense.[130] As bishops continued to staff the regal office of the church as successors of the Apostles, Newman argued that, "Prophets or Doctors *are* the interpreters of the revelation; they unfold and define its mysteries, they illuminate its documents, they harmonize its contents, [and] they apply its promises."[131] While its product was fallible, "irregular in its shape from its very profusion and exuberance," even sometimes "melting away into legend and fable," the production endured as an abiding constant, guaranteed by the presence of Christ in the church by the Holy Spirit.[132] This, above all, warranted the particular gathering together of Newman's now prophetical school at Oxford. They gathered "not merely from imitation and sympathy, but certainly from internal compulsion, from the constraining influence of their several principles."[133] As Newman saw it was the proper manifestation of their divine charism, calling the Church of England back to the

---

from those who went before" (i.e., in the scriptures, ancient liturgies, and traditions of early Christianity), while at the same time articulating that witness according to the "new conditions and new forms of life introduced into the modern world." John XXIII, "Allocutio Gaudet Mater Ecclesia, 11 October 1962," *Acta Apostolicae Sedis* 54 (1962): 790-91. It is important here that *aggiornamento* and *ressourcement* form, not distinct and separate actions, but a *single integrated movement*. In its work of updating, the church draws on ancient tradition to develop new insight into the contemporary movement of the Spirit. Newman exemplified John XIII's insight as will become clear.

129 John XXIII, "Allocutio Gaudet Mater Ecclesia, 11 October 1962," 298.

130 John XXIII, "Allocutio Gaudet Mater Ecclesia, 11 October 1962."

131 John XXIII, "Allocutio Gaudet Mater Ecclesia, 11 October 1962," 298. Emphasis mine.

132 John XXIII, "Allocutio Gaudet Mater Ecclesia, 11 October 1962."

133 Newman, *US*, new ed. (London: Rivingtons, 1880), 212.

indefectible core of apostolical truth as he saw it imperfectly reflected in Anglicanism's theological patrimony.

The sum of Newman's later Anglican work on behalf of his school can be profitably understood as an attempt at realizing this vocation. In his introduction to the *Lectures on the Prophetical Office of the Church*, he readily acknowledged how "English doctrine" was not yet fully "embodied in any substantive form, or publicly recognized in its details."[134] Its "champions and teachers . . . lived in stormy times; political and other influences have acted upon them variously in their day," and these had "obstructed a careful consolidation of their judgments."[135] All had been "given us in profusion," and it remained "to catalogue, sort, distribute, select, harmonize, and complete."[136] Whether we consider the latter *Tracts for the Times*, his own *Lectures on Justification* (1838), his contributions as editor of the *British Critic*, his published *Parochial Sermons* (1834-1845), the publication of *The Church of the Fathers* (1840), his collaboration with Keble to publish Froude's *Remains* (1838-1839), or, as we will see, his final *Tract 90*–this is to say, all Newman's latter efforts as an Anglican theologian–we see them arising from this impulse to constructively inventory the "vast inheritance" of the Church of England's treasures.[137]

This reading of Newman's broader intentions in the *Lectures on the Prophetical Office* is made clearer by tracing his practical involvement in the work of theological education at Oxford after 1835. In his July 1838 review of James Ingram's three-volume *Memorials of Oxford* for the *British Critic*, Newman voiced his admiration for the medieval form of the university and advocated openly for its return as a standard raised against the virtues and values of the day.

> If any of her children, who have no special claim to speak, may presume to offer her counsel, ours would be that she should never forget that her present life is but the continuation of the life of past

---

[134] Newman, *Pro*, 22.

[135] Newman, *Pro*, 24.

[136] Newman, *Pro*, 24.

[137] Newman, *Pro*, 24.

ages, and that her constituent members are, after all, in a new form and with new names, the Benedictines and Augustinians of a former day. The monastic principle, a most important element in the social character of the Church, lingers among them, while it has been absorbed elsewhere in the frivolous or selfish tempers and opinions of an advanced period of civilization. To the Universities is committed the duty of cherishing and exemplifying Christian simplicity, nobleness, self-devotion, munificence, strictness, and zeal, which have well-nigh vanished in other places. To them only it is allotted, especially if chapters are to be swept away, to show that the Christian can be deeply read in the philosophy of ancient truth, and serenely prescient of the future from his comprehension of the past. To them only it falls, as being out of the world, to measure and expose the world, and, as being in the heart of the Church, to strengthen the Church to resist it.[138]

Here Newman returned to themes first raised in his 1832 sermon on personal influence, but with a contra-mundane monastic community now circumscribing the twin values of theological orthodoxy and personal holiness, projecting for his prophetical school a recognized institutional form.

During his time in the Oriel tuition, Newman championed the precedent established by its fourteenth-century founder, Adam de Brome, with the "Head and the Fellows living together as a brotherhood, sharing a common table, all devoted to a life of study, and using their learning in the service of God."[139] This would reclaim, "that portion of the ancient college which had faded away, namely the idea of a resident body of Fellows engaged, not in teaching but in advanced theological study."[140] Now delivering his own theological lectures in the chapel bearing de Brome's name, Newman increasingly aimed to reincarnate such a

---

[138] Newman, "Medieval Oxford," in *HS* iii (London: Basil Montagu Pickering, 1872), 331.

[139] Peter Nockles, "An Academic Counter-Revolution: Newman and Tractarian Oxford's Idea of a University," in *History of Universities*, eds. L. Brockliss, and M. Curthoys, vol. 10 (Oxford: Oxford University Press, 1991), 167.

[140] A. Dwight Culler, *The Imperial Intellect* (New Haven, CT: Yale University Press, 1965), 90.

school by cultivating a spiritual and scholarly brotherhood in a new context outside the increasingly inhospitable Oxford colleges. In many ways, the Theological Society was the first realization of this impulse. As a result of that work, Pusey opened his home to young students on condition that they studied theology or subjects connected with theology. In 1837, Newman then purchased a house at St. Aldate's for "a sufficient number of men without Fellowships" who wished "to stay up regularly in the University."[141] The environment was described by John Mozley as "a reading and collating establishment," with Newman and Pusey collaborating together with the young men to produce the *Library of the Fathers* as an eventual result.[142] In the end, Newman's final Anglican attempt in this direction would end with a community coming together under his informal direction at Littlemore, but all of these represent attempts to realize the vocation discovered in his progress from imagining to inhabiting the *Prophetical Office of the Church*.

NEWMAN'S PROPHETICAL OFFICE OF THE CHURCH IN 1877

For the Anglican Newman of 1837, Roman Catholicism was borne of an over-realized eschatology that substituted genuine ecclesial unity, graced by the full "mind of the Spirit," for an oppressive, imposed authority. Rome had stamped its arbitrary gleanings from the church's prophetical heritage–the "*ruins* and *perversions* of Primitive Tradition," as he termed them–with its magniloquent imprimatur of infallibility.[143] In doing so, Rome squelched the full prophetical voice of the church by speaking completely from and for its manifold branches. Newman described this abuse by returning to the maternal image of the church that he invoked in his debate with Jager: "A child comes to his mother for instruction and she gives it. She does not assume infallibility, nor

---

[141] J. B. Mozley to Anne Mozley (19 November 1837), in Anne Mozley, ed. *Letters of the Rev. J. B. Mozley* (London: Rivingtons, 1885), 69.

[142] J. B. Mozley to Anne Mozley (27 April 1838), *Letters of the Rev. J. B. Mozley*, 78. Mark Pattison mistakenly recalled that the house at St. Aldate's was purchased by Pusey. *Memoirs*, 81.

[143] *Letters of the Rev. J. B. Mozley*, 240, 300-301.

is she infallible." While only a "very unpleasant temper in the child" would lead it to "doubt her word"–hence Newman's critique of private judgment–"sometimes, perhaps, she mistakes in lesser matters, and is *set right by her child*."[144] By this Newman described how the ostentatious claims of Rome's "apostolical" officers tended to repress "the elastic or creative force" of the church's full prophetical mind, eliminating in the process any possibility of beneficial reform.[145]

While it is certainly true that Newman was operating on a misunderstanding of the Roman claim to infallibility–that it meant something like a maximalist claim to immediacy as opposed to a minimalist claim of indefectibility–this latter observation suggests a powerful reason for Newman's republication of the *Lectures on the Prophetical Office* in 1877 with the all-important "Preface to the Third Edition" amplifying the church's perpetual manifestation of the *triplex munus Christi*. Newman had long since come around to Froude's suspicion that the apostolic office could indeed add to the church's fundamental doctrines through its processes of theological development. This was, after all, the basic theme of his 1845 *Essay on the Development of Christian Doctrine*. The present-day church might, as he argued, receive itself and its history with a creative fidelity. In this case, however, Newman's bold reassertion of the church's prophetical office challenged the rigid neo-ultramontanism of Henry Cardinal Manning. In a way very much like his younger Anglican self, the Catholic Newman of 1877 perceived anew tendencies in the apostolical office to "ambition, craft, cruelty and superstition." These neglected theology as "the fundamental and regulating principle of the whole Church system."[146] By reissuing his lectures, Newman reminded the "Regal" and "Sacerdotal" offices of the Roman hierarchy that they were the creation of the "Prophetical Office" and so were obliged to its "power of jurisdiction" as being of its own

---

144 *Letters of the Rev. J. B. Mozley*, 307. Emphasis mine.

145 *Letters of the Rev. J. B. Mozley*, 308.

146 Newman, "Preface to the Third Edition," in *VM* i, (London: Basil Montagu Pickering, 1877), xlvii.

creation.[147] As Newman put it in an important letter to William Maskell a few months prior to the promulgation of *Pastor Aeternus*,

> The Council cannot force things–the voice of the Schola Theologorum, of the whole Church diffusive, will in time make itself heard, and Catholic instincts and ideas will assimilate and harmonize into the credenda of Christendom, and the living tradition of the faithful, what at present many would impose upon us, and many are startled at, as a momentous addition to the faith.[148]

While Newman directed his 1877 preface to fellow Roman Catholics, we must never forget that they prefaced a theology that he forged as an Anglican. While the *Lectures on the Prophetical Office of the Church* had been lightly revised so that Newman retracted specific anti-Catholic statements, his conception of a prophetical office of the church remained fully intact. Newman merely extended to Roman Catholic theologians the rights and responsibilities he had once claimed as an Anglican for his school at Oxford. Seen against the backdrop of that history, Newman's Catholic writings on the prophetical office, on the *schola theologorum*, and on the ecclesial vocation of theologians generally, appear far thicker and in far greater continuity with the man he had been all along.

---

[147] Newman, "Preface to the Third Edition," *VM* i, xlvii.
[148] Newman to William Maskell (12 February 1871), *LD* xxv, 284.

CHAPTER 5

The Pros and Cons of Proving Canon
Tract 90 and the Fall of Newman's Anglican School

From the natal origins of his Anglican school through its final exile, Newman maintained a complicated disposition toward the Thirty-nine Articles. At times he unapologetically embraced them as "entirely Scriptural" and championed their unmitigated use as a confessional standard for the Church of England and the University of Oxford. On other occasions, he disparaged them as "not such favourites of mine" and complained that they "accidentally countenance[d] a vile Protestantism."[1] In a different world, Newman might have chosen to author a detailed commentary to make sense of his divergent opinions. There was, after all, ample precedent for such works in writings of many Anglican Divines. The *Apologia* even suggests a onetime aspiration to contribute one of his own,[2] but *Tract 90*, the last of the *Tracts for the Times* containing Newman's "Remarks on Certain Passages in the Thirty-nine Articles," was no such work.[3] As was often the case in his writings, public controversy rather than sober inquiry occasioned his work in January of 1841.

In this final chapter I argue that *Tract 90* consolidated a new stage in Newman's theological evolution, one in which he finally embraced the theologian's vocation to be an active agent in the development of

---

[1] Newman to R. F. Wilson (13 May 1835), *LD* v, 70.
[2] Newman, *Apo*, 158.
[3] Henceforth, I refer to the work simply as *Tract 90*.

church doctrine. *Tract 90* thus crowns Newman's understanding of the theological office–and of his own theological school at Oxford therein–as a creative interpreter of the church's witness to divine revelation, articulating that witness in a prophetic mode of discourse. Newman had long since embraced the prophetical office of theology as a proper counterpart to the regal office of the episcopate, but prior to 1839 he positioned the work as a passive enterprise. He would discern and describe the notes of England's apostolical heritage amid the discordant modern howls of private judgment. Having come to the realization that genuine apostolicity could yet remain uncatholic, however, Newman began in *Tract 90* to think of himself and his school as traditionary agents, actively forming the English Church in a project of rectification by development. From his early work in the Oriel tuition, through the construction and dissolution of his *via media*, Newman had written of what the Church of England had once been, and of what it might be, if only it would appropriate its historic patrimony. *Tract 90* was something different: a prospective exhortation urging the Church of England to harmonize, not simply with the apostolic church of the past, but also with the living catholic church singing presently in the voices of all the baptized faithful. *Tract 90* was thus a work of prophesy, challenging the English episcopate and the University of Oxford to affirm what it could not deny without standing self-condemned as a sect.

ALIENATED FROM HISTORY, CONTESTED AT OXFORD: LITERAL AND GRAMMATICAL SENSE AND THE DRAMA OF SUBSCRIPTION

William Pitt, Earl of Chatham, once famously quipped that the Church of England possessed "Calvinist Articles, a Popish Liturgy, and Arminian Clergy."[4] In fact, the Articles of Religion, or Thirty-nine Articles

---

[4] Pitt's quote is so ubiquitous that there are few works on the Thirty-nine Articles that fail to mention it. He made the remark during one of the debates for the repeal of the Toleration Act of William III in the House of Lords on 19 May 1772. The remark does not survive in the parliamentary reports of the day, but Edmund Burke recalled the remark while speaking in the House of Commons on 2 March 1790. William Gladstone remembered the remark as "A shallow witticism, little worthy

as they were popularly known, were as much the product of Tudor Anglicanism's appropriation of Lutheran influences as they were of the more zealous reforming instincts of Geneva. They had gradually developed over a period of thirty-five years beginning with the Ten Articles, drawn up at the request of Henry VIII to facilitate negotiations for a political alliance with German Lutheran princes in 1535. These were then approved by convocations of the English clergy at Canterbury and York. They became, for a time, the official teaching of the Church of England.[5] Amid a subsequent six-year period of theological negotiation between parties who alternatively favored the king's more traditional Catholic theology or a moderating Protestant reform, a renewed dialogue with the German Lutheran princes led in 1538 to the composition of the Thirteen Articles by Henry's Archbishop of Canterbury, Thomas Cranmer.[6] The work never saw publication, and the hoped-for doctrinal accord with the Germans failed, but the deliberately Lutheran flavor of work is, again, unmistakable.[7] Following the death of Henry VIII and the accession to the throne of his son, Edward VI, Cranmer's personal theological development under the influence of the South German reformer, Martin Bucer resulted in his moving the Church of England in a more clearly Reformed direction. Cranmer expanded the Thirteen Articles into The Forty-two Articles of 1552, but Edward's

---

of so illustrious a man." John Timbs, *Anecdote Lives of William Pitt, Earl of Chatham and Edmund Burke* (London: Richard Bentley and Son, 1880), 137.

[5] Charles Hardwick, *A History of the Articles of Religion* (London: George Bell and Sons, 1895), 32-42.

[6] Extant only in Latin, Cranmer's Thirteen Articles were discovered among his papers in the early nineteenth century and published in the Parker Society edition of Cranmer's works in 1846. Also discovered and published at the same time were three separate articles that appear to have been composed in the same period. Gerald Bray published an English translation of the Thirteen Articles in *Churchman* 106 (1992): 244-62. In addition to Cranmer's Thirteen Articles, this period between 1537 and 1543 produced the moderating Protestant *Institution of a Christian Man* or *The Bishops Book* in 1537, the so-called "Six Articles" of 1539, defending Henry VIII's own traditional Catholic faith and practice, and the likewise Catholic *Necessary Doctrine and Erudition for any Christian Man* of 1543.

[7] One notes here that the first three articles of the work are taken almost verbatim from the *Augsburg Confession*, while the articles on justification, baptism, the Eucharist, and penance similarly reflect Lutheran emphases.

death and the accession of his Roman Catholic half-sister, Mary I, effectively halted efforts to establish these as official doctrine. The Articles then fell into disuse until they were revived half a decade into the reign of Mary's Protestant sister, Elizabeth I. It was during Elizabeth I's reign that Archbishop Mathew Parker of Canterbury made use of the Lutheran *Confession of Wurtemburg* (1552) to further revise the Articles, tempering their more obviously Reformed teaching and pairing their number to thirty-nine in 1571.

The contested history of the Thirty-nine Articles was further complicated by the addition of a supplementary preface by Charles I in 1628. This "Declaration," as Newman characteristically referred to it, was intended to check a resurgent Reformed reception of the Thirty-nine Articles that followed in the wake of the Dutch Quinquarticular Controversy. It restricted interpretations of the Articles to their "plain and full . . . literal and grammatical" sense. The unintended effect of the Declaration, however, was an alienation of the Articles from their historical sense. While the compositional development and sometimes ambiguous wording of the Articles made them already liable to divergent interpretations by Anglicans who favored the various Lutheran, Calvinist, and Arminian influences of the continent, no one who considered their history could question their purpose to safeguard an essential Protestant identity for the Church of England. But Charles's preface removed the need for such considerations and opened the way for a new catholic-apostolical reception proposed by John Henry Newman.

While the broader Tractarian movement could trace its origins to the contested renegotiation of England's establishmentarian constitution and the resulting reforms of the Wellington-Peel Parliament from 1828-1832, these wider sociopolitical concerns both created and reflected a more discrete contest between alternative theological schools at the University of Oxford. As part of the 1662 *Book of Common Prayer*, the Thirty-nine Articles formed a key part of the Church of England's theological identity and so became an early skirmish line in Newman's efforts to establish the apostolic identity of the university. Prior to their emendation by the University Reform Act of 1854, the university statutes mandated that every student take an oath of subscription to the Articles at matriculation and again prior to the conferral of any degree. But having been made eligible for election by the repeal of the 1678 Test Act in 1829, the Unitarian Member of Parliament, G. W. Wood, introduced a bill in 1834 to vacate this religious test, thereby clearing the way for the admission of dissenting Protestants. The bill passed the House of Commons but was defeated in the House of Lords following the vigorous opposition of the Duke of Wellington. Newman and his Tractarian fellows joined the 1,900 members of convocation and over 1,050 undergraduates in signing the Oxford declaration against any attempt to modify the oath, but the mere existence of the bill stoked their fears that the newly elected coalition of dissenting Members of Parliament would eventually succeed in their efforts to fundamentally alter the confessional character of Oxford.

Amid the controversy, divisions within Oriel College appeared between those who signed the declaration and those who refused. Renn Dickson Hampden's perplexing decision to sign the bill despite his published advocacy for the removal of all doctrinal tests in the *Observations on Religious Dissent* (1834) was a particular irritant to Newman. Upon receiving a copy, he upbraided Hampden and predicted that its principles would "make shipwreck of Christian faith" and lead to the interruption of "that peace and mutual good understanding which has prevailed so long in this place."[8] Years later Newman noted that this letter "was the beginning of hostilities in the University." Perhaps ironically, these same hostilities would conclude with Newman's own dramatic *volte face* in 1841. There he would compose and contend for his own radical reappropriation of the Articles' doctrinal standard.

As Newman and his fellow Tractarians sought increasingly to wean the Church of England from its established dependence on the royal supremacy, they required a new ecclesiological center around which faithful churchman could gather. In his own contributions to the *Tracts for the Times*, Newman led the fight to locate that center in the Church of England's episcopate, in the stability of the *Book of Common Prayer*, and more broadly in the ancient "Apostolical" consensus of early

---

[8] Newman to Renn Dickson Hampden (24 June 1835), *LD* v, 84.

Christianity.[9] Newman judged that these resources possessed sufficient power to reclaim the Church of England from the enthusiasms of dissenting Protestantism and the liberalizing infidelities of the state. He grouped these enemies together under the odious banner of "private judgment." Newman's recollection of these experiences many years later evince no loss of the apocalyptic fervor he manifested at the time:

> That ancient religion had well-nigh faded away out of the land, through the political changes of the last 150 years, and it must be restored. It would be in fact a second Reformation:–a better reformation, for it would be a return not to the sixteenth century, but to the seventeenth. No time was to be lost, for the Whigs had come to do their worst, and the rescue might come too late. Bishopricks were already in course of suppression; Church property was in course of confiscation; Sees would soon be receiving unsuitable occupants. We knew enough to begin preaching upon, and there was no one else to preach.[10]

Finally centering their efforts in a distinct school at Oxford, Tractarian advocacy of close adherence to patristic form appeared in the eyes of friend and foe alike to circumvent the more immediate and demonstrable patrimony of the English Reformation and its final Elizabethan settlement as a Protestant communion. The more Newman and his

---

9 The "Caroline" Divines (from the Latin *Carolus* for "Charles") were Anglican Churchmen who lived and wrote during the reigns of Charles I (1600-1649) and Charles II (1630-1685). Most of the early Carolines were Cambridge dons, but their number increased rapidly under Stuart patronage, and they came to significantly influence the church of England as a "High Church" party. They were later called "Arminians" because of superficial resemblances the Dutch Reformed theologian, Jacobus Arminius, but they predated the latter's emergence as a controversial figure in the Reformed churches. Less concerned with Arminius's emphases on the role of human freedom in salvation, they emphasized the historical continuity of the English Church through the Reformation and manifested an appreciation for early Christian and Medieval liturgical, sacramental, and devotional piety. Above all, they were bound together in a desire to recover the eclipsed doctrine of the real presence of Christ in the Eucharist. Notable among the Caroline Divines were William Laud (1573-1645), Lancelot Andrewes (1555-1626), Izaak Walton (1594-1683), George Herbert (1593-1633), Henry Hammond (1605-1660), John Cosin (1594-1672), Thomas Ken (1637-1711), Herbert Thorndike (1598-1672), Thomas Sprat (1635-1713), Peter Heylyn (1599-1662), and Jeremy Taylor (1613-1667).

10 Newman, *Apo*, 113.

fellows championed the apostolic succession of the English bishops and the unique sacramental powers of the clergy, the more Roman Catholic they sounded in the ears of fellow churchmen. By midsummer 1834, accusations of "Popery" were already commonplace, and they were regularly derided by fellow churchmen as scattering "bigotry, Popery, and intolerance" from Oxford to the broader reaches of England.[11] Evangelical Anglicans might have been expected to react in this fashion, but would-be friends among the "old historic High Church school" likewise worried over the "papistical" and "more than semi-popish" tendencies they perceived in the *Tracts for the Times*. This rising tide of anti-Catholic critique led Newman to better develop his *via media* theory that the Church of England was, not a middle way between Roman Catholicism and Puritanism, but a middle way between Roman Catholicism and Protestantism as such.[12] In July and August of 1834, Newman defended this thesis in *Tracts 38* and *41*, "*Via Media* I" (25 June 1834) and "*Via Media* II" (28 August 1834). Following upon the yearlong debate with Abbé Jean-Nicolas Jager, he then began in May 1836 a series of mildly anti-Catholic lectures in Adam de Brome's Chapel of St. Mary the Virgin Church. These culminated his 1837 *Lectures on the Prophetical Office of the Church*. That Newman expected these works collectively to quell any suspicion of Roman Catholic sympathy is clear from thoughts he penned to his sister Jemima on 25 April 1837:

> It only shows how deep the absurd notion was in men's minds that I was a Papist; and now they are agreeably surprised. Thus I gain, as commonly happens in the long run, by being misrepresented– thanks to Record and Co. I shall take it out in an attack on popular Protestantism.[13]

Oncoming events would soon shake Newman out of his confidence.

---

[11] Wilks, *The Christian Observer*, iii. In a published letter dated 11 January 1837, Newman upbraided Wilks, writing that "The tone of that challenge, I must own, or rather the general conduct of your Magazine towards the *Tracts*, since their first appearance, has been an exception to its usual mildness and urbanity." *Tracts* iv, ix.

[12] James Dean to Newman (16 December 1833), *LD* iv, 144

[13] Newman to Mrs. John Mozley (25 April 1837), *LD* vi, 61.

RICHARD BAGOT'S ANIMADVERSIONS AND NEWMAN'S INDISCRETIONS

In his triennial Visitation Charge of 14 August 1838, Newman's bishop, Richard Bagot of Oxford, gave new voice to anti-Catholic criticisms in some "light animadversions" on the *Tracts for the Times*.[14] While he began by praising their work as valuable for the recollection of "truths" related to "the union, the discipline and the authority of the Church," he also registered concerns over abuse by younger "minds of a peculiar temperament." Recognizing their school as a school, Bagot lamented, "I have more fear of the Disciples than of the Teachers." As a remedy, he implored Newman and his fellow Tractarians "to be cautious, both in their writings and actions, to take heed lest their good be evil spoken of; lest in their exertions to re-establish unity, they unhappily create fresh schism; lest in their admiration of antiquity, they revert to practices which heretofore have ended in superstition."[15] Badly bruised by what sounded like round damnation ornamented with faint praise, Newman immediately offered to discontinue the series. Despite Bagot's reply with assurances of his approval, Newman later recognized in the incident a portending a much larger "collision with the nation, and that Church of the Nation, which it began by professing especially to serve."[16]

By 1839, Newman had additionally begun to lose confidence in his *via media* "paper religion."[17] This resulted partly from his own study of early conflicts over the doctrine of the incarnation and partly from an unexpected critique of the *Tracts for the Times* from the man who would one day become Newman's Roman Catholic bishop. Regarding

---

14 Newman, *Apo*, 157.

15 "Bishop of Oxford's Charge" (14 August 1838), *LD* vi, 285-86.

16 Newman, *Apo*, 157.

17 In his *Lectures on the Prophetical Office of the Church*, Newman had contrasted the theory of an Anglican *via media* with "Protestantism and Popery." While the latter were "real religions," he confessed that the *via media* had "never had existence except on paper." Of the *via media*, he concluded, "it is known, not positively but negatively, in its differences from the rival creeds, not in its own properties; and can only be described as a third system, neither the one nor the other, but with something of each, cutting between them, and, as if with a critical fastidiousness, trifling with them both, and boasting to be nearer Antiquity than either," 16.

the first, Newman began a study of early Christological debates in July of 1839. He observed there how the Councils of Nicea in 325 and Constantinople in 381 determined that Jesus Christ was both fully God and fully man, but Newman noted the remaining controversy as to how the divine and human natures related in the one person of the incarnate Son. The orthodox Dyophysite party taught that Jesus had two distinct natures in the one person. The Eutychians responded that the human and divine natures of Christ were at all times combined into one single nature in the one person. In the early decades of the fifth century, the Monophysite party opted for a *via media* between the extremes, arguing that Christ's human nature had been absorbed by his divine nature. Reflecting on the Monophysites' refusal to coalesce around the developed Catholic definition of Chalcedon in 451, Newman awakened to the consequence of his own *via media* between Protestantism and Roman Catholicism. If the Monophysites were truly heterodox and in schism, it would be difficult to exculpate the Church of England from the same charge. Newman's later recollections summarized his horror: "I saw my face in that mirror and I was a Monophysite."[18]

Nicholas Wiseman reviewed a four-volume collection of the first eighty-five *Tracts for the Times* in the *Dublin Review* in August 1839. The review's subtitle was "The Anglican Claim of Apostolical Succession," and Wiseman hoisted the Church of England by the same kind of historical petard that Newman was so fond of directing against Roman Catholics. In much the same way that Newman came to see his own Anglican face reflected in the sectarian Monophysites of the fifth century, Wiseman drew more dire connections from the fourth-century Donatist heresy. Unlike the Monophysites, the Donatists had not chosen a *via media* in preference to communion with Rome. They held to precisely the same doctrine and sacramental practice as did the Catholic party and only separated because they doubted the succession of holy orders from bishops who failed to persevere under persecution. The Church of England had actually committed itself in Article 26 to the Catholic settlement of this controversy, so Wiseman pressed his case on that account:

---

[18] Newman, *Apo*, 209.

> St. Augustine has a golden sentence on this subject, which should be an axiom in theology: "Quapropter SECURUS judicat orbis terrarum, bonos non esse qui se dividunt ab orbe terrarum, in quacumque parte orbis terrarum." Those cannot be possibly right who have separated themselves from the communion of distant Churches which remain still connected in the bond of unity.[19]

Under Wiseman's scrutiny Newman came to see that even a perfect realization of the church's natal, apostolic orthodoxy would be insufficient to claim a place in the true church. Reconciled communion would be the only alternative to the Church of England remaining a heretical sect. Wiseman's quotation of Augustine to this effect–*securus judicat orbis terrarium*–became a nagging symbol as Newman admitted at the time:

> I must confess it has given me a stomach-ache. You see the whole history of the Monophysites has been a sort of alterative, and now comes this dose at the end of it. It does certainly come upon one that we are not at the bottom of things.[20]

While Newman was slow to fully embrace St. Augustine's "infallible prescription" and "final sentence" for the Church of England, students and younger scholars in his Oxford school proved less willing to suffer the practical frictions of claiming Catholic identity in a Protestant church. This again exposed them to the accusations of "popery" that he sought to mitigate in 1837. When Henry Manning wrote to discuss one such case involving a young woman who was discerning a call to become Roman Catholic, Newman's reply said much of his fears for the final success of their cause within the Church of England: "Our blanket is too small for our bed." By this he meant that the Church of England–even in the form of his *via media*–lacked sufficient "provisions and methods by which Catholic feelings are to be detained, secured,

---

[19] Wiseman quotes Augustine's *Contra epistolam Parmeniani*, 3.3 here, and he supplies his own English translation: "Wherefore, the entire world judges with security, that they are not good, who separate themselves from the entire world, in whatever part of the entire world." Nicholas Wiseman, "Tracts for the Times: Anglican Claim of Apostolic Succession," *Dublin Review* 7 (1839): 154.

[20] Newman to Frederic Rogers (22 September 1839), *LD* vii, 154.

sobered and trained heavenwards." This, in turn, led him to fret openly over the ways that they were "raising longings and tastes which we are not allowed to supply" and thereby "tend[ing] to make impatient minds seek it where it has ever been, *in* Rome."[21] Writing to Samuel Wood on 29 September 1839, Newman even foresaw such conversions as a potential threat to the collaborative integrity of their school: "What I very much fear is our all not keeping together, *though* moving on the same road. Accident of one kind or other occasions this or that person to anticipate a truth to which others are advancing also–and his anticipating it throws others back."[22]

Newman's worries were immediately confirmed upon his return to Oxford following a month's travel. There he quickly learned of two sermons delivered by John Morris, a younger priest and Petrean Fellow of Exeter College, Oxford, who had been tasked to cover Newman's duties at St. Mary's. In his first sermon, Morris had treated the subject of fasting–something Newman described as the "one subject, for which [Morris] has a monomania."[23] Morris unashamedly urged the astonished faithful that even their domesticated animals were obliged to keep the church's fast days. Still worse was his sermon the following Sunday wherein Morris condemned the unbelief and carnality of anyone who failed to embrace the Roman doctrine of the mass.[24] These events led the Vice Chancellor of Oxford, Ashurst Turner Gilbert, to withdraw his family from further attendance at St. Mary's and so inflamed the university's Hebdomadal Board that Newman felt duty bound to bring the matter to his bishop's attention. The ink barely dry on Richard Bagot's reassuring response, Newman heard word that his young curate, John Bloxam, had prostrated himself at the elevation of the host while attending mass at a Roman Catholic chapel in Alton Towers. Though Bloxam offered assurances to the contrary, arguing that he had merely continued to kneel following his own recitation of morning prayer, Newman again felt obliged to report the matter. This time Bagot's reply took the

---

21 Newman to H. E. Manning (1 September 1839), *LD* vii, 133.
22 Newman to S. F. Wood (29 September 1839), *LD* vii, 156-57.
23 Newman to J. W. Bowden (4 November 1839), *LD* vii, 176-77.
24 Newman to J. W. Bowden (4 November 1839), *LD* vii.

form of two letters. The first told Newman that his report was unnecessary, but the second included a request that Newman use his "high and influential name" among the younger men to

> discourage by every means in your power indiscretions similar to Mr Bloxams's or any little extravagances, the results of youth–harmless perhaps in themselves, but which I am sure, when they occur, and are known, tend to retard the progress of sound and high Church principles.[25]

Newman later upbraided himself for his scrupulosity in continually referring such matters to Bagot. They reflected, in his words, "a great impatience of keeping things back and not letting all come out" and amounted to an "indiscretion" of his own.[26] Taken together, these twin indiscretions gave rise to a triplet, manifested in the events surrounding *Tract 90*.

A HAZARDOUS EXPERIMENT, LIKE PROVING CANNON

The ability to make sense of Newman's various and often contrary lines of inquiry in *Tract 90* turns on a prior understanding of what the work was intended to be. Is the work best understood as Newman's last attempt at to salvage his *via media*, or did it represent something new following upon the *via media*'s acknowledged collapse? This is not easy to judge, and Newman's own recollection in the *Apologia* leads in divergent directions.[27] The answer finally turns on a proper under-

---

25 Richard Bagot to Newman (26 December 1839), *LD* vii, 190; cf., Richard Bagot to Newman (25 November 1839), *LD* vii, 185.

26 In an undated notation on his 5 January 1840 letter to J. W. Bowden recounting the latter incident involving Bloxam, Newman wrote, "I ought not to have mentioned it to the Bishop. But this has really been the source of many of my indiscretions, a great impatience of keeping things back and not letting all come out. It was the cause of Number 90." *LD* vii, 201n2.

27 On one hand Newman justified his read on the Thirty-nine Articles as being commensurate with the Caroline Divines: "[One] might hold in the Anglican Church a comprecation with the Saints with Bramhall, and the Mass all but Transubstantiation with Andrewes, or with Hooker that Transubstantiation itself is not

standing of events as they occurred in the real-time reporting of Newman's letters. There we find that only a month prior to commencing his work on *Tract 90*, Newman wrote to John Keble seeking advice regarding a possible resignation of his living as Vicar of St. Mary's. While his charge afforded him a venue to exert strong influence at Oxford with only minimal interference from university authorities, Newman was anxious over his seeming inability to shepherd the lay townspeople who found themselves under his spiritual charge. "I do not know my Oxford Parishioners," he worried. "I am not conscious of influencing them; and certainly I have no insight into their spiritual state. I have no personal, no pastoral acquaintance with them."[28] Newman recognized in his own clerical ministrations some of the same practical clash he had identified in the "impatient minds" of younger protégés. He had spent nearly thirteen years clearing space for a very different way of being Anglican than was customary in Oxford. Though his introduction of daily services, a weekly communion, and a course of theological lectures in Adam de Brome's Chapel had been successful in securing the loyalty of students and prospective clergy–that is, the constituency of his *schola*–he was nevertheless conscious of the distance between his pastoral efforts and the expectations of his parishioners. He bemoaned the latter as expectations born of a "system of religion which has been received for 300 years, and of which the Heads of Houses are the legitimate maintainers in this place."[29]

Keble's response to the letter, by turns assuring him of his good effect and worrying that any withdrawal from pastoral ministry might detract from their efforts, did little to alleviate Newman's deeper sense of irresolution. A second letter to Keble announced his determination

---

a point for Churches to part communion upon, or with Hammond that a General Council, truly such, never did, never shall err in a matter of faith, or with Bull that man lost inward grace by the fall, or with Thorndike that penance is a propitiation for post-baptismal sin, or with Pearson that the all-powerful name of Jesus is no otherwise given than in the Catholic Church." Newman, *Apo*, 181. Alternatively, he indicated that *Tract 90* was the product of "moral sickness," wherein he was "neither able to acquiesce in Anglicanism, nor able to go to Rome." Newman, *Apo*, 143.

[28] Newman to John Keble (26 October 1840), *LD* vii, 416.
[29] Newman to John Keble (26 October 1840), *LD* vii, 417.

to relieve the intolerable tensions by bringing the Church of England to a moment of decision by "fair trial." He would force both the bishops and the university to self-identify as a part of the Catholic Church or accede to the truth that their church was but a sect. As Newman put the matter to Keble, such an undertaking would be his "hazardous experiment, like proving Cannon," but his forecast nevertheless remained hopeful:

> Yet we must not take it for granted the metal will burst in the operation. It has borne at various times, not to say at this time, a great infusion of Catholic Truth without damage. As to the result, viz whether this process will not approximate the whole English Church, as a body, to Rome, that is nothing to us. For what we know, it may be the providential means of uniting the whole Church in one, without fresh schismatising, or use of private judgment.[30]

This latter sentiment–that Newman's work could potentially establish a basis for Anglican unity with Rome without a provoking fresh schism in the English Church–suggests that he ultimately intended *Tract 90* to represent something new, constructed from the truly Catholic elements that lay scattered amid the ruins of his collapsing *via media*, while at the same time supplanting it. Until this point, Newman's theological work was centered on the recovery and reinforcement of Anglicanism's *apostolicity*. Now he would turn to a rectification of its lapsed *catholicity*.[31] The difference would lay in this new product being more than the

---

[30] Newman to John Keble (6 November 1840), *LD* vii, 433.

[31] Referring to the sermon, "Faith the Title for Justification," delivered at St. Mary's on 24 January 1841, Edwin Abbot noted Newman's increasingly frequent use of the biblical figure, Cornelius the Centurion, as a metaphor of orthodoxy seeking catholicity. Newman hopefully proclaimed, "Thousands who are in unconscious heresy or unwilling schism, still are, through faith, in the state of Cornelius, when his prayers and alms went up before God." Newman, *PS* vi, new ed. (London: Rivingtons, 1868), 172. Coming, then, to the letter of 25 December 1841 to R. W. Church wherein Newman wrote of being "very sanguine . . . that our prayers and alms will come up as a memorial before God," Abbot wrote, "and we see, at once, that Newman is putting himself and his party in the position of 'Cornelius'–not yet in the Church, but preparing, by alms and prayer, for admission into it." Edwin Abbott, *The Anglican Career of John Henry Newman*, vol. 2 (London: Macmillan & Co., 1892), 240.

discernment and description of a self-sufficient middle way, existing in practical schism with other branches of the universal church. Rather, it would be a development of Anglicanism into something genuinely *Catholic*–at once true to its apostolic patrimony and at the same time solicitous of reconciliation with those portions of the true church that lay outside England.

CATHOLICITY AS A HERMENEUTICAL DUTY IN *TRACT 90*

On first examination, the argument of *Tract 90* appears muddled. In places Newman appears content with the lax wording of the Articles, establishing a succession of deliberately broad and inclusive doctrines, codified by the Anglican Reformers and imposed by the Convocations of 1571 and 1662.[32] At other points, Newman unabashedly denied that the church of his own day possessed any interpretive obligation to their "original framers" and asserted instead the superseding authority of Holy Scripture as interpreted by the "ancient Church" and the "*Regula Fidei*" of late antiquity.[33] On occasions he severely restricted the Articles' condemnations of Roman Catholic "error" so they were only applicable to "actual existing errors" held within its communion "whether taken into its system or not."[34] On others, he proved so generous in the weighting of opinions held by individual Anglican Divines that he seemed ready to assume, in the words of one critic, "that every opinion . . . that had been once expressed by any one High Church Bishop or Divine, and that had not been authoritatively censured, at once became part of justifiable Anglican doctrine."[35] According to Newman, the first and second *Books of Homilies* were not to be considered part of a churchman's oath of subscription to the Articles–and this despite their being commended by Article 35 as containing "godly and wholesome doctrine, and necessary for these times." He judged it unreasonable to

---

[32] Newman, *Tract 90*, 80.

[33] Newman, *Tract 8*.

[34] Newman, *Tract 90*, 59.

[35] Abbot, *The Anglican Career of Cardinal Newman*, vol. 2, 247-48.

trouble the conscience with a "thick octavo volume, written flowingly and freely by fallible men" and considered such a proposition to be nothing less than "a yoke of bondage."[36] This judgment did not prevent him, however, from making authoritative use of those same homilies throughout the work as a high court of Catholic appeal to countermand the Articles' naturally Protestant language.

The single thread holding these competing arguments together is found in the first of his concluding remarks near the end of *Tract 90*. There Newman gave account of the theological rationale warranting his exploitation of the Articles' "elasticity" to explore "how far their text *could* be opened."[37] In the *Tract*, he pleaded for the "*duty* which we owe both to the Catholic Church and to our own, to take our reformed confessions in the most Catholic sense they will admit." He argued that this concern alone was sufficient to nullify "any duties toward their framers."[38] Newman's use of the word "duty" should be taken as clothing his interpretive creativity with the gravest sincerity. Now *catholicity* stood alongside apostolicity as a hermeneutical crux, committing the church to a self-understanding that accorded with the *contemporaneous* catholicity of the universal church.

Newman was embracing the responsibility to commend a genuinely *theological* reception of its formularies, one that reckoned with their contingency and contemplated the open possibilities of their subsequent reception and use. The particularities of grammar, history, authority, and context were thus made useful for his larger task. Ambiguities could be deployed to limit sectarian claims in the Articles. They could also function to open possible readings that better reflected ecumenical concord. It was this feature of *Tract 90* that led Newman himself to recognize in its pages a first opening in favor of what he

---

[36] Newman, *Tract 90*, 66.

[37] Newman, *Apo*, 160-61.

[38] Newman, *Tract 90*, 89. In the second edition of *Tract 90*, Newman mollified somewhat the sweeping implications of his statement by appending, "Nor do we receive the articles from their original framers, but from several successive convocations after their time; in the last instance, from that of 1662." Newman, *VM* ii, 344.

termed "the *principle* of doctrinal development."³⁹ In *Tract 90*, Newman embraced his prophetical vocation and, in an interpretive act of creative fidelity, moved to rectify the lapsed catholicity of the Church of England.

NEWMAN'S UNACKNOWLEDGEABLE DEBT: FRANCISCUS À SANCTA CLARA

Newman received some previously unappreciated assistance in his attempt to open the Thirty-nine Articles. It came in a source suggested to him in 1835 by Richard Hurrell Froude. In life, Froude had been indefatigable when urging fellow Tractarians to embrace his contempt for the Reformers. His opinions of the Thirty-nine Articles were especially influential to Newman. As early as November of 1833, Froude had confided that he could be "content to throw overboard the Articles keeping the Creeds" and spoke of his own present milieu as a time when he was firmly reconciled to the opinion.⁴⁰ While still in the throes of the controversies over subscription at Oxford and musing on the possibilities of visiting Rome during the upcoming Long Vacation of 1835, Froude additionally hinted at an alternative way of interpreting the Thirty-nine Articles that he had gleaned from a work of history by the Caroline Divine, Peter Heylyn:

> It occurred to me the other day that one might send a Latin petition to the Pope confessing one's interpretation of the 39 Articles (Which by the by the Jesuit Francis Sancta Clara showed to be "patient if not ambitious of a Catholic meaning" and apparently Laud did not think the interpretation over strained vid. Heylin) and opinions on divers subjects, and praying that one might be allowed to communicate in their Churches.⁴¹

Heylyn only briefly mentioned Franciscus à Sancta Clara and his exposition of the Thirty-nine Articles in *Cyprianus Anglicus: Or the History*

---

39 Newman, *Apo*, 161.
40 Richard Hurrell Froude to Newman (17 November 1833), *LD* iv, 112.
41 Richard Hurrell Froude to Newman (4 March 1835), *LD* v, 68.

of the Life and Death of William Laud (1668). Froude's use of Heylyn's summary of "Sancta Clara's" contribution–that the Thirty-nine Articles were "patient of a Catholic meaning"–is especially noteworthy for the way the phrase became something of a slogan for Anglo-Catholic reception of the Articles that followed in the wake of *Tract 90*.[42] Still more important was Sancta Clara himself.[43]

As his religious name suggests, Sancta Clara was a Franciscan who converted to Roman Catholicism sometime prior to his reception into the Order of Friars Minor at Ypres in October 1617. Born Christopher Davenport, he was admitted to Merton College, Oxford in 1613 where he studied under Samuel Lane. At some point he transferred to Magdalen Hall and took his degree in 1614. Francis then continued his studies at the English College in Douai and was ordained to the diaconate in 1619 and the priesthood in 1620. At Douai he also read philosophy, became Chief Reader of Divinity at St. Bonaventure's, and was finally named Professor of Sacred Theology. He later returned to his native England and served as "theologian" or "confessor" to Queen Henrietta Maria in the court of Charles I. There he gained the admiration of Catholics and Anglicans alike. His *Paraphrastica Expositio Articulorum Confessionis Anglicanae* (hereafter cited as *The Articles of the Anglican Church*) appeared in 1646 as an attempt at harmonizing the Thirty-nine

---

[42] Peter Heylyn, *Cyprianus Anglicus; Or the History of the Life and Death of William Laud* (London: A Siele, 1668), 252-53. Newman first used the explicit verbiage "*patient* of a Catholic interpretation" in a letter to Thomas Flanagan on 28 July 1857. *LD* xviii, 102. The words "patient, though not ambitious, of a Catholic interpretation" also appears in the 1877 Notice to *Tract 90* that appeared in *VM* ii, 265. R. W. Church later summarized Newman's position in *Tract 90* writing that the Articles were "*patient* of a Catholic meaning, but *ambitious* of a Protestant meaning; whatever their logic was, their rhetoric was Protestant. It was just possible, but not more, for a Catholic to subscribe to them." R. W. Church, *The Oxford Movement: 12 Years, 1833-1845* (London: MacMillan, 1891), 349. The inclusion of the phrase in what was the canonical history of the Oxford Movement until the late twentieth century guaranteed its durability.

[43] Francis à Sancta Clara is sometimes known as Santa Clara, Francis Hunt, Francis Doventrie, or Francis of Coventry. Hereafter, I will use the most common form, "Sancta Clara."

Articles with the teachings of the Roman Catholic Church.[44] Froude's reproduction of Heylyn's error, confusing an obvious Franciscan for a Jesuit, suggests that he had not read Sancta Clara's work directly, but Newman pursued Heylyn's comment back to the source.[45]

It is certain that Newman became intimately familiar with Sancta Clara's exposition of the Articles and that he eventually used the work as a primary resource for his own creative reception of the Thirty-nine Articles in *Tract 90*. Not long after Froude first made him aware of Sancta Clara by his letter of 4 March 1835, Newman secured a copy from the Oriel College Library on 27 November 1835 and kept it until 24 February of the following year.[46] Years later and just a few weeks after the publication of *Tract 90* in 1841, Newman again briefly confirmed his knowledge of Francis's identity and work in response to a nonextant inquiry of John Bowden.[47] Three weeks after this, Newman referred to Sancta Clara yet again in a reply to Charles Russell, a Roman Catholic correspondent who had written to clarify Newman's understanding the doctrine of

---

[44] For a detailed history of Sancta Clara's life, see John Dockery, *Christopher Davenport: Friar and Diplomat* (London: Burns & Oates, 1960). Owing in large part to the controversy stirred by *Tract 90*, Sancta Clara's work was republished in 1865 with an English translation by Frederick George Lee. Franciscus A. Sancta Clara, *Paraphrastica Expositio Articulorum Confessionis Anglicanae: The Articles of the Anglican Church Paraphrastically Considered and Explained*, trans. F. G. Lee (London: John T. Hayes, 1865). Quotes from Sancta Clara's work below are from this edition.

[45] I have spoken of Sancta Clara as an "unappreciated" resource deliberately. Vincent Ferrer Blehl's note that Sancta Clara's work "anticipated" *Tract 90* is common enough. See, *Pilgrim Journey: 1901-1856* (New York: Continuum, 2001), 154. Cf., W. G. Ward, *An Address to Members of Convocation* (London: Toovy, 1845), and E. M. Goulburn, *Reply to Some Parts of Mr. Ward's Defence* (Oxford, 1845), entitled "Dishonest Subscription," in *The Churchman's Monthly Review* (March 1845): 200-208, at 203. No author has made the case for Newman's direct familiarity with *Paraphrastica Expositio Articulorum Confessionis Anglicanae*, and his use of it as a source for his own treatment of the Articles.

[46] Kenneth Parker, *Newman's Oriel College Senior Library Record* (2014): digitalcollections.newmanstudies.org/library-records. The *Paraphrastica Expositio Articulorum Confessionis Anglicanae* was originally published separately but was later included at the end of Sancta Clara's *Deus, Natura, Gratia, Sive Tractatus de Predestinatione*, 2nd ed. (Lyons, 1635). Newman accessed the work in this form and edition.

[47] Newman wrote, "Santa Clara (Davenport) was the writer in Charles 1st's time you refer to about the Articles." Newman to J. W. Bowden (24 March 1841) *LD* viii, 115.

transubstantiation. As part of Newman's assurances of his familiarity with Catholic teaching on the subject, he explained that his object in *Tract 90* was not to defend Catholic doctrine so much as to defend the essential catholicity of the Thirty-nine Articles. He added that by doing so, he was "taking the line of your own writer Davenport or A Sancta Clara, who if I mistake not, commenting on this particular article says 'Capharnāitarum hæresim procul dubio spectat.'"[48] The inexact recollection of Francis's Latin here indicates that Newman did not have the work before him, but his improvised gloss of the original, "eos scilicet solum condemnare antiquum errorem Capharnaïtarum," suggests that he had thoroughly internalized the work and made it his own.[49]

Newman's first line of inquiry in *Tract 90* was aimed at establishing the proper sense and reference of the language used by the Articles. It was here that his treatment most clearly reflected the influence of Sancta Clara. Both men insisted on the necessity of treating Articles 6 (Of the Sufficiency of the Holy Scriptures for Salvation) and 20 (Of the Authority of the Church) together so that, in Newman's words, both Holy Scripture and the church are "adjusted with one another in their actual exercise" of "teaching revealed truth."[50] The two men were likewise of the same mind when observing that Article 6 does not categorically reject the canonical or liturgical place of the Apocrypha and when arguing that the "Rule of Faith" is not reducible to scripture alone. Newman argued the latter explicitly while Sancta Clara affirmed that the Article countenanced an idea that "the Church has the power to propose to our faith" certain "ordinances and traditions not contained in Scripture" but which "can be proved by Scripture."[51] Treating Article 11 (Of the Justification of Man), both men again emphasized the substantial continuity between the Church of England and the Church of Rome on the various "causes" of justification. When treating the

---

[48] "Undoubtedly looks to the Capharnaite heresy." Newman to Charles W. Russell (13 April 1841), *LD* viii, 174.

[49] "They only condemn the ancient error of the Capharnaites." Sancta Clara, *Articles of the Anglican Church*, 58.

[50] Newman, *Tract 90*, 5. Cf., *Articles of the Anglican Church*, 3-4.

[51] Sancta Clara, *Articles of the Anglican Church*, 31. Cf., Newman, *Tract 90*, 11.

classical division between Protestants and Catholics on the "formal" cause of justification, both resorted to the Articles' permitting a variety of ways that "faith alone" justifies. Where Sancta Clara wrote of how trust in God expresses itself by prayer and by works of charity, Newman stated more generally how "a number of means go to effect our justification."

Newman also emphasized the justifying power of the sacrament of baptism–a rite contextualized by the liturgical prayer of the church– and "newness of heart."[52] Coming to Articles 12 (Of Good Works) and 13 (Of Works Before Justification), Newman again followed Sancta Clara very closely, recognizing how their wording excluded the *de condigno* or "strict meriting" of justifying grace, but permitted a *de congruo* conception of merit wherein persons in an "intermediate state"–that is, neither "in light or in darkness" as regards the state of Christian justification–might be visited by "Divine influences, or by *actual* grace, or rather *aid*." These, then, were "the first-fruits of the grace of justification going before it."[53]

On the question of the relation of the "Roman Church" to the "Visible Church" in Article 19 (of the church), both men argued that the listing of Rome alongside Jerusalem, Alexandria, and Antioch allowed for the contemplation of Rome as a "local church" or a "national communion" that lacked an inviolable promise of indefectibility. Thus, both men inferred a difference between the Church of Rome severally and the "Universal" (Sancta Clara) or "Catholic" (Newman) Church, that is not said to err.[54] This manner of accord carried over into their reading of Article 21 (Of the Authority of General Councils). There, both men followed Robert Bellarmine carefully in distinguishing between "general councils"–qualified by Newman as merely "a thing of earth"– and "Catholic councils," that, as a "thing of heaven" are graced with an "express supernatural privilege, that they shall not err."[55] Each also reintroduced what had been previously argued when treating Articles 6

---

[52] Sancta Clara, *Articles of the Anglican Church*, 12-13. Cf., Newman, *Tract 90*, 13.

[53] Newman, *Tract 90*, 16. Cf., Sancta Clara, *Articles of the Anglican Church*, 14.

[54] Sancta Clara, *Articles of the Anglican Church*, 28-29. Cf., Newman, *Tract 90*.

[55] Newman, *Tract 90*, 21 Cf., *Articles of the Anglican Church*, 35-36.

and 20. Sancta Clara wrote that the church "does not trust to new revelations, but to the old ones, hidden in the Scriptures and in the words of the Apostles, as is the constant opinion of the Doctors."[56] Newman echoed the sentiment, arguing that an essential condition of the church "gathering 'in the Name of CHRIST'" is that "in points necessary to salvation, a council should prove its decrees by Scripture."[57]

Moving into matters of more practical controversy between Canterbury and Rome, Newman's imitation of Sancta Clara became still closer. Both noted the ambiguity of Article 22 (Of Purgatory) in speaking of "the *Romish* doctrine concerning purgatory, pardons, worshipping and adoration, as well of images as of relics, and also invocation of saints." Sancta Clara argued that the proper sense of "Romish" there is to be discovered, "not from the writings of Catholics, but from those of their opponents."[58] He then cited his experience with Anglicans who admitted that all of these practices were "agreeable to primitive antiquity."[59] Newman echoed his judgment, arguing both that what the Article opposed was "the *received doctrine* of the day" and that it was to be contrasted with "a primitive doctrine on all these points" that was "so widely received and so respectably supported, that it may well be entertained as a matter of opinion by a theologian now."[60] Likewise on the sacraments (Article 25), Newman followed Sancta Clara's contention that the distinction between Baptism and the Eucharist on one hand, and the other five sacraments on the other, did not absolutely deny that the latter might be contemplated as sacraments: "This Article does not deny the five rites in question to be sacraments, but to be sacraments *in the sense* in which Baptism and the Lord's Supper are sacraments; 'sacraments of *the Gospel*,' sacraments *with an outward sign ordained of* God."[61]

---

56 Sancta Clara, *Articles of the Anglican Church*, 37.

57 Newman, *Tract 90*, 22.

58 Sancta Clara, *Articles of the Anglican Church*, 39.

59 Sancta Clara, *Articles of the Anglican Church*, 41.

60 Newman, *Tract 90*, 23.

61 Newman, *Tract 90*, 43.

As indicated, Sancta Clara argued that the judgment of Article 28 (Of the Lord's Supper)–that is, that the doctrine of transubstantiation is "repugnant to the plain words of Scripture"–was rooted in what he called "the old error of the Capharnäites, namely, the carnal presence of Christ . . . as though Christ was present in a natural or carnal manner and were chewed by the teeth."[62] To this he added a reference to the "Canon (*Ego Berengarius*) in the Roman Council under Nicolas I."[63] Although Newman knew the error by the "Capharnäites" moniker, he did not opt for using the word and he corrected Sancta Clara's misattribution of the responsible pontiff, writing that the Article referred only to the "doctrine . . . imposed by Nicholas the Second on Berengarius." He then quoted the latter's confession in full.[64] Turning to the question of "Masses" in Article 31 (Of the One Oblation of Christ Finished on the Cross), Newman then replicated Sancta Clara's distinction between "masses" (plural) and the "Sacrifice of the Mass" (singular). The first could be understood as "sacrifices for sin distinct from the sacrifice of CHRIST's death," but the second established the Mass as a *re-presenting* of "the one oblation of CHRIST finished upon the Cross."[65] Both men also agreed that clerical celibacy was not imposed by "God's law." Rather, it was commended by the "Church's rule, or on vow," so the censure of Article 32 (Of the Marriage of Priests) did not apply.[66]

Finally, Newman and Sancta Clara were agreed in judging that Article 35 did not require strict subscription to "every word and clause" of the "Anglican Homilies." The Article intended, merely, that they "savor of sound doctrine" and should be read discerningly.[67]

Finally, concerning Article 37 (on the Bishop of Rome), Newman used an argument that paralleled that of Sancta Clara, noting that papal jurisdiction was providentially contingent, but there was a slight

---

62 Sancta Clara, *Articles of the Anglican Church*, 58.

63 Sancta Clara, *Articles of the Anglican Church*.

64 Newman, *Tract 90*, 50.

65 Newman, *Tract 90*, 59-60. Cf., Sancta Clara, *Articles of the Anglican Church*, 59-60.

66 Sancta Clara, *Articles of the Anglican Church*, 80; Cf., Newman, *Tract 90*, 64.

67 Sancta Clara, *Articles of the Anglican Church*, 83-84; Cf., Newman, *Tract 90*, 66.

difference in emphasis. While Sancta Clara tended to regard such contingency as a matter of pontifical discretion and disposition–which reflected an early modern ultramontane outlook–Newman adopted an argument influenced by Gallican theories, that made the intercommunion of national churches or the "confederacy of sees and churches" into a "natural duty," with its absence being no bar to genuine catholicity.[68]

It is not difficult to understand why Newman was careful to avoid any direct quotation of Sancta Clara's work in *Tract 90*. Still less mysterious is Newman's reticence to acknowledge Sancta Clara in the *Apologia*. To openly admit such a direct dependence on a Roman Catholic who had formerly been both an Anglican and a student of Oxford University would have been as disastrous for Newman's Tractarian prospects in 1841 as they would be for a winsome defense of his own personal and religious integrity in 1864. That being said, *our* recognition of Newman's unacknowledgeable debt to Franciscus à Sancta Clara is critical to any fair evaluation of *Tract 90*–particularly its claim that the Articles were "through God's good providence, to say the least, not uncatholic."[69] Far from an act of untethered exploitation, wantonly teasing at ambiguities to suit private judgment, *Tract 90* was the product of real theological collaboration. In reading the Articles *with* Sancta Clara, Newman was exploring the interpretive potential of a sectarian formulary in dialogue with a representative Catholic voice. In this, he was able to name possibilities for genuine accord within the prophetical tradition. The possibilities would still require discernment and approval by the apostolical office, of course, but Newman realized the proper task of his prophetical office by pressing the English bishops to recognize their duty to consult the *whole* body of the baptized faithful.

---

[68] Sancta Clara, *Articles of the Anglican Church*, 97; Cf., Newman, *Tract 90*, 78–79. Living as he did in a time when Gallicanism flourished without censure in France, Santa Clara likewise judged that the Article is no bar to a similar arrangement in England. Sancta Clara, *Articles of the Anglican Church*, 106–107. One also notes that this was the common position of recusant Catholics in England and was widely considered to be a matter of indifference (i.e., adiaphora) throughout western Europe. See Paul Valliere, *Conciliarism: A History of Decision-Making in the Church* (Cambridge: Cambridge University Press, 2012), 119–61.

[69] Newman, *Tract 90*, 4.

HARMONIZING THE CHURCH'S BODY OF TRUTH: ARTICLES, HOMILIES, AND THE *BOOK OF COMMON PRAYER*

Newman's instinct for the voice of the living church extended to his treatment of the first and second *Books of Homilies*.[70] While he did not believe that Article 35 required *ex animo* subscription to their contents, he nevertheless made use of them as exemplary fruits of a worshiping church. Read together with the *Book of Common Prayer*, the homilies thus bore witness to a larger body of divine truth within which the church might better hear and receive the Thirty-nine Articles. Harmonizing potentially discordant notes between these witnesses was, as Newman put it in *Tract 90*, "an object of the most serious moment for those who have given their assent to both formularies."[71]

In treating Article 11, Newman made use of Homily 11 in the second book ("Of Almsdeeds and Mercifulness Toward the Poor and Needy") to include good works alongside "justification by faith" as a means of justification.[72] When treating the Anglican understanding of the "visible church" in Article 19, he quoted at length from Homily 16 in the second book ("Concerning the Coming Down of the Holy Ghost and the Manifold Gifts of the Same") to demonstrate his contention that by "the visible Church" the Articles could mean "an *universal* congregation

---

[70] The *Books of Homilies* are two books of thirty-three sermons approved for use by the Church of England. The title of the collection is *Certain Sermons or Homilies Appointed to Be Read in Churches*. In the sixteenth-century Church of England, a sermon was required by the Order for the Holy Communion of the *Book of Common Prayer*. Sermons, however, could not be delivered by just any incumbent. Rather, a license was required, for which an MA degree (usually from Oxford or Cambridge) was a usual qualification. When no licensed preacher was available, the *Book of Common Prayer* prescribed that "After the Crede . . . one of the homelies already set forth, or hereafter to be set forth by commune auchthoritie." The rubric remained substantially unchanged in Newman's day. During the reigns of King Edward VI and Queen Elizabeth I especially, they were in wide use. The first book of twelve written sermons was published in the reign of Edward VI in 1547, and the second book of twenty-one was issued in the reign of Elizabeth in 1563. Archbishop Thomas Cranmer and Bishop John Jewel were principal contributors to their contents.

[71] Newman, *Tract 90*, 80.

[72] Newman, *Tract 90*, 12.

or fellowship of God's faithful and elect people," as opposed to "an abstract idea of a Church, which may be multiplied indefinitely in fact."[73]

In his treatment of Article 22, Newman made rich use of the *Books of Homilies* to justify his categorical distinction between "Romish" practices that were innovative, and valid early Christian practices of worship. The Articles, he argued, could not be read as condemning the latter. So, in treating early Christian relic veneration, he cited the Empress Helena's non-idolatrous veneration of the "True Cross," lauded in Homily 2 from the second *Book of Homilies* ("Against the Peril of Idolatry").[74] Newman then used this same homily's castigation of prayers for the dead–prayers specifically offered in the hope that God's might revoke a verdict of eternal damnation–to exempt both the ancient and Tridentine practice of praying for the faithful departed.[75] This use of the homilies carried over to his identification of "Romish" in Article 22 with what he considered to be the manifold errors and popular corruptions, authorized or suffered by the Roman Catholic Church prior to the Council of Trent. So, the long descriptions of popular folly and idolatry in the homily against idolatry and from Homily 5 in the first book (that is, "Of Good Works) became the selfsame "enormities" repented of and forbidden by the Tridentine Church of Rome.[76] Newman also used this latter move to restrict Article 22's derision of the "fond" practice of invoking the saints to the "the

---

[73] Newman, *Tract 90*, 18-20.

[74] Newman, *Tract 90*, 23-24. The same homily also records the testimony of valid miracles at the tomb of St. Epiphanius.

[75] Newman, *Tract 90*, 25-26.

[76] Newman quotes Session 25 of Trent in his own translation: "Into these holy and salutary observances should any abuses creep, of these the Holy Council strongly [*vehementer*] desires the utter extinction; so that no images of a false doctrine, and supplying to the uninstructed opportunity of perilous error, should be set up . . . All superstition also in invocation of saints, veneration of relics, and sacred use of images, be put away; all *filthy* lucre be cast out of doors; and *all wantonness* be avoided; *so that images be not painted or adorned with an immodest beauty*; or the celebration of Saints and attendance on Relics *be abused to revelries and drunkennesses*; as though festival days were kept in honour of saints by *luxury and lasciviousness*." Newman, *Tract 90*, 36.

superstitious use of invocations." In longer quotations from Homilies 7 and 8 from the second *Book of Homilies* (that is, "On Prayer" and "Of the Place and Time of Prayer"), Newman pleaded for the licit use of biblical Psalms to invoke angels and prescribed prayers like the *Benedicte* (that is, "O all ye Works of the Lord, bless ye the Lord") wherein the "spirits and souls of the righteous" are called upon to "bless the Lord." Newman likewise made such uses of the homilies throughout *Tract 90* to buttress his restriction of "Transubstantiation" in Article 28 to the "Capharnaite" or "carnal" understanding of the real presence and to validate the ecclesial discipline of clerical celibacy.

In his debate with Jager and in the *Lectures on the Prophetical Office of the Church*, Newman argued for the existence of a larger "body of Truth" that lay in a mass of written and unwritten sources. In *Tract 90* he consulted the *Books of Homilies* and the *Book of Common Prayer* as witnesses to that body taking concrete form in an unbroken continuity of Catholic worship. By this light, Newman argued that the Church of England was duty bound to understand itself and its codified formularies as a rule of belief in dialogue with a living, dynamic rule of prayer. This enabled him to inhabit the prophetic office, "harmonizing" discordant church teachings and even "setting right" mother church as a still-faithful and obedient child.

"IN NO WAY SANCTIONED": A PROPHETIC WORD REJECTED AT OXFORD

On the day he finished the composition of *Tract 90*, Newman additionally penned a letter to Robert Belaney, a fellow Anglican Catholic at Cambridge. There he included a summary of the seven years' work of his prophetical school at Oxford and expressed an unbridled optimism for its future prospects.

> The one thing I feared and deprecated years ago, when we began the *Tracts for the Times*, was utter neglect of us on the part of the Church. I was not afraid of being misrepresented, censured or illtreated–and certainly hitherto it has done no harm. Every attack hitherto has turned to good, or at least is dying a natural death. But *Controversy* does but delay the sure victory of truth by making people angry. When they find out they are wrong of *themselves*, a generous feeling rises

in their minds towards the persons and things they have abused and resisted. Much of this reaction has already taken place. Controversy too is a waste of time–one has other things to do. Truth can fight its own battle. It has a reality in it, which shivers to pieces swords of earth. As far as we are not on the side of truth, *we* shall shiver to bits, and I am willing it should be so. The only cause of the prevalence of fallacies for the last 300 years has been the strong arm of the civil power countenancing them. This can hardly continue now. I see too that in the rising generation the most influential and stirring men in Church and State have in them a root of Catholic principles.[77]

These sentiments suggest that Newman entertained no expectation that *Tract 90* would arouse the controversy it did–and this despite his recognition of the risks undertaken when "proving cannon." As his acerbic chronicler, Edwin Abbot, phrased it, "people who do that sort of thing are prepared for inconvenient explosions," and by year's end the theological cannon that Newman had been loading would finally burst asunder. As he would come to see it, the explosion would leave him and the school without a home in either the university or the Church of England. The shepherd being thus smitten, his "rising generation" of men would quickly divide into factions, and he would be left to reforge his cannon elsewhere.

When *Tract 90* appeared in late February 1841, Oxford was the first to register its protest. Newman's younger confederate, William Ward, was positively elated by the tract and immediately brought it to his fellow tutor, Archibald Tait of Balliol College. Tait later described to Arthur Stanley how he drowsily read over the pamphlet, "rather disturbed from time to time" by sentences about "working in chains" and "stammering lips," till he was startled awake by Newman's comments on Article 22.[78] Having been born a Presbyterian, Tait retained that particular form of Scots-Reformed antipathy for images and relics as a violation of the Second Commandment and so began to voice his outrage among friends around the university. About the same time,

---

[77] Newman to Robert Belaney (25 January 1841), *LD* viii, 23.

[78] Stanley's personal recollection appears in Rowland Prothero, *The Life and Letters of Dean Stanley* (London: Thomas Nelson, 1909), 155. Cf., Wilfrid Ward, *The Life of Cardinal Newman*, vol. 1 (London: Longmans, Green, and Co. 1912), 72.

Charles Golightly began making extensive use of *Tract 90* to further his longstanding crusade against the Tractarians. Quickly becoming the *Tract*'s largest single customer, Golightly presented copies to each of the Heads of Houses and then distributed them to key members of the Church of England's episcopate. When news of these activities finally reached Newman, he accused Ward of being a "false prophet" and railed helplessly over "Golightly . . . who is the Tony Fire-the-Faggot of the affair."[79]

With Tait at the lead, T. T. Churton of Brasenose College, H. B. Wilson of St. John's College, and John Griffiths of Wadham College addressed a joint letter of protest to Newman on 8 March 1841. These "four tutors" complained of Newman's "highly dangerous tendency" to receive "very important errors of the Church of Rome" as being licit in the Church of England.[80] While several resident Oriel fellows–Frederic Rogers, Charles Marriott, Richard Church, and John Christie, among them–rose to support Newman alongside the nonresident John Keble, Newman addressed a public letter of response to Richard Jelf, a former fellow of Oriel who was serving at that time as a canon of Christ Church, Oxford. The letter retraced Newman's steps in *Tract 90*, but with language condemning the systemic corruptions in Roman Catholicism. In Newman's words, these warranted "destruction" so as to accomplish "*its* [that is, the Roman Church's] reformation," but the controversy was, by then, too far out of hand to regain control.

---

[79] Newman to A. P. Perceval (12 March 1841), *LD* viii, 68-69. "Tony Fire-the-Faggot" reference is to a character in Sir Walter Scott's *Kenilworth*. Cf., Ward, *The Life of John Henry Cardinal Newman*, 72. Golightly had been an undergraduate of Oriel (1824-1828) and a pupil of Newman. Having taken orders, he had settled in Oxford. He had supported the campaign against Hampden, and Newman had offered to put him in charge of his new chapel at Littlemore, but following upon a row with Pusey over the latter's sermon on postbaptismal sin, the offer was withdrawn. Thereafter Golightly became an ardent opponent of Newman. His campaign against *Tract 90* was but one of many high-profile religious crusades in which he participated. See here Andrew Atherstone, *Oxford's Protestant Spy: The Controversial Career of Charles Golightly* (Milton Keynes: Paternoster Press, 2007).

[80] Letter from T. T. Churton and Others to the Editor of the "Tracts for the Times" (8 March 1841), *LD* viii, 59-60.

On 15 March, the Hebdomadal Board of the University Heads of Houses voted to censure Newman, judging that his "modes of interpretation" were "evading rather than explaining the sense of the Thirty-nine Articles." They added that "reconciling subscription to them with the adoption of errors, which they are designed to counter" defeated their object. As such, *Tract 90* was "inconsistent with the due observance of the [Statutes of this University]." Alongside this round condemnation, the resolution went still further to reference all the *Tracts for the Times* as "a series of anonymous publications purporting to be written by Members of the University, but which are in no way sanctioned by the University itself."[81] As far as the Hebdomadal Board was concerned, Newman's Apostolical school had no home at Oxford.

Positive action to purge the school from Oxford continued apace in the months following the Hebdomadal Board's decision. This signaled a new ascendancy of the Noetics at Oriel. Edward Hawkins made repudiation of *Tract 90* into a litmus test of eligibility for college office and preferment. When Richard Church informed Edward Hawkins of his concurrence with *Tract 90*, Hawkins reportedly said first that he "was a young man and did not know his own mind." He then offered to retain Church as tutor with the proviso that he not lecture on the Articles, but Church declined on the ground that the Oxford statutes made it the duty of tutors to teach the Articles. When Hawkins finally proposed laying things before Vice-Chancellor Philip Wynter, Church replied that he was competent to act by himself, adding that Wynter's decision against him was a foregone conclusion.[82]

Matters were likewise made difficult for senior adherents to the Tractarian school. In the Spring of 1842, a statute was submitted to the Convocation of Oxford to add chairs of ecclesiastical history and pastoral theology to the theological faculty. Edward Pusey's Hebrew chair professor occupied a position that made it doubtful whether he was a theology professor or a professor of language, so the proposed statute led him to request that Vice Chancellor Philip Wynter alter the

---

81 "Censure on Tract 90" (15 March 1841), *LD* viii, 77-78.

82 Frederic Rogers to Miss S. Rogers (27 June 1841), in Gordon Eden Marindin, ed. *The Letters of Frederic Lord Blachford* (London: John Murray, 1896), 105.

languages to explicitly recognize the theological character of his professorship. Wynter replied that the Hebdomadal Board did not wish to interfere with the existing arrangements for old professorships and gestured to Pusey's having a voice as Hebrew professor in the election of examiners. At the same time, however, Renn Dickson Hampden was also making an appeal to Wynter, urging him to remove even this provision from the statute. In a letter dated 27 April 1842, Hampden warned that granting such privilege to Pusey would empower a man who was "identified with a class of theological writers" who had "attracted to them the expostulations of several of our Bishops" and whose *Tracts for the Times* had been "censured by the Hebdomadal Board." In Hampden's opinion, such a person would undoubtedly be "unfriendly to the Reformation and the Protestant establishment of the Church."[83]

"I AM A FOREIGN MATERIAL AND CANNOT ASSIMILATE": A SCHOOL OF PROPHETS EXILED FROM THE CHURCH OF ENGLAND

The actions of the Heads of Houses created no small conflict for the Bishop of Oxford. Richard Bagot was being pressured to publicly condemn *Tract 90*, and the appearance of Newman's letter to Richard Jelf only added fuel to the fire. He wrote to Edward Pusey expressing his "regret" at the appearance of *Tract 90* and communicating his desire "that steps should be promptly taken for removing all grounds for the alarm and offence." While assuring Pusey that Newman would not be obliged "to put forth any opinion which he does not heartily believe," Bagot hinted that some word from Newman, correcting the more extreme implications of his words and adopting "respectful language (and the more cordial the better) in speaking of the formularies of the Church," would be preferable to a public censure delivered by himself

---

[83] Renn Dickson Hampden to Philip Wynter (27 April 1841), in Liddon, *Life of Edward Bouverie Pusey*, vol. 2, 285. W. R. Ward has written of the "consummate egotism" of Newman's read on such events as reflecting, in part, a determinate campaign to curb the influence of his school at Oxford, but one wonders how such lobbying might be interpreted otherwise. See here his *Victorian Oxford*, 110.

or by the English bishops in concert.[84] The letter also contained an attached backchannel communiqué to Newman himself. There Bagot expressed confidence in Newman's best intentions to make the Church of England "more Catholic (in its true sense) and more united," and also stated his "anxious wish that,–for the peace of the Church:–discussions upon the Articles should not be continued in the publications of the 'Tracts for the Times.'" Bagot also pledged that he would "not dispute upon what interpretations may or may not be put upon various articles." Newman accepted the twin correspondence as an offer of a gentleman's "understanding" that *Tract 90* would be allowed to stand without a public censure if he accepted Bagot's terms.[85] He immediately replied that he had no intention of further discussing the Thirty-nine Articles in public.[86] Two days later Newman wrote again, expressing his reasons for publishing *Tract 90* in words that closely adhered to Bagot's hinted expectations to Pusey:

> I assure your Lordship I was altogether unsuspicious that my Tract would make any disturbance. No one can enter into my situation but myself. I see a great many minds working in various directions and a variety of principles with multiplied bearings, I act for the best. I sincerely think that matters would not have gone better for the Church had I never written. And if I write I have a choice of difficulties. It is easy for those who do not enter into these difficulties to say, 'He ought to say this and not say that'; but things are so wonderfully linked together, and I cannot, or rather I would not, be dishonest. When persons too interrogate me, I am obliged in many cases to give an opinion, or I seem to be underhand. Keeping silence looks like artifice. And I do not like persons to consult or to respect me, from thinking differently of my opinions from what I know them to be. And again, to use the proverb, what is one man's food is another man's poison. All these things make my situation very difficult. Hitherto I have been successful in keeping people together–but that a collision must at some time ensue between members of the Church of opposite opinions [sentiments] I have long been aware. The time and mode

---

84 Richard Bagot to Edward Pusey (17 March 1841), *LD* viii, 93-94.
85 Richard Bagot to Newman (17 March 1841), *LD* viii, 94-95.
86 Newman to Richard Bagot (18 March 1841), *LD* viii, 95.

have been in the hand of Providence: I do not mean to exclude my own great imperfections in bringing it about, yet I still feel obliged to think the Tract necessary.[87]

He then concluded his letter with a pledge of willingness to voice "in print anything which I can honestly say to remove false impressions created by the Tract."[88]

Newman privately confided to friends that he had said all that could be said for *Tract 90* in the letter to Richard Jelf. He added only sincere hopes that the bishops would not press him to commit to a narrower view of the Articles.[89] Newman was afraid, too, as he told Pusey, that the older Noetic opponents of his school, the newly-installed Regius Professor of Modern History, Thomas Arnold being most prominent among them, were preparing an attack in order "to *drag out* things from me which I do not wish to say, and which the Bishops would not wish."[90] The danger was that if pressed into a corner, any semblances of equivocation on Newman's part would elicit contempt as well as suspicion, so he again made use of Pusey as a backchannel, confirming his trust that the Richard Bagot would not ask him "to commit myself on points on which I cannot."[91]

---

[87] Newman to Richard Bagot (20 March 1841), *LD* viii, 100-101.

[88] Newman to Richard Bagot (20 March 1841), *LD* viii, 101.

[89] An example both sentiments here would be Newman's letter to Walter Hook, the High Church Vicar of Leeds (19 March 1841), *LD* viii, 99.

[90] Newman to Edward Pusey (20 March 1841), *LD* viii, 103-104. Arnold had written to A. C. Tait on 11 March 1841, thanking him for sending a copy of the Four Tutors' letter and saying, "I am extremely glad that the Tract has been so noticed; yet it is to me far more objectionable morally than theologically; and especially the comment on the 21st Article, to which you have not alluded, is of such a character, that if subscription to the 21st Article, justified by such rules of interpretation, may be honestly practised, I do not see why an Unitarian may not subscribe the first Article or the second. The comparative importance of the truths subscribed to does not affect the question, I am merely speaking of the utter perversion of language shown in the Tract, according to which a man may subscribe to an article when he holds the very opposite opinions,--believing what it denies, and denying what it affirms." Randall T. Davidson and William Benham, *The Life of Archibald Campbell Tait, Archbishop of Canterbury*, vol. 1 (London: Macmillan, 1891), 86-87.

[91] Newman to Edward Pusey (20 March 1841), *LD* viii, 104.

Newman momentarily entertained a notion that "the storm," as he called it, would "blow over." Writing to Arthur Perceval, he conceded that there would inevitably be further "commotion in the country," but his expectation was that only "two or three Bishops" would publicly express themselves against his *Tract*.[92] Following a pressured consultation with Archbishop of Canterbury William Howley the following day, however, Bagot informed Pusey of his wish that the *Tracts* should cease, that *Tract 90* should not be reprinted, and that Newman himself should publish word that he was suppressing both at the behest of his bishop. Upon learning that Bagot had altered their implicit arrangement, Newman was initially ready to comply, but later expressed second thoughts. Withdrawing *Tract 90* was one thing–he had initially offered that very prize without reservation–but the obligation to submit publicly to his bishop's "virtual censure" was another matter entirely. In Newman's estimation, this would signal the bishop's concurrence with the Hebdomadal Board and would effectively outlaw his mode of interpreting the Thirty-nine Articles in the Church of England. As he put it, he was not simply acting on behalf of his own principles; he was representing "a vast number all through the country" who identified with his school and who had come under its influence.[93] If his school would suffer exile from its home in the church as well as in the university, Newman resolved that he would suffer exile along with it.

When Pusey conveyed Newman's sentiments a few days later, Richard Bagot retracted his request. Their negotiated settlement was that Newman would close the *Tracts* immediately rather than waiting for the appearance of two in preparation at the printer. Newman would also be obliged to acknowledge his bishop's judgment that *Tract 90* was "objectionable" for its tendency to "disturb the peace and tranquility of the Church," and agree to cease any further efforts to defend it. For his part, Bagot agreed not to condemn Newman's theological principles nor signal his concurrence with the Hebdomadal Board by forbidding a Catholic reception of the Thirty-nine Articles.

---

[92] Newman to A. P. Perceval (22 March 1841), *LD* viii, 113.
[93] Newman to E. B. Pusey (24 March 1841), *LD* viii, 115-16.

THE PROS AND CONS OF PROVING CANON 221

Newman was able to secure one additional private concession from Bagot and he provoked no small controversy when he publicly disclosed both its content and its practical breach in the *Apologia*. Newman wrote of an "understanding" between himself and Bagot–who, as he left implicit, was representing Archbishop Howley and the other English bishops. Newman would be allowed to continue *Tract 90* on sale and, though individual bishops would not be prevented from conveying opinions of it in their own dioceses, a synod of bishops would not be convened to condemn it. "I agreed to their conditions," Newman recalled, "My one point was to save the Tract."[94] Assessing the nature and reach of the understanding in Newman's report, Edwin Abbot was roundly skeptical, arguing first that there was a "strong *a priori* improbability that the Bishops would so commit themselves." Abbot added that the vague and speculative nature of Newman's report detracted from its veracity.[95] In a second edition of a republished version of *Tract 90*, however, Pusey validated Newman's recollection in a footnote to his "Historical Preface,"

> The fact that the Bishops would not, as a body, censure Tract 90, was told me by the late Bishop of Oxford (Bagot) . . . This Bishop Bagot said to me, not as his own opinion, but on authority (although he did

---

94 Newman, *Apo*, 175.

95 Abbot, *The Anglican Career of Cardinal Newman*, vol. 2, 272. Newman's report of the "understanding" confused friends as well as adversaries. Referring to Newman's account in the *Apologia*, John Coleridge wrote to Newman on 14 October 1864 complaining that the matter had not been explained to his satisfaction. He wondered specifically who had authority to tell Newman that *Tract 90* would not be condemned by his own bishop, Phillpotts of Exeter. Cf., *LD* xxi, 262n2. Newman's reply on 16 October reads, "As to the objection you offer about your own Bishop, the words on which I relied expressly said 'That perhaps *one* or two Bishops would charge, but that would be all–it would not be a general charging.' The Bishops contemplated I conceive to be John B. Sumner and H. Phillpotts." *LD* viii, 123-24n4; Cf., Newman to John Duke Coleridge (16 October 1864), *LD* xxi, 262. It seems that Newman had some vague understanding of a deal in the works by 22 March 1841 as the letter to Perceval above makes clear. This news might have very well come from Jelf, who Newman later said approached him "on the beginning of the row about [*Tract 90*], from Archbishop Howley to say that, if my friends would consent not to move, nothing should be done on the other side." See Newman to W. J. Copeland (1 July 1868), *LD* xxiv, 96.

not tell me what authority). I suppose that *that* authority had miscalculated. Yet it was a very grave matter; for the non-condemnation of Tract 90 was the inducement held out by him why (with materials for another year at least) we should close the series abruptly.[96]

In the end it seems that no gentleman's agreement could head off the mounting controversy. While Newman maintained his public silence and fulfilled his part of the agreement by penning a well-received letter to Bagot three days after their arrangement, he was unable to prevent other members of their school from mounting their own defenses in his stead.

In early April, John Keble released his *Case of Catholic Subscription to the Thirty-Nine Articles Considered: With Especial Reference to the Duties and Difficulties of English Catholics in the Present Crisis*. He argued that the Hebdomadal Board's declaration represented "no *authoritative* censure" of *Tract 90* on the part of the university. Were any similar action to be contemplated by Convocation, Keble warned that it would amount to the establishment of "a new test" and represent "no slight stumbling-block in the way of academical tutors" who might "think it their duty so to interpret ambiguous phrases in the Articles, as to bring them most nearly into conformity with the primitive Church, and to throw no unnecessary censure on other Churches."[97] Given that those serving in the university's tutorial system were "ordained to serve at God's Altar" and called to discharge their duties as "a branch of the Pastoral Care," such persons would be forced either to "teach Catholicism, or not teach at all."[98] Turning his attention to the episcopate of the Church of England, Keble challenged the right of sitting bishops to impose a "particular interpretation," which they might happen to put upon the Articles according to "their own private opinion."[99] Rather, he argued that they too were accountable to "the known judgment of

---

[96] E. B. Pusey, "A Historical Preface," in Newman, *Tract XC. On Certain Passages in the XXXIX Articles* (Oxford: Gilbert and Rivington, 1866), xxvii.

[97] John Keble, *Catholic Subscription to the Thirty-Nine Articles Considered* (Privately Printed, 1841), 11.

[98] Keble, *Catholic Subscription to the Thirty-Nine Articles Considered*, 12.

[99] Keble, *Catholic Subscription to the Thirty-Nine Articles Considered*, 13.

the primitive, and as yet undivided, Church" (that is, the standard of apostolicity). They were likewise obliged to interpret their formularies "so as to cast the least unnecessary censure on other portions of the existing Church" (that is, the standard of catholicity).[100]

The defenses of *Tract 90* mounted by William Ward and Frederick Oakeley were still more strident. In his *A Few Words in Support of No. 90* and *A Few More Words in Support of No. 90*, appearing in April and May of 1841 respectively, Ward moved beyond Newman's "patient of a Catholic interpretation" commonplace to argue that the English Church

> fails in one of her very principal duties, that of witnessing plainly and directly to Catholic truth; that she *seems* to include whom she ought to repel, to teach what she is bound to anathematize; and that it is difficult to estimate the amount of responsibility she year by year incurs on account of those . . . who remain buried in the darkness of Protestant error, because she fails in her duty of holding clearly forth to them the light of Gospel truth.[101]

In Oakeley's July pamphlet, *The Subject of Tract XC. Examined, in Connection with the History of the Thirty-Nine Articles, and the Statements of Certain English Divines*, he not only defended Newman's *Tract*, but also argued that for the English Reformers who had drafted the Articles, "Protestantism was . . . an *after-thought*."[102] Because their pressing concerns were political, rather than religious, he continued, the English reformers had not intended to advance "a comprehensive system." Unlike the Lutheran and Reformed churches, they rather had sought to "remodel the existing, and long-established, English Church."[103] That same month, Oakeley's article on Bishop Jewel appeared in the *British Critic*. He argued there that continued separation from Rome was an "evil" and "a most grievous penalty upon sin *somewhere*; upon

---

[100] Keble, *Catholic Subscription to the Thirty-Nine Articles Considered*, 14.

[101] William Ward, *A Few More Words in Support of No. 90* (Oxford: John Henry Parker, 1841), 29.

[102] Frederick Oakeley, *The Subject of Tract XC. Examined* (London: J. G. F. & J. Rivington, 1841).

[103] Oakeley, *The Subject of Tract XC. Examined*, 17, 26.

the corruption which provoked, or the sacrilege which assailed, or both together."[104] He cautioned, "Let us never plume ourselves upon our isolation, and call it independence" and even commended the Church of Rome as "our 'elder sister' in the Faith" and "our Mother; to whom, by the grace of God, we owe it that we are what we are."[105] Turning to the Thirty-nine Articles, he complained, "without some more stringent test of Catholicity than we are likely to obtain," the English Church would remain "[in the great body of her members,] the *apparent* representative of a very different principle."[106] He concluded that Catholics "must recede more and more from the principles, if any such there be, of the English Reformation."[107]

Although his position as Archbishop of Canterbury granted William Howley the sole authority to convene an episcopal synod, it was beyond his power to prevent bishops from speaking from and for their own charges. Between June 1841 and April 1842, six bishops denounced *Tract 90* in their triennial charges: Edward Maltby of Durham (August 1841), Charles Longley of Ripon (August 1841), John Sumner of Chester (September 1841), his younger brother Charles Sumner of Winchester (September 1841), and James Monk of Gloucester and Bristol (September 1841).[108] Edward Denison of Salisbury, John Beresford of Armagh, Richard Whately of Dublin, and Daniel Wilson of Calcutta likewise criticized it publicly, but it was the charge delivered by Richard Bagot on 23 May 1842 that did Newman the most damage. In his diocesan charge to an assemblage of clergy at St. Mary's that included Newman himself, Bagot again introduced his comments on the Oxford school with words of praise, both for pious aims–the commendation of "self-discipline

---

[104] Frederick Oakeley, "Bishop Jewell," *The British Critic* 30 (1841): 2.

[105] Oakeley, "Bishop Jewell," 3.

[106] Oakeley, "Bishop Jewell," 27.

[107] Oakeley, "Bishop Jewell," 45.

[108] These charges have been collected in an appendix to *LD* viii, 569-92. See also the helpful, if tendentious, work of Simcox Bricknell, *The Judgment of the Bishops on Tractarian Theology* (Oxford: J. Vincent, 1845). By quoting statements delivered by the English Episcopate made from 1837 to 1843, Bricknell makes a formidable case that the bishops of the church had condemned Tractarianism generally and in nearly all particulars.

and self-denial" and "deference to authority," etc.–and for the personal "moderation and forbearance" of its members.[109] Turning to *Tract 90* more particularly, however, he once again restated the sentiments Newman had published at his request, that it was "objectionable, and likely to disturb the peace of the Church." Critically, however, he also added that

> I cannot persuade myself, that any but the plain obvious meaning is the meaning which as members of the Church we are bound to receive; and I cannot reconcile myself to a system of interpretation, which is so subtle, that by it the Articles may be made to mean anything or nothing.[110]

In his letter to Keble the following day, Newman attempted to put the best possible face on Bagot's words, relating that the bishop's remarks were "favorable to us, or rather to our cause" and that any "censure" was applicable only to "*disciples* of the movement."[111] He communicated similar sentiments in letters to Thomas Mozley and Robert Wilberforce the same day and nearly a month later he told his sister, Jemima, of a planned friendly visit by Bagot to Littlemore, reflecting, "It is plain which way he leans, and every thing I hear goes the same way."[112] That same month, however, Bagot's charge set in motion an avalanche of new condemnations from the remainder of the English episcopate. These included Richard Mant of Down, Connor, and Dromore (June 1842); Thomas Musgrave of Hereford (June 1842); Christopher Pepys of Worcester (August 1842); John Kaye of Lincoln (August 1842); Thomas O'Brien of Ossory, Ferns, and Leighlin (September 1842); Edward Denison of Salisbury (September 1842); Henry Phillpotts of Exeter (September 1842); Connop Thirlwall of St. David's

---

[109] Richard Bagot, *A Charge delivered to the Clergy of the Diocese of Oxford*, LD ix, 609-13.

[110] Bagot, *A Charge delivered to the Clergy of the Diocese of Oxford*, LD ix, 608.

[111] Newman to John Keble (24 May 1842), *LD* ix, 14. In this letter Newman is highly selective and, though it is obvious that he made notes of the charge, he acknowledged Bagot's "delicate wording" in places and expressed his desire to see the transcription of the charge when published.

[112] Newman to Mrs. John Mozley (12 June 1842), *LD* ix, 30-31.

(October 1842); Edward Copleston of Llandaff (October 1842); and Charles Blomfield of London (October 1842).

Two bishops died before delivering their forecasted blasts. A fragment survives of the charge that was to be given by Charles Dickinson of Meath in Ireland on the day of his death, 12 July 1842. Although Meath had only written enough to introduce the "Oxford Tractarian School," his remarks portended a robust condemnation, noting the "irregularities" and "insobriety" of the movement and complaining that it "left me altogether doubtful, what it is that they would wish me to believe, or what it is that they themselves believe."[113] Philip Shuttleworth of Chichester died on 7 January 1842, but four years earlier he had written against the Tractarian use of Hawkins's thesis on unauthoritative tradition. Shuttleworth was likewise remembered by Edward Purcell as being "stubborn and rough of tongue toward the Tractarians."[114] Despite the fact that his charge did not survive him, it may be safely assumed that his treatment of *Tract 90* would have been entirely critical.[115]

By the end of 1842, nothing more could be done, and Newman was finally forced to recognize that the cannon had burst. Less than a year following the last of the episcopal charges condemning *Tract 90*, Newman summarized his view of things to Henry Manning:

> The nearest approach I can give to a general account of them is to say that it has been caused by the general repudiation of the view contained in Number 90 on the part of the Church. I could not stand against such an unanimous expression of opinion from the Bishops, supported as it has been by the concurrence, or at least silence, of all classes in the Church, lay and clerical. If ever there was a case in

---

113 Charles Dickinson, *The Remains of the Most Reverend Charles Dickinson, D.D., Lord Bishop of Meath* (London: B. Fellowes, 1845), 217, 219.

114 Edward Purcell, *The Life of Cardinal Manning*, vol. 1 (London: Macmillan and Co., 1896), 196.

115 Like Newman, Shuttleworth made use of patristic sources, but marshaled them to argue that appeals to "floating tradition, containing articles of belief *in addition* or in contradiction to the records of holy writ" better resembled the strategies of heretics–particularly Gnostic heretics–than they did the Catholic fathers. Philip Shuttleworth, *Not Tradition, But Revelation* (London: Rivington, 1838), 2.

which an individual has been put aside, and virtually put away, by a community, mine is one. No decency has been observed in the attacks upon me from authority, no protests have appeared against them. It is felt, I am far from denying justly felt, that I am a foreign material–and cannot assimilate with the Church of England.[116]

Part VI of the *Apologia* begins, "From the end of 1841, I was on my death-bed, as regards my membership with the Anglican Church, though at the time I became aware of it only by degrees."[117] Looking to the Arian controversy that provoked his initial efforts to found a school of traditional religion, he saw anew the very parallel that confronted him while studying the Monophysites in 1839. Now, "the pure Arians were the Protestants, the semi-Arians were the Anglicans, and that Rome now was what it was."[118] Finding no home for his school in Oxford or in the Church of England, Newman slowly reconciled himself to a season of wilderness wandering.

THE JERUSALEM BISHOPRIC: THE ABOMINATION THAT DESOLATES AND PROPHESY FULFILLED

In Newman's reckoning, the Church of England's great sectarian tribulation began on 5 October 1841 with the proposed creation of a Protestant bishopric in Jerusalem.[119] As he later framed it, the move was

---

116 Newman to H. E. Manning (14 October 1843), *LD* ix, 573.

117 Newman, *Apo*, 257.

118 Newman, *Apo*, 243.

119 Copious research has been done on the history of Jerusalem Bishopric and its reception by members of the Oxford Movement. The most recent studies include those of Rowan Strong, "The Oxford Movement and the British Empire: Newman, Manning, and the 1841 Jerusalem Bishopric," in *The Oxford Movement: Europe and the Wider World 1830-1930*, ed. Stewart Brown and Peter Nockles (Cambridge: Cambridge University Press, 2012), 78-98; and Charlotte Van der Leest, "Conversion and Conflict in Palestine: The Missions of the Church Missionary Society and the Protestant Bishop Samuel Gobat" (PhD diss., Universiteit Leiden, 2008). See also Henry Smith, *The Protestant Bishopric in Jerusalem; Its Origins and Progress. From the Official Documents Published by Command of his Majesty the King of Prussia, and from Other Authentic Sources* (London: B. Wertheim, Aldine Chambers, 1847); Paulus

nothing less than an "abomination," signaling the Church of England's determined embrace of Protestantism while it simultaneously acted "to eject from their communion" all who held Catholic doctrine.[120] As Charlotte van der Leest has rightly argued, the conception and creation of the Protestant bishopric in Jerusalem can only be rightly understood from the perspective of the extant rivalries between European Protestants and Roman Catholics. The Prussian diplomat and European Protestant leader, Christian Karl Josias von Bunsen, first conceived the idea in the wake of his deep involvement in the *Kölner Wirren* or "Cologne Troubles" while serving as Prussian envoy to the papal court between 1834 and 1838. Having failed to persuade the Catholic archbishop of Cologne to dispense with a requirement that children from mixed marriages receive a Catholic education, Bunsen had him thrown in prison. When Pius IX remained intransigent, adding his refusal of any further negotiations with Bunsen, the situation became untenable, and in 1838 he was removed from his post. The now stridently anti-Catholic Bunsen then proposed the Jerusalem plan as a means for securing a multinational Christian unity against the Church of Rome. Having gained the approval of the sympathetic Prussian King Frederick William IV, he quickly found support among British evangelicals. Prominent among them was the stalwart anti-Catholic, anti-Tractarian, Lord Anthony Ashley Cooper, who believed that the work would hasten millenarian expectations for the restoration of the Jews to Palestine and the Second Coming of Christ.[121]

Cassel, *Das Bisthum von Jerusalem: Aegypten und Palästina* (Berlin: Kühl, 1882); William Hechler, *The Jerusalem Bishopric: Documents with Translations* (London, 1883); R. W. Greaves, "The Jerusalem Bishopric 1841," *The English Historical Review* 64 (1949): 328-52; P. J. Welch, "Anglican Churchmen and the Establishment of the Jerusalem Bishopric," *Journal of Ecclesiastical History* 8 (1957): 193-204; Abdul Tibawi, *British Interests in Palestine, 1800-1901: A Study of Religious and Educational Enterprise* (Oxford: Oxford University Press, 1961); Owen Chadwick, *The Victorian Church: An Ecclesiastical History of England*, vol. 1 (Oxford: Oxford University Press, 1970), 189-93; Martin Lückhoff, *Anglikaner und Protestanten im Heiligen Land: Das gemeinsame Bistum Jerusalem, 1841-1886* (Wiesbaden: Otto Harrassowitz, 1998).

120 Newman, *Apo*, 264.

121 Van der Leest, "Conversion and Conflict in Palestine," 58; Greaves, "The Jerusalem Bishopric," 332-33. Ashley's reputation as a conspicuous opponent of the

According to Bunsen, it was Ashley who "set the Jerusalem plan a-going" in England, as he made arguments to gather politicians and Church of England prelates to the cause.[122] The plan itself called for a bishop in Jerusalem to take charge of Anglicans, German Lutherans, and any others who elected to come under his jurisdiction. Incumbents would be nominated alternately by the British and Prussian governments with a monetary endowment coming equally from the two countries. Consecrated according to the Anglican Ordinal, he would be authorized to ordain both Anglicans and Lutherans provided that the latter embraced the Thirty-nine Articles as well as their Prussian Church's Augsburg Confession. Support for the plan was immediate and widespread in England, with politicians regarding it as a means of asserting British presence in the Near East, where France and Russia had long enjoyed special prestige as protectors of the Roman Catholic and Orthodox Churches. High Churchmen were pleased with the bequeathal of episcopacy in apostolic succession to Prussia, while Anglican evangelicals were delighted by prospects for a pan-Protestant connection in Europe. Theological liberals rejoiced at the doctrinal compromise such a link necessitated.

Reception of the idea in Tractarian circles proved more complex. William Gladstone, a close supporter of the Tractarians who had journeyed to Oxford to cast his vote against the condemnation of *Tract 90*, was initially supportive. Having been taken into the counsel of Archbishop Howley and Bishop Charles Blomfield of London–the latter being Ordinary to the Anglican Churches of Europe–Gladstone even

---

Oxford Movement was on clear display in 1841-1842 when he served as chairman of the committee that successfully promoted the election of James Garbett over Isaac Williams for the Oxford professorship of poetry. He also campaigned against High Church tendencies within the Church of England, and in 1845 condemned the passing of the Maynooth Act that increased the annual grant from the British government to a Roman Catholic seminary in Ireland. John Wolffe, "Cooper, Anthony Ashley, Seventh Earl of Shaftesbury (1801-1885)," in *Oxford Dictionary of National Biography*, eds. H. C. G. Matthew and Brian Harrison (Oxford: Oxford University Press, 2004).

122 Bunsen to his wife, Frances (13 July 1841) in Frances Waddington Bunsen, *A Memoir of Baron Bunsen*, vol. 1 (London: Longmans Green and Co., 1868), 608.

initially agreed to become a trustee of the Jerusalem Bishopric.[123] Samuel Wilberforce–a less dependable friend than Gladstone, but someone whom Richard Church nevertheless praised as a "thoroughly sincere man, with a very lofty idea of the religious aims to which he devoted all his life"–was likewise persuaded by Blomfield's enthusiastic advocacy.[124] Still more significant was Edward Pusey's welcome of the proposal on the High Church rationale that introduction of apostolic succession in Europe was a desideratum.

Eventually, Gladstone and Pusey both repudiated the project. Gladstone did so on the ground that it appeared to bind the Church of England to objectionable doctrines in the Augsburg Confession, and Pusey because of Bunsen's heterodox views on scripture.[125] Newman, however, was notably constant in his opposition. Upon receiving word of the plan from John Walter III, a fellow of Exeter College, whose father

---

[123] Gladstone communicated his support for the plan and his agreement to serve as a trustee in letters to Blomfield, 28 October 1841, and to Bunsen, 8 November 1841. *Correspondence on Church and Religion of William Ewart Gladstone*, ed. D. C. Lathbury, vol. 1 (New York: Macmillan, 1910), 236-38, 244-47. Cf., P. J. Welch, "Anglican Churchmen and the Establishment of the Jerusalem Bishopric," 196. Pusey's essay, "Bunsen on the Chronology of Holy Scripture," was part of the *Christian Remembrancer*'s more general case that the plan would "Judaize" and "Protestantize" the Church of England. *The Christian Remembrancer* 12 (1846): 298-324.

[124] R. W. Church to Dr. Asa Gray, 25 July 1873, in Richard Church, *The Life and Letters of Dean Church*, 239-40. Blomfield's enthusiasm for the Jerusalem Bishopric was driven by his commitment to the evangelization of the Jewish people. He even published his 4 May 1843 sermon on the subject, delivered before the London Society for Promoting Christianity amongst the Jews. There he argued (interestingly, borrowing the words of the millenarian Baptist minister Andrew Fuller) that "There is *nothing in the religion of the Jews, or at least in that which they profess*, to disqualify them altogether for embracing the Gospel." Charles Blomfield, *God's Ancient People Not Cast Away* (London: B. Fellowes, 1843), 14. Cf., Andrew Fuller, *Jesus the True Messiah*, 3rd ed. (London: B. R. Goakman, 1810), 15; Welch, "Anglican Churchmen and the Establishment of the Jerusalem Bishopric," 193-96.

[125] Gladstone particularly objected to language in the Augsburg Confession that condemned anyone denying that it is a sin to doubt their own pardon and acceptance by God (Cf., Article 20). William Gladstone to Charles Blomfield, 30 November 1841, in Lathbury, *Correspondence on Church and Religion of William Ewart Gladstone*, 249-54. Pusey's letter, "Bunsen on the Chronology of Holy Scripture," appeared alongside "Judaism and the Jerusalem Bishoprick," *The Christian Remembrancer* 12 (1846): 298-324, 222-88.

was editor of the *Times*, Newman immediately shared it with Keble, attaching his own cover letter:

> I inclose you, what will be no consolation, but think you ought to see it. It really does seem to me as if the Bishops were doing their best to uncatholicize us–and whether they will succeed before a rescue comes, who can say? The Bishop of Jerusalem is to be consecrated forthwith–perhaps in a few days–Mr Bunsen is at the bottom of the whole business, who, I think I am right in saying, considers the Nicene Council the first step in the corruption of the Church.[126]

Newman and Froude had met Bunsen at Rome in 1833. His remark regarding the latter's opinion of the Council of Nicea probably arose from his recollection of a letter he had received from Thomas Dyke Acland while the latter was in Bologna during May of 1834. Acland reported Bunsen's having read *Arians of the Fourth Century* and commenting that "the council of Nicaea was the beginning of Popery, of adding an authority to Scripture."[127] As for Lord Ashley, Newman had once recognized his potential value as a cobelligerent in the controversy with Hampden but knew him primarily as an opponent who had been a source of considerable vexation.[128]

In the end, Newman judged that the Church of England was "courting an intercommunion with Protestant Prussia and the heresy of Orientals" while forbidding him "any sympathy or concurrence with the church of Rome."[129] This move recapitulated the English Reformers' subverting collaboration with continental Protestant advisors in the 1540s, but it went still further in giving them an unprecedented, anti-ecclesial form. As he put things to his sister, Jemima, "The Church [was] actually *changing* her position, by forming a special league ... with the foreign Protestants."[130] Such high stakes led Newman to breaking his self-imposed silence following the *Tract 90* episode. The

---

[126] Newman to John Keble (5 October 1841), *LD* viii, 286,

[127] Thomas Dyke Ackland to Newman (11 May 1834), *LD* iv, 257.

[128] Newman to E. B. Pusey (29 March 1840), *LD* vii, 283.

[129] Newman, *Apo*, 248.

[130] Newman to Mrs J. Mozley (21 November 1841), *LD* viii, 340.

conclusion of his formal protest portended far more than Newman's estimation of the Jerusalem Bishopric:

> I in my place, being a priest of the English Church and Vicar of St Mary the Virgin's, Oxford, by way of relieving my conscience, do hereby solemnly protest against the measure aforesaid, and disown it, as removing the English Church from her present ground [as "a branch of the Catholic Church"] and tending to her disorganization.[131]

Only a few days prior to the anniversary of Bagot's remarks on *Tract 90*, Newman confided to Keble his consideration that "the Roman Catholic Communion [was] the Church of the Apostles, and that what grace is among us (which, through God's mercy, is not little,) is extraordinary, and from the overflowings of His Dispensation."[132] Within months Newman resigned the vicarate of St. Mary's, and two years after, he resigned as a fellow of Oriel College, leaving him free to continue his theological sojourn elsewhere.

In keeping with his understanding of the prophetical office, *Tract 90* proposed a way for the Church of England to embrace a developed self-understanding and to thereby reconcile apostolicity and catholicity within its confines. The Jerusalem Bishopric was important to Newman for the way that it confirmed the Church of England's determinate sectarian course. Far from representing a move toward Christian unity in Europe or the bequeathal of apostolic succession to Lutheranism, Newman saw the Jerusalem Bishopric as a decisive embrace of Protestantism and the triumph of a very different school from that for which he had been contending.

A PROPHET FINALLY WELCOMED

John Henry Newman was a theological dissident throughout his Anglican sojourn, and this mode of prophetic existence would continue through most of his life as a Roman Catholic. His commitment to catholicity standing alongside apostolicity as a theological duty

---

[131] "Protest Against the Jerusalem Bishopric" (11 November 1841), *LD* viii, 328.
[132] Newman to John Keble (II) (4 May 1843), *LD* ix, 328.

stirred controversy in both Christian communions. As an Anglican, his attempt to rectify the Church of England's self-understanding in a new, Catholic reception of the Thirty-nine Articles was met with official condemnation and exile by the University of Oxford and by the English episcopate. As a Roman Catholic, Newman's commitment to the theological consultation of the laity and a corresponding resistance to neo-ultramontanist usurpations by the regal office of the church, led to a similar disapproval and exile. These condemnations, official and unofficial, and his consequent exiles came to something of a conclusion as he approached his seventy-seventh birthday.

On 14 December 1877, Newman received an invitation from S. W. Wayte, President of Trinity College, Oxford, to accept an honorary fellowship. This was no small honor as Wayte's letter read, "I may mention that if you should do so, you will be the first person in whose case the College will have exercised the power which was given to it in 1857, and that at present it is not contemplated to elect another Honorary Fellow."[133] Having satisfied himself of the compatibility of the honor with his vows as an Oratorian and encouraged by his bishop, William Ullathorne, to accept the offer with its pledge of "a renewal of good feeling between your old College and yourself," Newman agreed. In February of 1878 he visited the university wherein he first made his home as a young man. While there, he called on his friend, Edward Pusey, surveyed the newly-founded Keble College, and visited Oriel College.

Just prior to his restoration to favor at Oxford, Pope Pius IX died and was succeeded on 20 February 1878 by Leo XIII. The Birmingham Oratory was then enjoying something of a revival with the reception of several new novices and several Catholic laypersons. The Duke of Norfolk, Edward Howard, and the Marquis of Ripon, George Frederick Samuel Robinson, being prominent among them, proposed that the Holy See should honor Newman by making him a cardinal. Margaret Dunn, who was then employed at the French Embassy in Rome, was subsequently introduced to Leo XIII as a penitent of Newman's during a papal audience. The new pope entrusted her with a gift to Newman of

---

[133] Samuel William Wayte to Newman (14 December 1877), *LD* xxviii, 279n4.

an autographed picture of Our Lady of Lourdes from his breviary.[134] This gift was followed by the offer of the cardinalate at the end of January 1879. Following an agonizing six-week interim–the delay resulting from stalwart opposition by neo-ultramontanist oppugners–Newman received the official Biglietto announcing the honor on 18 March 1879. Leo XIII's words to Lady Sophia Palmer during a papal audience on 26 January 1888 makes clear that the honor was intended as commendation of Newman as a *catholic* theologian: "My Cardinal! it was not easy, it was not easy. They said he was too liberal, but I had determined to honour the Church in honouring Newman. I always had a cult for him. I am proud that I was able to honour such a man."[135]

Newman's restoration at Oxford and his elevation to the Roman Catholic Cardinalate are significant for the way that they signal the reclamation of a school as well as the recovery of a man. Though neither act functioned to revoke previous judgments or alter church teaching, both signaled the possibility of a new reception of Newman and of his expression of the prophetical office. That this possibility was in some fashion embraced by representatives of the apostolical office–the Bishop of Rome being most prominent among them–illustrates the durability of Newman's three-office ecclesiological schema. In honoring such a man, Leo XIII opened a way to honor Newman's prophetical school to speak again. Developments toward apostolic and catholic concord in doctrine between the Church of England and the Church of Rome testify to its ongoing fruitfulness.

---

134 *LD* xxviii, 435n1. The picture is still present in Newman's room at the Birmingham Oratory.

135 Lady Laura Ridding, *Sophia Matilda Palmer, comtesse de Franqueville, 1852-1915, A Memoir* (London: Macmillan, 1919), 190. Cf., Appendix I, *LD* xxix, 426.

CONCLUSION

A School *and* An Agitating Party

> We have nothing which deserves the name of a School among us; but we have, in that lamentable absence, one large active agitating Party, bound together, not (as a School) by common views founded on learning, but by common vulgar mischievous feelings based in ignorance. And to oppose this, what have we? Nothing but individual and isolated efforts of solitary students, and the somewhat low tone of the mass. There is no value for deep learning or for thorough knowledge of Antiquity; and still less for those great Catholic principles on which alone (under God's blessing) reliance can be placed. There are no heads to guide, no strong hand to rule us. We are like sheep without a shepherd. The very magnitude of the evil has produced something of a reaction and feeling after a better state of things.
>
> –Hugh James Rose to Edward Bouverie Pusey, 30 April 1836[1]

As I argued previously, John Henry Newman hoped that his two *Tracts* against Romanism would finally immunize his Tractarian school against accusations of Roman Catholic sympathy. While prosecuting his case, however, he could not resist a corresponding inclination to chasten the Church of England for its neglect of key early Christian teachings and practices. Despite Newman's hastening to add that the neglect was less blameworthy than the positive errors introduced by Rome, he stalwartly maintained that

---

[1] This letter appears in John William Burgon, *The Lives of Twelve Good Men*, vol. 1 (London: John Murray, 1889), 207. Rose's side of this exchange with Pusey and later with Newman does not appear in Liddon's biography of Pusey or in Newman's *Letters and Diaries*.

the English Reformation had bequeathed an "incomplete and defective" settlement, leading to a "false meaning" England's reception of the Christian faith.[2] Here Newman went so far as to concede that the church of his baptism was "*incomplete* even in its formal doctrine and discipline."[3]

This habitual comingling of anti-Roman and anti-Protestant sentiment in Newman's critique provoked as much consternation in his day as it has in our own. Where Frank Turner has made Newman's remarks an occasion to argue the attack on Protestantism was Newman's true intent all along, Hugh Rose stood to defend the integrity of English High Churchmanship and denied that Newman's Apostolicals could function as a "*substantive* School of Divinity" unto itself.[4] Rose had long been fearful that the unrestrained appeal to antiquity might lead to his abandonment of the "older and sounder views" of traditional High Churchmanship. To his mind, Newman's intentions were overambitious and courted political disaster. As things stood, Newman was laboring so far ahead of the skirmish lines as to be mistaken for an enemy.

Rose's concerns notwithstanding, Newman could not be moved from his conviction that "the Anglican system of doctrine" was in fact "not *complete*." There were "hiatuses which [had] never been filled up" so that one wished for more.[5] Not content with arguing for a simple *ressourcement* in the "system of divinity" bequeathed by England's venerable Divines, Newman was advancing a genuine *aggiornamento* wherein his Tractarian school would "grant . . . one or two points which in *our private judgments* might be added."[6] As Newman put it, "The 1688 Protestantism will upset us, if we confine ourselves to it. Again it strikes

---

2 Burgon, *The Lives of Twelve Good Men*, vol. 3, 30.

3 Newman, *Tract 71*.

4 Hugh James Rose to Edward Bouverie Pusey, 30 April 1836, in Burgon, *The Lives of Twelve Good Men*, vol. 1, 207. Rose's side of this exchange with Pusey and later with Newman does not appear in Liddon's biography of Pusey or in Newman's *Letters and Diaries*.

5 Burgon, *The Lives of Twelve Good Men*.

6 Burgon, *The Lives of Twelve Good Men*. Emphasis mine.

me, if we *are* reviving things, why not, while we are about it raise them a peg or two higher, if the position gained be truer and securer?"[7]

This brief *tête-à-tête* between Rose and Newman is instructive for the clear alternatives it presents–alternatives in sentiment and in vision that explain the impossibility of any long-term, fruitful collaboration between the Tractarians and traditional High Churchmen. The cleavage was there from the initial meeting at Rose's rectory in Hadleigh, of course, but it steadily widened as Newman's school progressed from noble idea to embodied form. While Rose was laboring on a project of recovery, championing a return to High Church virtues and values as the hope of English Christianity, Newman was pressing toward a constructive end–a properly theological end that, while grounded in history and its traditionary religion, also contemplated much more than his understated "one or two points," raised "a peg or two higher." Newman's attainment of a "truer and securer" foundation for the faith required the rectification of false developments in doctrine so that faithful developments–*catholic* as well as *apostolic* developments–might emerge in their place. His willingness to positively commend the collective product of his schools' "private judgments" (plural), using terminology that had been so repugnant to him from the late 1820s, is a powerful indicator of his intentions by the time he commenced the theological lectures in Adam de Brome Chapel.

John William Burgon's editorial comment on their exchange could not have been more critical, but his exasperated conclusion at Newman's thinking that theology's purpose was "to *exaggerate* sacred Truth" and "to *startle* mankind" unwittingly gestures at the crowning breakthrough of Newman's theological career.[8] Newman did, in fact, believe that the "office of a theologian" or "the business of a Divine" was prophetic in nature and form. Simply put, the prophetic disclosure of the rule and reign of God characteristically sounds like startling exaggeration and distressing agitation in the ears of those who are comfortable

---

[7] Burgon, *The Lives of Twelve Good Men*, vol. 5, 295.

[8] Burgon, *The Lives of Twelve Good Men*, vol. 1, 224.

and contented in with the status quo.[9] So Rose's alternative, that is, a "School" or "a large active agitating *Party*," is a false alternative.

But this leaves the problem of how of how the church is to discern between the private judgment of a school of prophets in service to apostolic and catholic truth and the private judgment of false prophets in service to liberalism and apostasy. For Newman, this began with a proper distinction between the prophetical office and the apostolical office and the proper place of both within the church.

PLACING THE PROPHET WITHIN THE PROPHETICAL OFFICE OF THE CHURCH

Throughout this book I have attempted to highlight the genesis and early development of Newman's conception of theologians–St. Vincent's "doctores" or "tractatores"–as proper heirs of the prophets in the Hebrew Bible, the New Testament, and in early Christianity. While it is not always easy to see which came first–the concept or the man–it remains important to observe how they sprang up together in Newman's imagination. I have charted Newman's early evangelical awakening as shepherded along by Walter Mayers's suggested reading. Thomas Scott's twin passion for doctrinal orthodoxy and personal holiness combined with Joseph Milner's narrations of God's providential effusions of grace to set a context for a young man with a divine mission in the world. Newton's *Dissertation on the Prophesies* could only heighten Newman's sense that the present moment could be charged with kairotic significance. While the rigors of Oriel College occasioned a theological departure from the evangelical school, it did little to extinguish the evangelical fervor in the man. Whether combating the heretical subversions of his brothers and students or taking arms against the liberal subversion of Christian England, Newman's life continued to manifest the unmistakable stamp of the onetime hothouse evangelical. By the time he penned *The Arians of the Fourth Century*, he had long surpassed Milner's elementary lessons in the Christian history, but he never lost Milner's sense that the same God was at work in all history–especially

---

[9] Burgon, *The Lives of Twelve Good Men*, vol. 1, 224.

his own. This warranted his prophetic rhetoricisations, delivered in the apocalyptic register of a man who could liken himself to a new Athanasius or Gregory Nazianzus, summoning a new generation of Ambrosian bishops to the proper governance of the church.

It was finally in the fires of his meandering controversy with Abbé Jean-Nicolas Jager that Newman's instincts were crowned with a proper name. In the rhetorical hopscotch from John Jebb and Alexander Knox to Vincent of Lérins, Newman neglected to mention that it was from the latter that he first drew inspiration to speak of theology as a prophetical office, an office distinct from the regal office of church's apostolic episcopate and its sacerdotal office of priests. Far from risking artificiality, as Paul Misner has feared, Newman stumbled on a rich inheritance that preceded Vincent by over 400 years, finding warrant at the font of the Christian faith in the earliest writings of the New Testament.[10]

---

10 Vincent's connection between Christian prophesy and the theological office of the church is demonstrably viable from a historical-critical point of view. Rudolf Bultmann was the first to break with the highly influential thesis of Adolf von Harnack that there was in early Christianity a hard distinction between the catholic-charismatic offices of early Christian apostles, prophets, and teachers and the parochial-pedestrian offices of local bishops, presbyters, and deacons. See, Adolf von Harnack, "Die Lehre der zwölf Apostel: Prolegomena," in *Texte und Untersuchungen zur Geschicte der altchristlichen Leteratur*, vol. 2 (Leipzig: J. C. Hinrichs, 1884), 88-158. See also his *Die Mission und Ausbreitung des Christentums in den ersten dre Jahrhunderten*, 4th ed., vol. 1 (Leipzig: J. C. Hinrichs, 1924), 354. Making use of the form critical method (*Formgeschichte*) pioneered by Old Testament scholar, Herman Gunkel, Bultmann rejected Harnack's bifurcation of "church offices (*Kirchenämter*) and community offices (*Gemeindeämter*), arguing instead that early Christianity recognized no clear distinction between directly-inspired charismatic utterances of the Holy Spirit through the prophets and the sayings of the historical Jesus as they were transmitted by traditional means. The latter, as Bultmann argued, were not "the pronouncements of a past authority, but sayings of the risen Lord who is always a contemporary for the Church." Rudolf Bultmann, *The History of the Synoptic Tradition*, trans. John Marsh (Oxford: Blackwell, 1963), 127-28. This opened the door for Bultmann's student, Ernst Käsemann, to argue that the proper *Sitz im Leben* of New Testament prophetic speech was that of the church, with its apocalyptic expectation of an imminent end and its prophet-leaders expounding the *kerygmatic* testimony of Jesus as "holy law." By "holy law" here he meant words of guidance, instruction, admonition, and encouragement derived from the church's remembrances of the words and works of Jesus. Hence, as Käsemann put it, "primitive Christian prophesy 'judges' the messianic people of God, as one the old prophets 'judged' Israel." As he more succinctly put it, these "sentences of holy

To these insights we then add Newman's efforts after 1835 to act as the faithful child, attempting to "set right" mother church, without diminishing "her prerogative of teaching," nor shirking his duty of receiving it dutifully.

This carefully configured balance, faithful child to mother church, is important in Newman's overall thinking. His prophet only finds a proper role within the prophetical office of the church. This, I think, is what finally distinguishes his school's collective private judgment from the radically autonomous, even anti-ecclesial, private judgment he associated with evangelicalism and liberalism.

---

law"–the products of New Testament prophesy–marked "the beginnings of Christian theology." Ernst Käsemann, "Sentences of Holy Law in the New Testament," in *New Testament Questions of Today*, trans. W. A. Montague (Philadelphia: Fortress, 1969), 79. See also his "The Beginnings of New Testament Theology," in *New Testament Questions of Today*, trans. W. A. Montague (Philadelphia: Fortress, 1969), 82-107. David Hill, Eugene Boring, Thomas Gillespie, and more recently, Michael Bird have each gone on to develop Käsemann's fundamental insight, adding texture and depth to this hypothesis and strengthening it in significant ways. All of them strongly validate Newman's attempt to name the early Christian consensus linking the ministry of the prophets in the Hebrew Bible and in the New Testament to the sub-Apostolic office of Christian theology. See, Eugene Boring, "Christian Prophesy and the Sayings of Jesus: The State of the Question," *New Testament Studies* 29 (1983): 104-12; Eugene Boring, *The Continuing Voice of Jesus: Christian Prophesy and the Gospel Tradition* (Louisville, KY: Westminster/John Knox Press, 1991); Eugene Boring, *Sayings of the Risen Jesus: Christian Prophesy in the Synoptic Tradition* (Cambridge: Cambridge University Press, 1982); David Hill, "Christian Prophets as Teachers or Instructors in the Church," in *Prophetic Vocation in the New Testament and Today*, ed. J. Panagopolous (Leiden: E. J. Brill, 1977); David Hill, *New Testament Prophesy* (Atlanta: John Knox Press, 1979); David Hill, "On the Evidence for the Creative Role of Christian Prophets," *New Testament Studies* 20 (1973-1974): 262-74. Michael F. Bird, *The Gospel of the Lord: How the Early Church Wrote the Story of Jesus* (Grand Rapids: Eerdmans, 2014), 119-24. While Boring, Hill, and Bird have concentrated on the Gospels, Gillespie's work is especially important for his concentration on an even earlier stratum of New Testament teaching in the works of the Apostle Paul. Thomas Gillespie, *The First Theologians: A Study in Early Christian Prophesy* (Grand Rapids: Eerdmans, 1994).

CONCLUSION

LOCATING THE SCHOOL IN NEWMAN'S *SCHOLA THEOLOGORUM*

If we must properly place the prophets as a counterpoint to the apostles within the church, so too must we locate Newman's exemplary Anglican school as a thickening precedent to his Roman Catholic understanding of the *schola theologorum*. His school of Anglican theologians, gathered deliberately and principally at Oxford, marked the genesis point, proving ground, and ever-present milieu for Newman's evolving thought on the ecclesial vocation of the theologian. I have highlighted the importance of the Oriel Noetics as a second school, helping to see the limits of evangelicalism while remaining unable of itself to ultimately escape the dangers of liberal apostasy. I have also traced Newman's attempts to reform the Oriel tutorial system under the pastoral banner of theological orthodoxy and personal holiness. This effort marked his first theological challenge to the *saeculum* and so it became, with Keble and Froude close at hand, his school's natal form. Newman's rhetoricisations of early Christian history in *The Arians of the Fourth Century* established a precedent for his own school of traditionary religion at Oxford. I have shed light on the witnesses to the university's key importance as a place and a counterpointed ecclesial power in Newman's reckoning.

While Newman's theological development took center stage in my fourth chapter, the school at Oxford never entirely receded. Newman conceived his role in the debate with Jager as that of an Oxford theologian. His key developments in the course of the debate were prompted by the contributions and critique of fellow schoolmen, Froude and Harrison. These gave rise to theological lectures and a theological society that would have been impossible outside his university context. Chapter five chronicled Newman's final work as an Anglican, attempting to fully embody his prophetical office within a prophetical school, illuminating the Church of England's documents, harmonizing its contents, and applying its promises. When his efforts were finally and undeniably rejected by Oxford and the English episcopate together, Newman's prophetical school–at least the portion he recognized as his own–followed him into exile at Littlemore and then on to Rome.

Given that individual theologians are not omnicompetent, nor alike focused on the same set of *loci communes theologici*, Newman believed that they ought to consult, collaborate, and contend with one another as part of their theological work. His close companionship with Froude and Keble is, of course, key in this respect, but so also is his collaboration with Harrison and Sancta Clara and his contention with Jager and Hampden. While Newman's later Benedictine and Augustinian monastic exemplars are less accessible in a modern context, there is yet something to be learned from what he spoke of as the "monastic element" in theological work. At Oriel and again at St. Aldate's and Littlemore, Newman aimed to create a culture of mutual implication and filial trust that extended beyond the professional social interactions that characterize contemporary academic life and its processes of peer review. This thick description of Newman's progress as an Anglican, joining his prophetical office of the church to an embodied *schola theologorum* at Oxford, prefigures all that he wrote on the latter subject as a Roman Catholic.

Stephen Sykes has quipped that "Newman was constitutionally incapable of reflecting any tradition of discourse without at the same time transforming it."[11] I wonder, however, if that is not an apt description of all theologians who are worthy of the name. As Catherine Clifford and Richard Gaillardetz have said, "the work of theology goes beyond the merely catechetical to consider how the legitimate interpretations of the pronouncement are to be appropriated, particularly in historical and cultural contexts often quite different from those in which the formulations first emerged."[12] Newman's project exemplified this impulse, pushing the Church of England to listen, to remember, to reflect, and to rectify an underdeveloped self-understanding. His project continued to exemplify this impulse in a new, Roman Catholic home wherein he lived out the second half of his life. Newman's best testimony to his vision for the ecclesial vocation of a prophet-theologian was his own life, struggling through times of exclusion and embrace, assuming the burden of being labeled a sometimes-false, sometimes true-prophet, and facing the seasons of exile and return that inevitably came with it.

---

[11] Stephen Sykes, *The Identity of Christianity* (Philadelphia: Fortress, 1984), 102.

[12] Catherine Clifford and Richard Gaillardetz, "Re-Imagining the Ecclesial/Prophetic Vocation of the Theologian," *CTSA Proceedings* 65 (2010): 58.

BIBLIOGRAPHY

ARCHIVAL SOURCES

"Theological Society Rules and Bye Laws." *Pusey Papers*. Pusey House: Oxford University.

Kenneth L. Parker, Oriel College Senior Library Records. *NINS Digital Collections*. https://digitalcollections.newmanstudies.org/library-records.

PRINT SOURCES

Abbott, Edwin. *The Anglican Career of John Henry Newman*. 2 vols. London: Macmillan and Co., 1892.

Acheson, Alan. *Bishop John Jebb and the Nineteenth-Century Anglican Revival*. Toronto: Clements Academic, 2013.

Allen, Louis, ed. *John Henry Newman and the Abbé Jager*. London: Oxford University Press, 1975.

Anonymous. *Ritual Notes on the Order of Divine Service*. Oxford: Mowbray, 1894.

Aquino, Frederick D. *Communities of Informed Judgment: Newman's Illative Sense and Accounts of Rationality*. Washington, DC: Catholic University of America, 2004.

Atherstone, Andrew. *Oxford's Protestant Spy: The Controversial Career of Charles Golightly*. Milton Keynes: Paternoster Press, 2007.

Avis, Paul. *Anglicanism and the Christian Church: Theological Resources in Historical Perspective*. Revised and expanded edition. London: T and T Clark, 2002.

Balleine, George Reginald. *A History of the Evangelical Party in the Church of England*. London: Longmans, Green, and Co, 1908.

Barr, Colin. *Paul Cullen, John Henry Newman, and the Catholic University of Ireland, 1845-1864*. Notre Dame, IN: University of Notre Dame Press, 2003.

Barr, James. *Semantics of Biblical Language*. Oxford: Oxford University Press, 1961.

Beale, G. K. *The Book of Revelation*. New International Greek Testament Commentary. Grand Rapids, MI: Eerdmans, 1999.

Bebbington, David. *Evangelicalism in Modern Britain: A History from the 1730s to the 1980s*. 2nd edition. London: Routledge, 1989.

Bentley, James. *Ritualism and Politics in Victorian Britain: The Attempt to Legislate for Belief*. Oxford: Oxford University Press, 1978.

Berger, Peter. *The Heretical Imperative*. New York: Anchor/Doubleday, 1979.

Biemer, Günter. *Überlieferung und Offenbarung: die Lehre von der Tradition nach John Henry Newman*. Freiburg: Herder, 1961.

Blehl, Vincent Farrar. *Pilgrim Journey: John Henry Newman 1801-1845*. New York: Paulist, 2001.

Blomfield, Charles. *God's Ancient People Not Cast Away*. London: B. Fellowes, 1843.

Boff, Leonardo. *Church: Charism and Power: Liberation Theology*. New York: Crossroad, 1985.

Boyle, John. *Church Teaching Authority: Historical and Theological Studies*. Notre Dame, IN: University of Notre Dame Press, 1995.

Bricknell, Simcox. *The Judgment of the Bishops on Tractarian Theology*. Oxford: J. Vincent, 1845.

Brilioth, Yngve. *The Anglican Revival: Studies in the Oxford Movement*. London: Longmans, Green, 1925.

Bromiley, Geoffrey, trans. *Theological Dictionary of the New Testament*, ed. G. Kittel and G. Friedrich, 10 vols. Grand Rapids, MI: Eerdmans, 1964-1976.

Brown, Desmond. *Paul Cardinal Cullen and the Shaping of Modern Irish Catholicism*. Dublin: Gill and Macmillan, 1983.

Bunsen, Frances Waddington. *A Memoir of Baron Bunsen*. 2 vols. London: Longmans, Green, and Co., 1868.

Burgon, John William. *Lives of Twelve Good Men*. 2 vols. 2nd edition. London: John Murray, 1888.

Capps, Donald. "John Henry Newman: A Study of Vocational Identity." *Journal for the Scientific Study of Religion* 9, no. 1 (Spring 1970): 33-51.

Carson, Donald A. *Evangelicalism: What is it and is it Worth Keeping*. Wheaton, IL: Crossway, 2012.

Cassel, Paulus. *Das Bisthum von Jerusalem: Aegypten und Palästina*. Berlin: Kühl, 1882.

Chadwick, Owen. *From Bossuet to Newman.* 2nd edition. Cambridge: Cambridge University Press, 1987.

———. *The Mind of the Oxford Movement.* Library of Modern Religious Thought. London: A. and C. Black, 1960.

———. *Newman.* Oxford: Oxford University Press, 1983.

———. "The Oxford Movement and its Reminiscencers." In *The Spirit of the Oxford Movement: Tractarian Essays.* 135-53. Cambridge: Cambridge University Press, 1990.

———. *The Victorian Church: An Ecclesiastical History of England.* 2 vols. Oxford: Oxford University Press, 1970.

Church, Richard. *Life and Letters of Dean Church.* Edited by Mary C. Church. London: Macmillan, 1894.

———. *The Oxford Movement: Twelve Years, 1833-1845.* London: Macmillan and Co., 1891.

Clark, J. C. D. *English Society, 1660-1832: Religion, Ideology, and Politics During the Ancien Regime.* 2nd ed. Cambridge: Cambridge University Press, 2000.

Clifford, Catherine and Richard Gaillardetz. "Re-Imagining the Ecclesial/Prophetic Vocation of the Theologian." *CTSA Proceedings* 65 (2010): 43-62.

Coleridge, John Taylor. *A Memoir of the Rev. John Keble, M. A., Late Vicar of Hursley.* 2 vols. 2nd edition. New York: Pott and Amery, 1869.

Congar, Yves Congar. "Sur la Trilogie 'Prophète-Roi-Prêtre.'" *Revue des Sciences Philosophiques et Théologiques* 67, no. 1 (1983): 97-116.

Congregation for the Doctrine of the Faith. *Donum Veritatis: On the Ecclesial Role of the Theologian.* Vatican City: Librereia Editrice Vaticana, 1990.

———. "Instruction on the Ecclesial Vocation of the Theologian." *Origins* 20 (5 July 1990): 117-26.

Coulson, John. *Newman and the Common Tradition: A Study in the Language of Church and Society.* Oxford: Clarendon, 1970.

Coulson, John, ed. *On Consulting the Faithful in Matters of Doctrine.* New York: Sheed and Ward, 1961.

Coulson, John and A. M. Allchin. *The Rediscovery of Newman: An Oxford Symposium.* London: Sheed and Ward/S.P.C.K., 1967.

Cunningham, Lawrence, "Review of Frank Turner's *John Henry Newman: The Challenge to Evangelical Religion.*" *Horizons* 30, no. 1 (Spring 2003): 144-46.

Curran, Charles E. and Richard A. McCormick, S.J., eds. *Readings in Moral Theology.* No. 3: *The Magisterium and Morality.* New York/Ramsey NJ: Paulist, 1982.

———. *Readings in Moral Theology*. No. 6: *Dissent in the Church*. New York/ Mahwah NJ: Paulist, 1988.

Cutler, A. Dwight. *The Imperial Intellect: A Study of Newman's Educational Ideal*. New Haven, CT. Yale University Press, 1955.

Daley, Brian. "The Church Fathers." In *The Cambridge Companion to John Henry Newman*. Edited by Ian Ker and Thomas Merrigan, 29-46. Cambridge: Cambridge University Press, 2009.

Davidson, Randall T. and William Benham, *The Life of Archibald Campbell Tait, Archbishop of Canterbury*. 2 vols. London: Macmillan, 1891.

Davies, Horton. *Worship and Theology in England*. 5 vols. Princeton, NJ: Princeton University Press, 1961-1975.

Dawson, Christopher. *The Spirit of the Oxford Movement*. Reprint. London: St. Austin, 2001.

Denzinger, Heinrich, Adolf Schönmetzer, and Peter Hünermann. *Enchiridion symbolorum, definitionum et declarationum de rebus fidei et morum*. 43rd edition. San Francisco: Ignatius, 2012.

De Saussure, Ferdinand. *Course in General Linguistics*. Translated by R. Harris. Peru, IL: Open Court, 1986.

Dessain, Charles Stephen. *John Henry Newman*. London: Thomas Nelson, 1966.

———. "Newman's First Conversion." *Newman Studien* 3 (1957): 44-59.

Dickinson, Charles. *The Remains of the Most Reverend Charles Dickinson, D.D. Lord Bishop of Meath*. London: B. Fellowes, 1845.

Dockery, John B. *Christopher Davenport: Friar and Diplomat*. London: Burns and Oates, 1960.

Donovan, Leo, ed. *Cooperation Between Theologians and the Ecclesial Magisterium*. Washington DC: Canon Law Society of America, 1982.

Dulles, Avery. *John Henry Newman*. New York: Continuum, 2002.

———. "Newman and the Hierarchy." *Newman Studies Journal* 2, no. 1 (Spring 2005): 8-19.

Ellis, Heather. *Generational Conflict and University Reform: Oxford in the Age of Revolution*. Leiden: Brill, 2012.

Femiano, Samuel. *Infallibility of the Laity: The Legacy of Newman*. New York: Herder, 1967.

Flemming, Amelia, "The Role of the Theologian, *Donum Veritatis*, and Newman." *Irish Theological Quarterly* 69, no. 3 (September 2004): 263-79.

Forrester, Charles, ed. *Thirty Years' Correspondence Between John Jebb, D.D., F. R. S., Bishop of Limerick, Adfert, and Aghadoe and Alexander Knox, Esq., M. R. I. A.*, 2 vols. Philadelphia: Carey, Lea, and Blanchard, 1835.

Froude, J. A. *Short Studies on Great Subjects.* New edition. 4 vols. New York: Charles Scribners, 1883.

Froude, Richard Hurrell, and James Bowling Mozley. *Remains of the Late Reverend Richard Hurrell Froude.* 4 vols. Derby: Henry Mozley and Sons, 1838-1839.

Fuller, Andrew. *Jesus the True Messiah.* 3rd edition. London: B. R. Goakman, 1810.

Gaillardetz, Richard. *Witnesses to the Faith: Community, Infallibility, and the Ordinary Magisterium of Bishops.* New York/Mahwah, NJ: Paulist, 1992.

———. *Teaching with Authority: A Theology of the Magisterium in the Church.* Collegeville, MN: Michael Glazier/Liturgical Press, 1997.

Gaillardetz, Richard, ed. *When the Magisterium Intervenes: The Magisterium and Theologians in Today's Church.* Collegeville, MN: Liturgical, 2012.

Greets, Clifford. "Thick Description: Toward an Interpretative Theory of Culture." In *The Interpretation of Cultures.* 3-13. New York: Basic Books, 1973.

Gilley, Sheridan. *Newman and His Age.* London: Darton, Longman, and Todd, 1990.

Gladstone, William. "Ritualism and Ritual." *Contemporary Review* 24 (October 1874): 663-81.

———. *The Vatican Decrees and their Bearing on Civil Allegiance.* London: Longmans, 1875.

Greaves, R. W. "The Jerusalem Bishopric, 1841." *The English Historical Review* 64, no. 252 (July 1949): 328-52.

Gres-Gayer, Jacques M. "The Magisterium of the Faculty of Theology of Paris in the Seventeenth Century." *Theological Studies* 53, no. 3 (September 1992): 424-50.

Griffiths, Paul. "Theological Disagreement: What It Is and How to Do It." Paper presented at the Catholic Theological Society of America. San Diego, CA. 6 June 2014.

Guitton, John. *The Church and the Laity: From Newman to Vatican II.* New York: Alba House, 1964.

Hall, Joseph. "The Peace-Maker: Laying Forth the Right Way of Peace in Matters of Religion." In *The Works of Joseph Hall.* Volume 7. Oxford: D. A. Talboys, 1837.

Hampden, Renn Dickson, *Observations on Religious Dissent*. S. Collingwood: Oxford, 1834.

Hardwick, Charles. *A History of the Articles of Religion*. London: George Bell and Sons, 1895.

Harnack, Adolf von. "Die Lehre der zwölf Apostel: Prolegomena." In *Texte und Untersuchungen zur Geschicte der altchristlichen Leteratur*. Volume 2. 1-274. Leipzig: J. C. Hinrichs, 1884.

———. *Die Mission und Ausbreitung des Christentums in den ersten dre Jahrhunderten*, 4th edition. 2 vols. Leipzig: J. C. Hinrichs, 1924.

Hawkins, Edward. *A Dissertation upon the Use and Importance of Unauthoritative Tradition as an Introduction to the Christian Doctrines*. London: SPCK, 1819.

[Hawkins, Edward and Edward Pusey]. *Subscription to the Thirty-nine Articles*. Baxter: Oxford, 1835.

Hechler, William. *The Jerusalem Bishopric: Documents with Translations*. London, 1883.

Heylyn, Peter. *Cyprianus Anglicus; Or the History of the Life and Death of William Laud*. London: A Siele, 1668.

Hill, Edmund, O.P. *Ministry and Authority in the Catholic Church*. London: Geoffrey Chapman, 1988.

Hilton, Boyd. *A Mad, Bad, Dangerous People? England 1783-1846*. Oxford: Clarendon, 2006.

Hylson-Smith, Kenneth. *High Churchmanship in the Church of England*. Edinburgh: T and T Clark, 1993.

Imberg, Rune. *In Quest of Authority: The "Tracts for the Times" and the Development of the Tractarian Leaders, 1833-1841*. Lund: Lund University Press, 1987.

———. *Tracts for the Times: A Complete Survey of All the Editions*, Bibliotheca Historico-Ecclesiastica Lundensis. Lund: Lund University Press, 1987.

Jager, Jean-Nicolas (Abbé) and John Henry Newman (Cardinal). *Le Protestantisme aux prises avec la Doctrine catholique, ou Controverses avec plusieux Ministres Anglicains, Membres de l'Université d'Oxford*. Paris: Debécourt, 1836.

Jebb, John. "Appendix: The Character of the Church of England." In *Sermons on Subjects Chiefly Practical*. 3rd edition. London: T. Cadell, 1824.

———. *Pastoral Instructions on the Character and Principles of the Church of England*. London: Duncan, 1831.

Jewell, John. "Apologia pro Ecclesia Anglicana." In *The Works of John Jewell*. Edited by John Ayre. Volume 3. Cambridge: Cambridge University Press, 1848.

John XXIII. "Allocutio Gaudet Mater Ecclesia, 11 October 1962." *Acta Apostolicae Sedis* 54 (26 November 1962): 786-95.

Jones, H. S. *Intellect and Character in Victorian England: Mark Pattison and the Invention of the Don*. Cambridge: Cambridge University Press, 2007.

Keble, John. *Catholic Subscription to the Thirty-Nine Articles Considered*. Privately Printed, 1841.

———. *National Apostasy Considered: In a Sermon Preached in St. Mary's Oxford, Before His Majesty's Judges of Assize, On Sunday, July 14, 1833*. Oxford: J. H. Parker, 1833.

Ker, Ian. *John Henry Newman: A Biography*. Oxford: Oxford University Press, 1988.

———. "Newman Can Lead Us Out of Our Post-Vatican II Turmoil." *The Catholic Herald* 10 (July 2009).

———. *The Achievement of John Henry Newman*. Notre Dame, IN: University of Notre Dame Press, 1990.

———. "The Father of Vatican II." *L'Osservatore Romano* (22 July 2009): 7.

King, Benjamin. "'In Whose Name I Write': Newman's Two Translations of Athanasius." *Zeitschrift für Neuere Theologiegeschichte* 15, no. 1 (July 2008): 32-55.

———. *Newman and the Alexandrian Fathers: Shaping Doctrine in the Nineteenth Century*. Oxford: Oxford University Press, 2009.

Küng, Hans. *Infallible? An Inquiry*. New York: Doubleday, 1971.

Lash, Nicholas. *Newman on Development: The Search for an Explanation in History*. Shepherdstown, WV: Patmos, 1975.

———. "Was Newman a Theologian?." *Heythrop Journal* 17, no. 3 (July 1976): 322-25.

Lathbury, D. C. ed. *Correspondence on Church and Religion of William Ewart Gladstone*. 2 vols. New York: Macmillan, 1910.

Liddon, Henry Parry, and J. O. Johnston. *Life of Edward Bouverie Pusey: Doctor of Divinity, Canon of Christ Church; Regius Professor of Hebrew in the University of Oxford*. 4 vols. London/ New York: Longmans, Green, and Co., 1893-1897.

Linnan, John. "The Evangelical Background of John Henry Newman: 1816-1826." STD dissertation. Catholic University of Louvain, 1965.

———. "The Search for Absolute Holiness: A Study of Newman's Evangelical Period." *The Ampleforth Journal* 73, no. 2 (Summer 1968): 161-74.

Lückhoff, Martin. *Anglikaner und Protestanten im Heiligen Land: Das gemeinsame Bistum Jerusalem, 1841-1886*. Wiesbaden: Otto Harrassowitz, 1998.

Manning, Henry Edward. *The Vatican Council and its Definitions: A Pastoral Letter to the Clergy*. London, 1870.

Marindin, Gordon Eden ed., *The Letters of Frederic Lord Blachford*. London: John Murray, 1896.

Matthew, H. C. G. "Noetics, Tractarians, and the Reform of the University of Oxford in the Nineteenth Century." *History of Universities* 9 (1990): 195-225.

Mayers, Walter. *Sermons by the Late Rev. Walter Mayers, A. M.* London: James Nisbet, 1831.

McClymond, Michael. "Continual Self-Reflection: John Henry Newman's Critique of Evangelicalism." In *Tradition and Pluralism: Essays in Honor of William M. Shea*. Edited by K. L. Parker, P. A. Huff, and M. J. G. Pahls, 303-28. Lanham, MD: University Press of America, 2009.

McCulloh, Gerald. *Christ's Person and Life-Work in the Theology of Albrecht Ritschl*. Lanham, MD: University Press of America, 1990.

McDougall, Hugh. "Newman–Historian or Apologist?." *CCHA Study Sessions* 35 (1968): 91-101.

Members of the University of Oxford. *Tracts for the Times by Members of the University of Oxford*. 6 vols. London: J. G. and F. Rivington, 1841.

Merrigan, Terrence. "Newman and Theological Liberalism." *Theological Studies* 66, no. 3 (September 2005): 605-21.

Milner, John. *The End of Religious Controversy: In a Friendly Correspondence between a Religious Society of Protestants and a Roman Catholic Divine. Addressed to Dr. Burgess, Lord Bishop of St. David's, in Answer to His Lordshi's "Protestant Catechism."* Catholic Book Society, 1842.

Middleton, Arthur. *Fathers and Anglicans: The Limits of Orthodoxy*. Herfordshire: Gracewing, 2001.

Middleton, Conyers. *Inquiry into the Miraculous Powers, Which are Supposed to have Subsisted in the Christian Church, from the Earliest Ages Through Several Successive Centuries*. London: Mamby and Cox, 1749.

Middleton, Robert. *Newman at Oxford: His Religious Development*. Oxford: Oxford University Press, 1950.

Migne, Apud J.-P., ed. *Sancti Patris Nostri Maximi Confessoris, Opera Omnia. Patrologia Graeca* 91. Paris, 1863.

Milner, Joseph. *The History of the Church of Christ: Volume the First Containing the Three First Centuries*. York: G. Peacock, 1794.

Misner, Paul. *Papacy and Development: Newman and the Primacy of the Pope*. Leiden: E. J. Brill, 1976.

Morgan, Drew. "The Rise and Fall of Newman's Anglican School: From the Caroline Divines to the *Schola Theologorum*." *Newman Studies Journal* 6, no. 1 (Spring 2009): 20-35.

Mortimer, Sarah. *Reason and Religion in the English Reformation: The Challenge of Socinianism*. Cambridge: Cambridge University Press, 2010.

Mosheim, Johann Lorenz von. *An Ecclesiastical History, Ancient and Modern, from the Birth of Christ to the Beginning of the Eighteenth Century*. Translated by Archibald Maclaine. London: Vernor and Hood, 1803.

———. *Institutiones Historiae Ecclesiasticae*. Helmstad, 1764.

Mozley, Anne, ed. *Letters of the Rev. J. B. Mozley*. London: Rivingtons, 1885.

Newman, Francis. *Phases of Faith, Or, Passages from the History of My Creed*. London: J. Chapman, 1850.

Newman, John Henry. *Apologia Pro Vita Sua: Being a Reply to a Pamphlet Entitled "What, Then, Does Dr. Newman Mean."* London: Longman, Green, Longman, Roberts, and Green, 1864.

———. *The Apologia Pro Vita Sua and Six Sermons*. Edited by Frank Turner. New Haven: Yale University Press, 2008.

———. *The Arians of the Fourth Century: Their Doctrine, Temper and Conduct Chiefly Exhibited in the Councils of the Church 325-381*. London: J. G. and F. Rivington, 1833.

———. "Art. VIII.–Lyra Innocentium; Thoughts in Verse on Christian Children, their Ways and their Privileges." *The Dublin Review* (1846): 434-61.

———. *Certain Difficulties Felt by Anglicans in Catholic Teaching Considered*. 2 vols. London: Longmans, Green, and Co., 1900.

———. *The Church of the Fathers*. London: J. G. F. and J Rivingtons, 1840.

———. "The Church of the Fathers, No. I." *The British Magazine* 4 (1833): 422-28.

———. "The Church of the Fathers, No II." *The British Magazine* 4 (1833): 540-45.

———. "Contemporary Events-Home Affairs." *The Rambler* n.s.1 (May 1859): 117-32.

———. *The Correspondence of John Henry Newman with John Keble and Others, 1839-1845*. London: Longmans Green, 1917.

———. *Elucidations of Dr Hampden's Theological Statements*. W. Baxter: Oxford, 1836.

———. *An Essay in Aid of a Grammar of Assent*. London: Burns and Oates, 1870.

———. *An Essay on the Development of Christian Doctrine*. London: James Toovey, 1845.

———. *An Essay on the Development of Christian Doctrine*. New edition. London: University of Basil, Montagu, and Pickering, 1878.

———. *Essays: Critical and Historical*. 2 vols. London: Longmans, Green, and Co., 1871.

———. *Fifteen Sermons Preached Before the University of Oxford Between 1826 and 1843*. 3rd edition. London: Rivingtons, 1872.

———. *Fifteen Sermons Preached Before the University of Oxford Between 1826 and 1843*. New edition. London: Rivingtons, 1880.

———. *The Idea of a University*. London: Basil, Montagu, Pickering, 1873.

———. *John Henry Newman, Autobiographical Writings*. Edited by Henry Tristram. New York: Sheed and Ward, 1956.

———. *Lectures on Justification*. London: J. G. and F Rivington, 1838.

———. *Lectures on the Prophetical Office of the Church*. London: J. G. and F. Rivington, 1837.

———. *Letters and Correspondence of John Henry Newman During His Life in the English Church*. Edited by Anne Mozley. 2 volumes. London: Longmans Green, and Co., 1890.

———. *The Letters and Diaries of John Henry Newman*. Volumes 1-8. Edited by Ian Ker, Thomas Gornall, and Gerard Tracey. Oxford: Clarendon, 1987-1999. Volumes 11-31. Edited by Charles Stephen Dessain, Edward Kelley, and Thomas Gornall. Oxford: Clarendon, 1961-1972.

———. "Memorials of Oxford." *The British Critic* 24 (July 1838): 133-46.

———. "On Consulting the Faithful in Matters of Doctrine" *The Rambler* 1, new series (1859): 198-230.

———. *Parochial and Plain Sermons*. New edition. 8 volumes. London: Rivingtons, 1868.

———. "Preface." In *Sacra Privata: The Private Meditations, Devotions and Prayers of the Right Rev. T. Wilson, D.D.*, v-vii. Oxford: J. H. Parker, 1838.

———. *The Speech of His Eminence, Cardinal Newman on His Reception of the Biglietto*. Rome: Libraria Spithöver, 1879.

———. "Questions and Answers." *The Rambler* 1 (May 1859): 105-109.

———. *The Via Media of the Anglican Church*. 2 vols. London: Longmans, Green, and Co., 1891.

Newsome, David. "Justification and Sanctification: Newman and the Evangelicals." *Journal of Theological Studies* 15, no. 1 (April 1964): 3-53.

Newton, Thomas. *Dissertations on the Prophesies, Which Have Been Remarkably Fulfilled and are at This Time Being Fulfilled*. 3 volumes. 2nd edition. London, J and R Tonsond, 1759-1760.

Nockles, Peter. "An Academic Counter-Revolution: Newman and Tractarian Oxford's Idea of a University." *History of Universities* 10 (February 1991): 137-97.

———. "Anglicanism 'Represented' or 'Misrepresented'? The Oxford Movement, Evangelicalism, and History: The Controversial Use of the Caroline Divines in the Victorian Church of England." In *Victorian Churches and Churchmen*, ed. Sheridan Gilley and Vincent Alan McClelland, 308-69. Suffolk, England: Boydell Press, 2005.

———. "Continuity and Change in British High Churchmanship, 1792-1850." D.Phil. thesis, University of Oxford, 1982.

———. "Newman and Early Tractarian Politics." In *By Whose Authority? Newman, Manning and the Magisterium*. Edited by V. Alan McClelland, 79-111. Bath: Downside Abbey, 1996.

———. "Survivals or New Arrivals? The Oxford Movement and the Nineteenth Century Historical Construction of Anglicanism." In *Anglicanism and the Western Christian Tradition: Continuity, Change, and the Search for Communion*. Edited by Stephen Platten, 144-91. Norwich: Canterbury, 2003.

———. "The Oxford Movement: Historical Background, 1780-1833." In *Tradition Renewed: The Oxford Movement Conference Papers*. Edited by Geoffrey Rowell, 24-50. Allison Park, PA: Pickwick, 1986.

———. "The Oxford Movement in an Oxford College: Oriel as the Cradle of Tractarianism." In *The Oxford Movement: Europe and the Wider World, 1830-1930*. Edited by Stewart Brown and Peter Nockles, 11-36. Cambridge: Cambridge University Press, 2012.

———. *The Oxford Movement in Context: Anglican High Churchmanship, 1760-1857*. Cambridge: Cambridge University Press, 1994.

———. "Oxford, Tract 90, and the Bishops." In *John Henry Newman: Reason, Rhetoric, and Romanticism*. Edited by D. Nicholls and F. Kerr, 28-87. Carbondale, IL: Southern Illinois University Press, 1991.

———. "'Lost Causes . . . and Impossible Loyalties': The Oxford Movement and the University." In *The History of the University of Oxford*. Volume VI: *Nineteenth-Century Oxford*. Part 1. Edited by M. G. Brock and M. C. Curthoys, 195-276. Oxford: Clarendon, 1997.

Oakeley, Frederick. "Bishop Jewell." *The British Critic* 30 (July 1841): 1-46.

———. *The Subject of Tract XC. Examined, In Connection with the History of the Thirty-Nine Articles, and the Statements of Certain English Divines.* London: J. G. F. and J. Rivington, 1841.

O'Faolain, Sean. *Newman's Way: The Odyssey of John Henry Newman.* New York: Devin-Adair, 1952.

Orsy, Ladislas. *The Church: Learning and Teaching: Magisterium, Assent, Dissent, Academic Freedom.* Willmington, DE: Michael Glazier, 1987.

Overton, John. *The Anglican Revival.* Chicago: Herbert Stone, 1898.

———. *The English Church in the Nineteenth Century.* London, Longmans, Green, and Co., 1894.

Page, John. *What Will Dr. Newman Do? John Henry Newman and Papal Infallibility, 1865-1875.* Collegeville, MN: Michael Glazier/Liturgical Press, 1994.

Pahls, Michael J. G. "Beyond Ideology and Utopia: Towards a Post-Critical Historical Theology." *Credo ut Intelligam* 2 (January 2009): 1-8.

Palmer, William. *Aids to Reflection on the Seemingly Double Character of the Established Church, with Reference to the Foundation of a "Protestant Bishopric" at Jerusalem.* Oxford: John Henry Parker, 1841.

———. *A Narrative of Events Connected with the Publication of the Tracts for the Times: With an Introduction and Supplement Extending to the Present Time.* London: Rivingtons, 1883.

Parker, Kenneth. "Coming to Terms with the Past: The Role of History in the Spirituality of John Henry Newman." In *Newman and Life in the Spirit: Theological Reflections on Spirituality for Today.* Edited by John Connolly and Brian Hughes, 51-74. Minneapolis: Fortress, 2014.

———. "Newman's Individualistic Use of the Caroline Divines." In *Discourse and Context: An Interdisciplinary Study of John Henry Newman.* Edited by Gerard Magill, 33-42. Edwardsville, IL: Southern Illinois University Press, 1993.

Parker, Kenneth and Michael J. G. Pahls, eds. *Authority, Dogma, and History: The Role of the Oxford Movement Converts in the Papal Infallibility Debates.* Betthesda, MD: Academica, 2009.

Pattison, Mark. *Memoirs.* London: Macmillan, 1885.

———. "Philosophy at Oxford." *Mind* 1, no. 1 (January 1876): 82-97.

Pattison, Robert. *The Great Dissent: John Henry Newman and the Liberal Heresy.* Oxford: Oxford University Press, 1991.

Peel, Robert. *The Speeches of the Late Right Honourable Sir Robert Peel, Bart. Delivered in the House of Commons.* Volume 2. London: George Routledge and Co., 1853.

Perceval, A. P. *A Collection of Papers Connected with the Theological Movement of 1833*. London: Rivington, 1842.

Pereiro, James. *'Ethos' and the Oxford Movement: At the Heart of Tractarianism*. Oxford: Oxford University Press, 2008.

Podmore, Frank. *Robert Owen: A Biography*. 2 vols. London: Huchinson and Co., 1906.

Pollard, Arthur. "Scott, Thomas (1747-1821)." In *Oxford Dictionary of National Biography*. Edited by Lawrence Goldman. Oxford: Oxford University Press. http://www.oxforddnb.com/view/article/24919.

Powell, Baden. "Reasons for not Joining in [the] Declaration." *British Magazine* 5 (1834): 592-95.

Purcell, Edward. *The Life of Cardinal Manning*. 2 vols. London: Macmillan and Co., 1896.

Pusey, Edward Bouverie. "A Historical Preface." In *Tract XC: On Certain Passages in the XXXIX Articles*, v-xviii. Oxford: Gilbert and Rivington, 1866.

———. "Bunsen on the Chronology of Holy Scripture. *The Christian Remembrancer* 12, no. 53 (July 1846): 298-324.

Rannie, David Watson. *Oriel College*. London: F. E. Robinson, 1900.

Rausch, Thomas, S.J. *Authority and Leadership in the Church: Past Directions and Future Possibilities*. Willmington, DE: Michael Glazier, 1989.

Rees, Thomas, trans. *The Racovian Catechism*. London: Longmans, Hurst, Rees, Orme, and Brown, 1818.

Ricoeur, Paul. *Lectures on Ideology and Utopia*. Edited by George H. Taylor. New York: Columbia University Press, 1986.

Ridding, Lady Laura. *Sophia Matilda Palmer de Franqueville, 1852-1915: A Memoir*. London, 1919.

Rigg, J. H. *Oxford High Anglicanism and its Chief Leaders*. London: C. H. Kelly, 1895.

Robbins, William. *The Newman Brothers: An Essay in Comparative Intellectual Biography*. Cambridge: Harvard University Press, 1966.

Roberts, J. M. "The Idea of a University Revisited." In *Newman After A Hundred Years*. Edited by Ian Ker and A. G. Hill, 193-222. London, Clarendon, 1990.

Rowell, Geoffrey. *The Vision Glorious: Themes and Personalities of the Catholic Revival in Anglicanism*. Oxford: Oxford University Press, 1983.

Rowlands, J. H. L. *Church, State, and Society: The Attitudes of John Keble, Richard Hurrell Froude, and John Henry Newman, 1827-1845*. Worthing: Churchman Publishing Ltd., 1989.

Rule, Philip. "Newman and the English Theologians." *Faith and Reason* 15, no. 4 (December 1989): 65-90.

Rutler, George. "The Rise of Opus Dei." *New Oxford Review* 119 (1983): 19-23.

Ryan, Alvan, ed. *Newman and Gladstone: The Vatican Decrees*. Notre Dame, IN: University of Notre Dame Press, 1962.

Ryle, Gilbert. *Collected Papers*. 2 vols., New York: Barnes and Noble, 1971.

Sancta Clara, Franciscus A. *Deus, Natura, Gratia, Sive Tractatus de Predestinatione*. 2nd edition. Lyons, 1635.

———. *Paraphrastica Expositio Articulorum Confessionis Anglicanae: The Articles of the Anglican Church Paraphrastically Considered and Explained*. Translated by F. G. Lee. London: John T. Hayes, 1865.

Schaff, Philip, ed. *Athanasius: Select Works and Letters*. The Nicene and Post-Nicene Fathers, Second Series. New York: Christian Literature Publishing Co., 1892.

Schillebeeckx, Edward. *Jesus: An Experiment in Christology*. New York: Crossroad, 1974.

Schwartz, Eduard, Johannes Straub, and Rudolf Schieffer. *Acta Conciliorum Oecumenicorum*. Berolini/Berlin: Walter de Gruyter, 1914.

Scott, John. *The Life of the Rev. Thomas Scott, D.D.* Boston: Samuel T. Armstrong and Crocker and Brewster, 1822.

Scott, Thomas. *The Force of Truth*. 10th edition. Brookfield: E. Merriam and Co. 1817.

Sheridan, Thomas. *Newman on Justification*. New York: Alba House, 1967.

Scott, William, et. al., "Judaism and the Jerusalem Bishoprick." *The Christian Remembrancer* 12 (July 1846): 222-88.

Short, Edward. *Newman and His Family*. London: Bloomsbury, 2013.

Short, Thomas Vowler. *A Letter Addressed to the Very Reverend Dean of Christ Church on the State of the Public Examinations in the University of Oxford*. Oxford: Oxford University Press, 1822.

Shuttleworth, Philip. *Not Tradition, But Revelation*. London: Rivington, 1838.

Silva, Moisés. *Biblical Words and Their Meaning: An Introduction to Lexical Semantics*. Revised edition. Grand Rapids: Zondervan, 1994.

Sinkewicz, Robert, trans. *Evagrius of Pontus: The Greek Ascetic Corpus*. Oxford: Oxford University Press, 2003.

Smith, Henry. *The Protestant Bishopric in Jerusalem; its Origins and Progress. From the Official Documents Published by Command of his Majesty the King of Prussia, and from Other Authentic Sources.* B. Wertheim, Aldine Chambers: London, 1847.

Stagaman, David, S.J. *Authority in the Church.* Collegeville, MN: Michael Glazier/ Liturgical Press, 1999.

Stanley, Arthur Penrhyn and Thomas Arnold. *The Life and Correspondence of Thomas Arnold, D.D.: Late Head Master of Rugby School, and Regius Professor of Modern History in the University of Oxford.* 2 vols. London: B. Fellowes, 1844.

Strong, Rowan. "The Oxford Movement and the British Empire: Newman, Manning, and the 1841 Jerusalem Bishopric." In *The Oxford Movement: Europe and the Wider World.* Edited by Stewart Brown and Peter Nockles, 78-98. Cambridge: Cambridge University Press, 2012.

Stunt, T. C. F. "John Henry Newman and the Evangelicals." *Journal of Ecclesiastical History* 21, no. 1 (January 1970): 65-74.

Sullivan, Francis, S.J. *Magisterium: Teaching Authority in the Catholic Church.* New York/ Ramsey, NJ: Paulist, 1983.

Stephen Thomas, *Newman and Heresy: The Anglican Years.* Cambridge: Cambridge University Press, 1991.

Sykes, Stephen Sykes, *The Identity of Christianity.* Philadelphia: Fortress, 1984.

Thomasset, Alain. *L'Ecclésiologie De John Henry Newman Anglican (1816-1845).* Leuven: Peters, 2006.

Tibawi, Abdul. *British Interests in Palestine, 1800-1901: A Study of Religious and Educational Enterprise.* Oxford: Oxford University Press, 1961.

Toon, Peter. *Evangelical Theology 1833-1856: A Response to Tractarianism.* Atlanta: John Knox, 1979.

Tristram, Henry. "In the Lists with the Abbé Jager." In *Newman Centenary Essays.* London: Burns, Oates, and Washbourne, 1945.

Turner, Frank. *John Henry Newman: The Challenge of Evangelical Religion.* New Haven, CT: Yale University Press, 2002.

Turpin, K. C. "The Ascendency of Oriel." In *The History of the University of Oxford.* Volume VI: *Nineteenth-Century Oxford.* Part I. Edited by M. G. Brock and M. C. Curthoys, 183-92. Oxford: Clarendon, 1997.

Tyrrell, George. "Introduction." In Henri Brémond, *The Mystery of Newman,* ix-xvii. London: Williams and Norgate, 1907.

Van der Leest, Charlotte. "Conversion and Conflict in Palestine: The Missions of the Church Missionary Society and the Protestant Bishop Samuel Gobart." Ph.D. dissertation. Universiteit Leiden, 2008.

Valleiere, Paul. *Conciliarism: A History of Decision-Making in the Church*. Cambridge: Cambridge University Press, 2012.

Vincentius Lerinensis. "Commonitorivm." In *Foebadivs, Victricivs, Leporivs, Vincenivs Lerinensis, Evagrivs, Rvricivs. Corpus Christianorum*. Series Latina 63, 146-95. Tvrnholti: Typographi Brepols Edotres Pontifioi, 1985.

Walgrave, Jan-Hendrik. *Newman, Le Developpement du Dogme*. Tournai-Paris: Casterman, 1957.

Ward, Bernard. *The Dawn of the Catholic Revival in England 1781-1803*. 2 vols. London: Longmans, Green, and Co., 1909.

———. *The Eve of Catholic Emancipation: Being the History of the English Catholics During the First Thirty Years of the Nineteenth Century*. London: Longmans, Green, and Co., 1912.

Ward, G. R. M. and James Heywood, eds. *The Oxford University Statutes: The University Statutes from 1767 to 1850*. London: William Pickering, 1851.

Ward, W. R. *Victorian Oxford*. London: Frank Cass, 1965.

Ward, Wilfrid. *The Life of John Henry Newman Based on His Private Journals and Correspondence*. 2 vols. London: Longmans, Green, and Co., 1912.

Ward, William. *A Few Words in Support of No. 90 of the Tracts for the Times, Partly with Reference to Mr. Wilson's Letter*. Oxford: John Henry Parker, 1841.

———. *A Few More Words in Support of No. 90*. Oxford: John Henry Parker, 1841.

Weaver, Mary Jo, ed. *Newman and the Modernists*. Lanham, MD: University Press of America, 1985.

Welch, P. J. "Anglican Churchmen and the Establishment of the Jerusalem Bishopric." *Journal of Ecclesiastical History* 8, no. 2 (October 1957): 193-204.

Whatley, Richard. *Letters on the Church. By an Episcopalian*. London, 1826.

———. *Christianity Independent of the State*. New York: Harper and Brothers, 1837.

Weidner, H. D. "Editor's Introduction." In John Henry Newman, *The Via Media of the Anglican Church*, edited by H. D. Weidner, xiii-xxxii. Oxford: Oxford University Press, 1990.

———. "Newman's Idea of the *Via Media*: An Introduction to the Lectures on the Prophetical Office of the Church." D.Phil. dissertation. University of Oxford, 1984.

Wilberforce, Henry. *The Foundations of Faith Assailed* in *Oxford*. London, 1835.

Wills, Gary. *Papal Sin: Structures of Deceit*. New York: Doubleday, 2000.

Wilks, Samuel Charles. *The Christian Observer Conducted by Members of the Established Church for the Year 1833*. London: J. Hatchard and Son, 1833.

Williams, Rowan. "Introduction." In *The Arians of the Fourth Century*. Birmingham Oratory Millennium edition. Volume 4. Notre Dame, IN: University of Notre Dame Press, 2001.

———. "Introduction: Images of a Heresy." In *Arius: Heresy and Tradition*. Revised edition. Grand Rapids: Eerdmans, 2001.

———. "Newman's *Arians* and the Question of Method in Doctrinal History." In *Newman After One Hundred Years*. Edited by Ian Ker and Alan G. Hill. Oxford: Clarendon, 1990.

Wiseman, Nicholas. "Tracts for the Times: Anglican Claim of Apostolic Succession." *Dublin Review* 7 (August 1839): 139-80.

Witham, Larry. *Curran vs. Catholic University: A Study of Authority, Freedom, and Conflict*. Riverdale, MD: Edington-Rand, 1991.

Wolffe, John. "Cooper, Anthony Ashley, Seventh Earl of Shaftesbury (1801-1885)." In *Oxford Dictionary of National Biography*. Edited by H. C. G. Matthew and Brian Harrison. Oxford: Oxford University Press, 2004. http://www.oxforddnb.com/view/article/6210.

Wood, T. W. *A Guide to Ordination in the Church of England with Instructions to Candidates for Holy Orders*. London: Bremrose and Sons, 1878.

Yates, Nigel. *Anglican Ritualism in Victorian Britain, 1830-1910*. Oxford: Oxford University Press, 2000.

Index

1877 Preface, 7-10, 14-15, 27

A
Acacius of Caesarea, 134
Acland, Thomas Dyke, 35, 231
Act of Supremacy, 62
Activism, 32
Acton, Lord, 7-9, 93, 129
Alexandria, 3, 9, 16, 86-92, 134, 207
    Catechetical School at Alexandria, 31, 83
Alton, 36
Analogy of Religion, Natural and Revealed, 51, 71, 110
Anglican, 8-1, 17, 20-23, 27-28, 68, 94, 125, 135, 139, 141, 147-151, 153, 157, 163, 171, 173, 178-79, 184-86, 190, 192, 194-95, 198-99, 204, 208-11, 213, 232-33, 236, 242
    School, 13-14, 30, 33-34, 187, 241
    Church, 171, 173, 227, 229
    Divines, 187, 201
    Ecclesiology, 15, 18
    Episcopal oversight, 9
    Evangelical, 8, 87, 193, 229
    Reformers, 42, 201
    Unity with Rome, 200
    work, 3, 10, 16, 182
Anglicanism, 8, 17, 19-23, 139-140, 144, 151-52, 179, 182, 189, 199-201
    ritualism in, 1
    evangelical, 58
ante-Nicene schools, 87, 89
Antioch, 3, 16, 85-90, 108, 133-34, 207
Apologia Pro Ecclesia Anglicana, 152
Apologia Pro Vita Sua, 14, 22, 32-33, 35, 39-40, 48, 51-52, 68, 82, 84-85, 96, 101, 112, 187, 198, 210, 221, 227
apology, 130
    apologist, 42,
    apologetic, 2, 42, 92
apostasy, 22, 41, 53, 55, 87, 99, 101, 238, 241
apostate, 31, 115
Apostles, 6, 18, 35, 49, 91, 103, 105, 107, 111, 115, 122, 132, 157, 159, 161-62, 175, 181, 208, 232, 239
Apostles' Creed, 159, 165-69, 172, 175, 178
Apostolic, 19, 59, 119, 151, 190, 196, 201, 237
    Apostolicals, 99-100, 124, 137, 236
    Apostolicity, 202, 223, 232
    bishops, 104, 109, 111-12
    Church, 107, 111, 137, 153, 188
    episcopate, 239
    office, 11, 162, 168-69, 175, 179-80, 185, 210, 234, 238, 240
    school, 72, 111, 125, 139-41, 216
    succession 5, 42, 99, 105, 113, 115, 138, 146, 163, 193, 229, 232
    tradition, 46, 159, 160-64, 174
Apostolical ethos. *See* ethos
Apostolical *munus*. *See* munus
Apostolic Preaching Considered in an Examination of St. Paul's Epistles, 49
Apostolical Society of Oxford, 137

Archdeacon of Oxford, 170
  Robert Froude, 95
Arian, 31, 84-85, 91, 106, 134, 166-67
  Arianism, 52, 86, 91, 134
  Arius, 85-86, 88, 92, 133
  Controversy, 227
  Crisis, 132
  Party, 108, 133
Articles of the Anglican Church, 204
Arians of the Fourth Century, 3, 16, 27, 31, 83, 85-86, 90-92, 94-95, 102, 105, 133-34, 166, 170, 231, 238, 241
Aristotle, 47, 71, 87
Articles of Religion. *See* Thirty-nine Articles
Arnold, Thomas, 46, 127, 219
Athanasius, 43, 45, 82-83, 91, 133-134, 166-67
Athanasian Creed, 159, 166, 168
Aunt Elizabeth, 33, 44, 53
Autobiographical Memoir, 51-52, 78
Auxentius, 106

B

Bagot, Richard, 120, 122-123, 194, 197-198, 217-25, 232
Baptism, 32, 49-51, 54, 58-59, 133, 152, 158-59, 163, 166, 207-208, 236
Barclay the Quaker, 33
Basilica at Milan, 109
  Church of Milan, 105
Belaney, Robert, 213
Bellarmine, Robert, 207
Bible, 32-33, 43, 48-49, 56, 58, 90-91, 144, 178, 238, 240
  Bible-Christianity, 165
Biblicism, 32, 87
Biglietto, 68, 90, 234
Birmingham Oratory, 38, 40, 233
Bishops, 8, 11-13, 15-16, 18, 24, 60, 93, 99, 106, 108-109, 111-13, 115, 117, 119, 123, 125, 127, 129-30, 134, 139, 160, 163-64, 181, 193, 195, 200, 210, 217-22, 224, 226, 231, 239
Bloxam, John, 197-98
Book of Common Prayer, 33, 99, 114, 150, 190-91, 211, 213
Books of Homilies, 201, 211-13
Bowden, John William, 84, 138-39, 169, 198, 205
Boyle, John, 10-12, 27
Branch theory, 153
British Critic, 16, 182, 223
British Magazine, 104, 107-110, 124-25, 164, 171
Bucer, Martin, 189
Bulteel, Henry Bellenden, 58-60
von Bunsen, Christian Karl Josias
Burton, Edward, 228-31
Butheric, 109

C

Calvinism, 33, 38, 40, 46, 49, 65
  Calvinist, 18, 36, 58, 138, 190
  Calvinistic antinomianism, 40
  Calvinistic influences, 33
  Calvinistic preaching, 59
Cambridge, 124-25, 149, 192, 211, 213
Canonization, xi, 2
Canterbury, 189
Capes, John Moore, 129
Cardinal, 25, 33, 68, 233-34
  See Manning, Henry Edward
  See Dulles, Avery
Caroline Divines, 13-15, 149-51, 192, 198
Catholic, 6, 15, 19, 23-24, 27, 30, 50, 71, 90, 95-96, 108, 129-30, 134, 137, 152-53, 158, 161, 167, 172-74, 176, 186, 188-90, 194, 196-97, 201-207, 213-14, 218, 226, 233, 235, 237-38, 242
  Catholicism, xii, 14, 19-20, 22, 43, 92, 117, 138-39 ,144, 178, 184, 193, 195, 204, 215

INDEX

Catholicity, 22, 72, 200-203, 206, 210, 223-24, 232
Catholics, 1, 12, 61, 66, 68, 143-44, 157, 208, 228
Conversion, xii, 1, 35
    Church, xii, 5, 11, 68, 93, 147, 154-55, 199-200, 212, 232
    Doctrine, 43, 51, 157, 206, 228
    Emancipation, 63-64, 84
    Liberal Catholics, 7
    Newman, xiii, 3-4, 8-9, 11, 17-18, 21, 25, 28, 30, 94, 101, 135, 140-41, 185, 232-33
    Party, 106, 133, 195
    Teaching, 156-57, 206
    Theologians, 4-5, 24, 149, 234
Catholic Anglicanism, 22
Catholic Rome, 44
Charism, 30, 101, 135, 181
Charles I, 190, 192, 204
Chief Justice Edward Lord Pennefather, 58
Christ, xi, 11, 32, 38-41, 49, 91, 101, 105-106, 111, 115-17, 160, 162, 175, 179, 195, 208-209, 228
    Christ Church, 50, 128, 141, 215
    Presence, 7-8, 181, 192
    Minister of, 72-75
Christian, 3, 30, 39, 41-42, 52, 67, 73 87, 89-91, 103, 109, 124, 144, 147, 156, 164, 166-67, 169, 176, 180, 183, 207, 212, 228, 232-33, 238-40
Christianity, 14, 19, 21, 28, 37, 48, 53, 57, 61, 83-84, 86, 96, 119, 165, 181, 192, 237, 239
Conversion. *See* conversion
    Doctrine. *See* doctrine
    Faith, 135, 157, 160, 191, 236, 239
    History, 16, 43, 45, 72, 101, 238, 241
    Orthodoxy, 34
    Tradition, xii, 149
    Truth, 65, 93
Christian Observer, 138

Christian Year, 35, 108
Christie, John, 215
Church, xi-xiii, 1, 3, 6-12, 14-18, 21, 24, 28, 30, 32, 35, 37, 41-42, 46, 48-49, 51, 65-67, 82-85, 88-90, 93-96, 99-107, 116, 119, 123, 130-32, 135, 146-47, 149, 152-56, 158-61, 165-69, 173, 175, 183-86, 194, 196, 201-202, 205-213, 220, 238-41
    Doctrine, 17
    History, xii, 85-87, 103, 150
    Teaching, 4, 6, 177-8, 234
Church of England, 3, 14, 19-22, 33, 45, 58-63, 66, 72, 81, 84, 90-91, 99-101, 104-106, 109-112, 115, 125-26, 128, 137-39, 142-46, 151, 153, 156, 163, 169, 172, 181-82, 187-96, 200, 203, 206, 211, 213-18, 223-24, 227-35, 241-42
    Disestablishment, 22, 99, 104, 115
    Episcopate, 191, 215, 222
    Independence, 59, 191
    Theological identity, 190
Church of England Newspaper. *See* The Record
Church of Rome, xv, 116, 131, 137, 142, 144, 146-47, 154, 179, 206-207, 212, 215, 224, 228, 234
    See apostolic
    See church
Church of the Fathers, 104, 109-110, 182
Church, Richard, 66, 215-16, 230
Church, R. W., 47, 204
Churchman's Manual, 145
Clerke, Charles Carr, 122, 170
Coleridge, Samuel Taylor, 7, 101, 221
Commonitorium, 144-45, 154-56, 161-62, 164, 177
Confession of Wurtemburg, 190
Conversion, xi-xiii, 1, 22, 32, 35-37, 39, 40, 51, 56, 58, 88, 197
    Convert, 1, 23, 34, 88, 93, 141, 158

Convocation, 62, 113, 126, 128, 189, 201, 222
Convocation of Oxford, 63, 216
  Members of, 66, 124
Cooper, Lord Anthony Ashley, 228-31
Copleston, Edward, 36, 76-77, 81, 226
Coulson, John, 6-14, 27
Council of Nicea, 167, 195, 231
Council of Trent, 161, 212
County Clare, 63
Cranmer, Thomas, 189
Crucicentrism, 32
Cullen, Paul, 131

D

Darby, John Nelson, 58
Dartington, 165
Davenport, Christopher.
  See Franciscus à Sancta Clara
Davison, John, 46, 116
Diocese, 7, 125, 221
Diodorus, 134
Disciplina arcani, 88-89
De Brom, Adam, 183
The Decline and Fall of the Roman Empire, 41
Doctor, 132, 161-62, 165, 181, 208
  Of Divinity, 93
  Of the Church, 25
Doctrine, 17, 37-38, 40-44, 48-51, 57-59, 65, 68, 72, 94, 88, 127, 130-32, 134, 146, 148, 151-57, 159-60, 163, 166-67, 171-76, 178, 180, 182, 185, 190, 192, 195, 197, 201, 208-209, 212, 228, 230, 236
  Development of, xiii, 4, 17-18, 85, 139, 155-59, 163, 169, 174, 177, 187-188, 203, 234, 237
  Doctrinal authority, 2, 32, 46, 154, 164, 157
  Doctrinal compromise, 229
  Disputes, 16-17, 194

Tests/notes, 85, 124, 191
  See church
Dogma, 1-2, 17, 24, 37, 90, 133, 153
  Dogmatic constitution, 1
Donatist Controversy, 163, 195
Dornford, Joseph, 78-79
Dublin Review, 195
Dulles, Avery Cardinal, 12-13, 34, 69
Dunn, Margaret, 233

E

Ealing, 36-37, 58, 73
Ecclesia docens, 132-33
Ecclesial, 1, 24, 49, 72, 99-100, 107, 109, 135, 159, 166, 179-80, 184, 213, 231, 240
  Authority, xiii, 18, 55
  Vocational, 140, 186, 241-42
  Ecclesiology, 4, 10, 15, 18, 30, 153
Edward VI, 189, 211
Elizabeth I, 72, 190, 211
End of Religious Controversy, 143
England, 32-34, 61, 84, 96, 99, 104-105, 129, 188, 190, 193, 204, 210, 229, 236, 238
  See Anglicanism
English Catholics, 1, 130
  See Anglican Catholics
  English Church, 150, 188, 192, 200, 223-24
English Reformation, 21, 192, 223-24, 231, 236
Episcopal tradition, 8, 164
Episcopate, 4, 15, 99, 101, 103-104, 111, 119, 120, 133, 135, 162, 164, 188, 191, 215, 222, 224-25, 233, 241
Essay on the development of Christian Doctrine, 134, 185
  See development
Ethos, 46-47, 71-72, 82-83, 89, 126, 170
Eucharist, 21, 192, 208

Eusebian Communion, 134
Evangelical, 32, 37-38, 40, 42-43, 56, 59-60, 86, 102, 138, 238
   See Anglican
   See Calvinism
   Doctrines, 42, 49
   Faith, 37
   School, 32, 34-35, 38, 40-41, 44-45, 52, 55, 61, 71, 87, 238
   Evangelicalism, 30-32, 34-35, 45, 49, 54-56, 58, 67, 69, 90, 240-41
   Evangelism, 32
   Evangelicals, 45-46, 52, 87, 228-29
Examination Statute of 1800, 47, 62, 81
Exeter College, 58, 197, 230

F

Faith, 2, 4-5, 17, 29-30, 32, 88-89, 91, 96, 108, 133-34, 144, 147, 154-56, 158, 160, 162, 172, 178, 191, 199, 206-207, 211, 236-37
   Faithful, 4, 17, 24, 87, 100, 104, 109, 111, 113, 123, 130-32, 135, 188, 197, 210, 212
Faussett, Godfrey, 170
Ferguson, Thomas, 90, 92
First conversion. *See* conversion
First Vatican Counsel, 2, 7, 93
Flavian, 134
The Force of Truth, 38, 40
Forgiveness, 51
The Forty-Two Articles of 1552, 189
Franciscus à Sancta Clara, 203-210, 242
Freedom, 89, 192
   Mental, 1
   Moral, 1
Friedrich, Gerhard, 26
Friends of the Church, 113, 116-17
Fries, Heinrich, 9
Froude, Richard Hurrell, 44, 53, 63, 65, 72, 75-76, 78-80, 82, 95, 99, 101, 112, 114, 116, 119, 151, 164-69, 172, 177-78, 182, 203-205, 231, 241-42
   Froude's suspicion, 185
Froude, Robert (Archdeacon), 95
Fundamental doctrines, 57, 152-53, 156, 159, 163, 175, 178, 185. *See also* doctrine

G

Gaisford, Thomas, 128
Gibbon, Edward, 41
Giberne, Maria, 94
Gilbert, Ashurst Turner, 197
Gillow, John, 130-31
Gladstone, William, 1-2, 188, 229-30
Golightly, Charles, 53, 101, 215
Grace, 32, 37, 42, 49, 51, 199, 207
Grammar of Assent, 135
Groves, Anthony Norris, 58

H

Hadleigh, 83, 100, 113, 237
   Hadleigh Group, 112-14
Hall, Joseph, 151
Hampden, Renn Dickson, 46, 123-28, 168, 191, 215, 217, 231, 242
Harrison, Benjamin, 141-43, 145-48, 151, 156, 164, 169, 171-78, 241-42
Hawkins, Edward, 46, 49, 54, 62-63, 65-66, 76-82, 89, 96, 126, 152, 216, 226
Hawkins, Edwin, 74
Heads of Houses, 126, 199, 215-17
Hebdomadal Board, 126, 128, 168, 197, 216-17, 220, 222
Henry VIII, 189
Heresy, 42, 87-88, 128, 163, 195, 200, 231
   Heresies, 86, 171
   Heretical imperative, 34, 90
   Heterodoxy, 127, 134
Heretical Power, 91

Heylyn, Peter, 203-205
Hierarchy of truths, 157, 160
High Church, 50, 193, 201, 230, 237
    Anglicans, 45, 150
    Clericalism, 46
    Oxford Faculty, 3, 46, 141
    Party, 19, 192
High Churchmanship, 20, 22, 236
    High Churchmen, 20, 62, 78, 83, 110, 120, 123, 170, 229, 237
Highwood, 54
Hinds, Samuel, 46, 127
Historicism, 43, 87
History of the Church of Christ, 41
Holy See. *See* pope
Howard, Edward, 233
Howley, William, 113, 220-21, 224, 229

I

Idea of a University, 3, 93
Individual conscience, 8
Infallible, 2, 7, 24, 130-32, 144, 147, 160, 178, 185
    Definitions, 10
    Infallibility, 1-2, 5, 7, 24, 130, 132, 158, 165, 179-80, 184-85
    Prescription, 196
    Tradition, 165
Inglis, Sir Robert, 65-66
Interpretation, 2, 12, 19, 23, 124, 144-45, 148, 159, 162, 166, 178, 190, 203, 218, 222-23, 225
Irish Church Temporalities Bill, 95-96, 100-101, 113
Irish Gallican Tradition, 131

J

Jager, Abbé Jean-Nicolas, 103, 135, 139, 141-69, 171-73, 177-78, 184, 193, 213, 239, 241-42
Jebb, John, 139-40, 141-48, 152, 154, 156-57, 239

Jelf, Richard, 215, 217, 219, 221
Jewel, John, 151, 211, 223

K

Keble College, 233
Keble, John, 35, 62-63, 65, 73, 76, 79, 92, 99, 101, 108, 113-14, 116, 118-19, 126-27, 138, 170-71, 182, 199-200, 215, 222, 225, 231-32, 241-42
    Keble's parish, 112
Kittel, Gerhard, 26
Knox, Alexander, 140, 239
Kölner Wirren, 228

L

L'Univers, 142, 145, 147-48, 151, 155, 157
Lady Margaret, 169-70
Lady Simeon, 2
Laity, 8, 13, 108, 111, 115, 131, 133-35, 158, 233
    Laypeople, 13
Lane, Samuel, 204
Latitudinarianism, 25
Le Moniteur religieux, 157, 158, 161
Lecture on Anglican Difficulties, 132
Lectures on Justification, 182
Lectures on the Prophetical Office of the Church, 3, 7-9, 11, 14, 18, 27, 178-79, 182, 185-86, 193-94, 213
Leonforte, 96
Leontius, 133-34
Letter to the Duke of Norfolk, 1, 9-10, 162
Letters on the Church, 48
Lexicography, 26
Liberalism, 18, 30-36, 49, 52-55, 60-61, 67-69, 90, 175, 177, 238, 240
Library of the Fathers, 184
Littlemore, 117, 184, 215, 225, 241
Lloyd, Charles, 50
London, 36, 59, 66-67, 230

INDEX

Long Vacation, 41, 53, 55, 82, 147, 169, 203
Lucian, 86
Lyall, William Rowe, 83, 92
Lyra Apostolica, 108

M

Magisterium, 4-5, 12-16, 18, 24, 160
  Office of the magisterium, 8
Manning, Henry Edward (Cardinal), 2, 9, 185, 196
Marriott, Charles, 215
Marshall-Hacker, Edward, 114
Mary I, 190
Maurice, Frederick Denison, 7
Mayers, Walter, 36-37, 46, 58, 73, 238
McDougall, Hugh, 42, 45
Medieval schools, 16, 182
Meletius of Antioch, 134
Memorials of Oxford, 16, 182
Merrigan, Terrence, 69
Middleton, Conyers, 52
Melbourne, Lord, 126
Milner, Joseph, 41-42, 82, 86, 89, 238
Ministerial priesthood, 15
Miracles, 52, 110, 212
Misner, Paul, 9-12, 27, 239
Monophysites, 195-96, 227
Moral subjects, 77
Morgan, Drew, 13-15, 27
Morris, John, 197
von Mosheim, Johann Lorenz, 41-42, 87, 143
Mozley, John, 33, 184
Mozley, Thomas, 96, 225
Munus, 3, 13, 28, 72, 103
  Triplex munus Christi, 8, 15, 179, 185

N

The Nature of Faith in Relation to Reason, 29
Nazianzen, Gregory, 43, 94-95, 176, 239
Neo-Thomism, 4
Neo-ultramontanism, 7, 185
  Neo-ultramontanist party, 10
  Neo-ultramontanist regime, 8
Newman family, 32-34, 36, 55-56
  Financial struggles, 36, 53, 55
Newman studies, xi, 22, 25
Newman, Charles, 54-58, 60, 88, 90
Newman, Francis, 33, 54-55, 58-61, 87, 90
Newman, Harriet, 59, 74, 79-80
Newman, Jemima, 44, 60, 64, 193, 225, 231
Newman, John, 33, 36-38, 45, 55
Newman, John Henry, 1-18, 21-141, 143, 147-227, 230-242
  Anglican, xiii, 3, 8-11, 16-18, 22-23, 25, 27, 30, 94, 135, 140-41, 153, 182, 184, 186, 232-33, 241-42
  Catholic, xii-xiii, 3-4, 8-9, 11, 17-18, 21-25, 27-28, 30, 68, 93-94, 101, 129, 135, 137-41, 185-86, 196, 232-34, 241-42
  Illness, 53-54
  Ordained, 72
  Tractarian, 21, 23, 25, 62, 66, 78, 104, 133, 191, 194, 210
Newman, Mary, 54
Newton, Benjamin Wills, 58
Newton, John, 33, 38
Newton, Thomas, 43-44
Nicene Council, 167, 195, 231
Nicene Creed, 159, 166, 168
Nicomachean Ethics, 71. *See also* Aristotle
Nockles, Peter, 19-22, 31, 47, 78, 81, 151
Noetic, 46, 219

School, 49, 54-55, 60-61
Noetics, 31, 46, 50, 55, 63, 65, 82, 88, 125, 216, 241
Norwood, 36

O

O'Connell, Daniel, 63
Oakeley, Frederick, 170, 223
Observations on Religious Dissent with Particular Reference to the Use of Religious Tests in the University, 124, 127
On Consulting the Faithful in Matters of Doctrine, 131
Ordinary reason, 29
Oriel, 61-63, 65, 74-75, 81, 83, 96, 114, 117, 149
　Fellows, 55, 215, 232
　Noetics, 88, 125, 216, 241
Oriel College, 6, 21, 44-47, 50, 53, 59, 67, 72, 82, 151, 191, 205, 233, 238, 242
　Tuition, 78, 91, 123, 183, 188
　Tutorial system, 71, 76, 102, 241
Original tradition, 45
Owen, Robert, 56-57
Oxford, 3, 16, 31, 37, 47, 58, 61-66, 72-73, 81, 96-100, 111-14, 119-20, 123-26, 128, 135, 139, 141, 147-49, 164-65, 169-71, 181-82, 184, 186-93, 196-97, 199, 203, 210, 213-17, 224, 227, 229, 233-34, 241-42
　Christ Church, 50, 128, 141, 215
　Exeter College, 58, 197, 230
　Merton College, 204
Oriel College. *See* Oriel
　St. Alban's Hall, 48, 74
　System, 76-80
　Trinity College, 37, 233
　Worcester College, 58, 110
Oxford Church Missionary Society Auxiliary, 59
Oxford committee, 65

Oxford Movement, xiii, 3, 14, 19-21, 24, 27, 30, 78, 92, 101, 111, 151, 171, 227, 229
　Studies, 17-22,
Oxford Tractarian School, 192, 226
Oxford Tracts. *See Tracts for the Times*
Oxonian theological integrity, 65

P

Paine, Thomas, 35
Palmer, William, 101, 111-15, 118, 153
Papal
　Definitions, 7
　Infallibility, 1-2, 5, 7, 24
　Office, 9
　Statements. 7
　Teachings, 7
Parker, Matthew, 190
Parochial Sermons, 182
Pastor Aeternus, 1-2, 186
Pastoral Charge, 80
Peace-Maker, 151
The Peculiar Character of the Church of England; as distinguished, both from other branches of the Reformation, and from the modern Church of Rome, 139, 143
Peculiars, 44
Peel, Robert, 63-67
　Peel election, 46, 66
Perceval, Arthur, 111-15
Pereiro, James, 44, 71-72, 177
Philpot, Joseph, 58
Pope, 2, 7, 11-12, 16, 24, 43-44, 133, 143, 146, 203, 233
　Benedict XVI, 5, 12, 160
　Francis, xi, xiii, 5
　John XXIII, 24, 180
　Leo XIII, 233
　Pius IX, 93, 233
　Popery, 138, 144, 153, 175, 177, 193-94, 196, 231

INDEX

Powell, Baden, 46, 125
Priests, 5, 72, 94, 96, 125
  Priestly office, 8-9, 12, 179, 239
Private judgment, 31, 34, 49, 55, 60, 69, 71, 86, 90, 145-46, 148, 153, 156-57, 164, 176, 178, 185, 188, 192, 200, 210, 237-38, 240
Private Lectures, 77-78
Prophetic office, xiii, 4, 6, 8, 10-11, 15, 17-18, 21, 27-28, 103, 137, 140-41, 162, 168-69, 171, 179-81, 185-86, 210, 213, 232, 234, 238-42
  Prophetical office of theology, xiii, 13, 15, 162, 180, 188
Prophetic tradition, 8, 159-65, 168, 173-75, 179, 210
Prophetical Office of the Church, 184
Prophetical school, 181, 183, 234, 241
Prophetical vocation, 203
Prophets, 159, 161-62, 164, 181, 238-41
Protestant, 3, 5, 20-21, 43, 87, 109, 172, 189-90, 196, 202, 204, 217, 229, 231, 236
  Doctrine, 42, 49
  Evangelicalism, 30
  Protestantism, 20, 32, 34, 68, 139, 144, 153, 156, 173, 178-79, 187, 192-95, 223, 228, 236
  Protestants, 35, 120, 147, 167, 191, 207, 227
Protestant bishopric in Jerusalem, 228
Public liturgy, 12
Purcell, Edward, 226
Puritanism, 20, 139, 193
Pusey, Edward Bouverie, 3, 50-51, 110, 119, 126, 128, 169-71, 176, 184, 215-21, 230, 233

R

The Rambler, 129-31
Real presence, 21, 192, 209, 213
Reason, 29-30, 57, 86

Reasons for not joining in the Declaration, 125
The Record, 106, 137
Reflections concerning the Expediency of a Council of the Church of England and the Church of Rome, 143
Reformation, 21, 42-43, 153, 156, 192, 224, 236
Reformers, 42, 201, 203, 223
Regal office, 18, 28
  Of the church, 9, 181, 233
  Of the episcopate, 188
  Of the magisterium, 8, 13
  Ruling episcopate, 15
Regius Professor of Hebrew, 170
Regius Professor of Divinity, 169
  See Burton, Edward
  See Lloyd, Charles
Remains, 182
Remarks on Certain Passages in the Thirty-nine Articles, 187
rhetoricisation, 42, 44, 68, 89, 134, 239, 241
Rickards, Samuel, 74, 116-17
Ritual and Ritualism, 1
Robinson, George Frederick Samuel, 1, 233
Rogers, Frederic, 108, 215
Roman Catholic, 3, 173, 201, 232
  Cardinalate, 234
  Church, 5, 68, 147, 212, 229
  Priest, 93
  Roman Catholic Relief Act, 61
  Teaching, 5, 156-57, 205
  Theologians, 4-5, 24, 186
Roman Catholicism, 14, 19-22, 35, 92, 138-39, 144, 153, 184, 193, 195, 204, 215
Roman Catholics, 6-7, 23-24, 61, 63, 139, 144, 157, 186, 190, 194-95, 205, 210, 228
Roman Church, 154, 207, 215

Romanise, 1
Rome, 10, 14, 17, 44-45, 94-96, 139, 146-47, 153, 156, 179, 184-85, 195, 200, 203, 207-208, 223, 227, 231, 233-35, 241
Römische Geschichte, 45
Romish, 208, 212
Rose, James Hugh, 83, 85, 92, 100, 104, 110, 112, 115-16, 125-26, 235-38
Russell, Charles, 205
Rule, Philip, 150

S

Sacerdotal
    Office, 11, 15, 28, 180, 185, 239
    Priesthood, 8
Sacrament, 37, 49, 72, 105, 115-16, 127, 146, 207-208
    Sacramental authority, 115
    Sacramentality, 46
Sacred Congregation for the Doctrine of the Faith (CDF), 4-5
Salvation, 32, 37, 50, 54, 127, 147-48, 155, 158, 192, 206
de Saussure, Ferdinand, 26
Schism, 14, 18, 42, 65, 179-180, 194-95, 200-201
Schismatics, 65
Schola Theologorum, xii-xiii, 1-4, 6, 8, 9, 11-18, 21-22, 24-28, 30, 111, 186, 241-42
    School of theologians, 92, 111, 164
Scott, Thomas, 38-41, 66, 74, 238
Scripture, 145-49, 152, 154, 156-60, 165-67, 173-76, 178-79, 201, 206, 208, 230
    Scriptural authority, 59, 145-46, 167, 201, 230-31
Second Council of Nicaea, 152
Second Vatican Council, 12-13, 23-24, 93, 152, 157, 180
    Post-Vatican II Church, 12
    Post-Vatican II era, 10

Prior to, 23
Turn away from neo-Thomism, 4
Shuttleworth, Philip, 226
Sibthorp, Richard Waldo, 59
Sin, 36-38, 40, 51, 60, 110, 127, 163, 199, 209, 223
Socinian, 38, 66, 175, 177-78
Socinianism, 39
Sola scriptura, 49, 172
St. Aldate's, 184, 242
St. Benet Fink, 33
St. Ebbe's Church, 59
St. Ambrose, 41-43, 82, 104-111
St. Mary's, 55, 177, 197, 199-200, 224, 232
    Adam de Brome Chapel, 177, 183, 193, 199, 237
Stanley, Arthur, 214
Stephen, James, 35
The Subject of Tract XC. Examined, in Connection with the History of the Thirty-Nine Articles, and the Statements of Certain English Divines, 223
Suggestions in Behalf of the Church Missionary Society, 59

T

Tait, Archibald, 214-15, 219
Temperance Societies, 137
Ten Articles, 189
Theodosius, 86, 108-110
Theologian, xi, xiii, 4, 8, 11-12, 17, 22, 24, 28, 44, 91, 94, 135, 186-87, 238, 241-42
Theological
    Development, 21, 185, 189, 241
    Lexicography, 26
    Liberalism, 18, 30, 35-36, 229
    Munus, 13
    Office, 9, 22, 135, 180, 188, 239
    School, 3, 9, 14, 135, 188, 190

INDEX

Work, 3, 83, 129, 177, 200, 242
Theological Society, 169, 171, 173, 184
Theology, xi-xiv, 3-4, 15, 18, 28, 44, 50, 85, 93-94, 103, 127, 129, 134, 169, 184-86, 189, 196, 237, 240, 242
   Office of theology, 3, 13, 15, 135, 140, 162, 180, 188, 239
   Liberation theology, 5
   Vocation of, xiv, 1-4, 94, 140, 181, 186-87
Thirteen Articles, 189
Thirty-nine Articles, 58, 61-62, 84, 125-26, 139, 158, 161, 168, 187-91, 198, 201-206, 210-12, 216, 218-20, 222-24, 229
   "Article 6," 158, 206-207
   "Article 11," 172, 206, 211
   "Article 12," 207
   "Article 13," 207
   "Article 19," 207, 211
   "Article 20," 206, 208
   "Article 21," 207, 219
   "Article 22," 208, 212-14
   "Article 25," 208
   "Article 26," 163, 195
   "Article 28," 209, 213
   "Article 31," 209
   "Article 32," 209
   "Article 35," 201, 209, 211
   "Article 37," 209
   Reception of the, 233
Times, 231
Toleration Act, 188
Toon, Peter, 32
Tractarian, 4, 18, 31, 99, 110, 151
   movement , 48, 69, 72, 190
   school, 41, 55, 79, 216, 226, 235-36
   Tractarianism, 3, 19-22, 30, 71, 78, 82, 141, 224
   Tractarians, 14, 19-21, 46, 71, 78, 120, 191, 194, 203, 215, 229, 237
Tractatores, 161, 164, 238

Tractators, 161, 162
Tracts against the Old Testament, 35
Tracts for the Times, 3, 115-19, 137-39, 142-43, 164, 171, 182, 187, 191, 193-95, 213, 216-18, 220, 235
Tract 5, 118
Tract 6, 119
Tract 10, 115
Tract 15, 118
Tract 38, 139, 193
Tract 41, 139, 193
Tract 80, 171
Tract 87, 171
Tract 90, 3, 21-22, 182, 187-88, 198-206, 210-26, 229, 231-32
Tradition, xi, xiii, 6, 49, 132, 146-48, 152-57, 165-67, 173, 175, 178-79, 181
   Anglican approach, 153
   Respect of, 145
Transubstantiation, 146, 163, 198, 206, 209, 213
Tridentine Church of Rome, 212
Trinitarian orthodoxy, 38, 40
Triplex munus Christi, 8, 15, 179, 185
Turner, Frank, 23, 30, 34, 46, 67-69, 90, 236
Tyrrell, George, 22, 24-25

U

Ullathorne, William Bernard, 130-31, 233
Ultramontanism, 7, 131
Underwood, Weston, 38
Universal church, 16-17, 154, 201-202, 207
Universal jurisdiction, 7
Universities of Paris and Bologna, 16
University
   Education, 21, 81
   Of Munich, 9
   Of Oxford. *See* Oxford

University Reform Act of 1854, 190
Utilitarians, 64-65

V
Valentinian I, 106
Valentinian II, 107
Via Media, 14, 20, 139, 144, 149, 151, 153, 157, 165, 171, 178, 188, 193-96, 198, 200
　Via Media I, 139, 193
　Via Media II, 139, 193
　The Via Media of the Anglican Church, 7
Vincent of Lérins, 140, 145, 162, 239
Voltaire, 35

W
Walter III, John, 230
Ward, William George, 214-15, 223
Wayte, Samuel William, 233

Wellesley, Arthur, 64
Whately, Richard, 46, 48-49, 53, 63, 74, 99, 127, 224
White, Joseph Blanco, 46, 127
Wilberforce, Henry, 53, 81-82, 124
Wilberforce, Robert, 54, 75-76, 78, 225
Wilberforce, Samuel, 230
Wilks, Samuel Charles, 138
William IV, Frederick, 228
Williams, Isaac, 120, 171, 229
Williams, Rowan, 85, 87-88, 89, 91-92
Wilson, Bishop Thomas, 119
Wiseman, Nicholas, 72, 96, 163, 195-96
Wood, G. W., 191
Wood, Samuel, 177, 197

X
Xs. See Peculiars